D1478954

FROM THE LIBRARY OF
BERKELEY COLLEGE

New York:
NYC (Midtown and Lower Manhattan)
Brooklyn • White Plains

New Jersey:
Newark • Paramus • Woodbridge
Woodland Park

Berkeley College Online:
BerkeleyCollege.edu/Online

From Chinese Brand Culture to Global Brands

From Chinese Brand Culture to Global Brands

Insights from aesthetics, fashion, and history

Wu Zhiyan, Janet Borgerson,
Jonathan Schroeder

First published 2013 by
PALGRAVE MACMILLAN

Palgrave Macmillan in the UK is an imprint of Macmillan Publishers Limited,
registered in England, company number 785998, of Houndmills, Basingstoke,
Hampshire RG21 6XS.

Palgrave Macmillan in the US is a division of St Martin's Press LLC,
175 Fifth Avenue, New York, NY 10010.

Palgrave Macmillan is the global academic imprint of the above companies
and has companies and representatives throughout the world.

Palgrave® and Macmillan® are registered trademarks in the United States,
the United Kingdom, Europe and other countries.

ISBN 978–1–137–27634–6
This book is printed on paper suitable for recycling and made from fully
managed and sustained forest sources. Logging, pulping and manufacturing
processes are expected to conform to the environmental regulations of the
country of origin.

A catalogue record for this book is available from the British Library.

A catalog record for this book is available from the Library of Congress.

This book is dedicated
to our parents.

Contents

List of Figures and Tables

Figures

Tables

About the Authors

Zhiyan Wu, a native of China, has worked in the Chinese garment manufacturing sector, and was a marketing supervisor at CUIPPC, an intellectual property firm in Beijing. She has a B.A. in English from Beijing Foreign Studies University, an M.Sc. in International Management and a Ph.D. in Management from University of Exeter, UK. She currently is an Assistant Professor at the School of Management, Shanghai Institute of Foreign Trade.

Janet Borgerson works on issues related to culture, identity, and experience at the intersections of philosophy and consumption. She has held tenured faculty positions at Stockholm University and the University of Exeter Business School, and is currently a Visiting Scholar in the Department of Philosophy at Rochester Institute of Technology. Borgerson received a Ph.D. in Philosophy from the University of Wisconsin, Madison, and completed postdoctoral work at Brown University. She has served as Malmsten Visiting Professor at Gothenburg University, Sweden, Research Fellow at University of Auckland, New Zealand, and Visiting Professor at Walailak University, Thailand, and at the Shanghai Institute of Foreign Trade.

Jonathan Schroeder is the William A. Kern Professor at Rochester Institute of Technology in New York. He has published widely on branding, communication, consumer research, and identity. He is the author of *Visual Consumption*, editor of *Conversations on Consumption*, and co-editor of *Brand Culture* and the *Routledge Companion to Visual Organization*. He is editor in chief of the interdisciplinary journal *Consumption Markets & Culture*. He has held visiting appointments at Wesleyan University, Göteborg University, University of Auckland, Bocconi University, Milan, Indian School of Business, Hyderabad, Stockholm University, Shanghai Institute of Foreign Trade, and Walailak University, Thailand.

Acknowledgments

Thanks to the team at Palgrave Macmillan, including Tamsine O'Riordan, Anna Keville, Stephen Rutt, Eleanor Davey Corrigan, Hannah Fox, and Ursula Gavin. Also thanks to Dannie Kjeldgaard, Eminigül Karababa, Robin Canniford, Søren Askegaard, Ming Lim, Giana Eckhardt, Russ Belk, Sunny Tsai, Xin Zhao, Kelly Tian, and Sid Levy for helpful comments on this project, to Tanvi Mehta for editorial assistance, to Catherine Burch at Cambridge Publishing Management Limited for manuscript production, to Joe Laredo for proofreading, and to Rachel Crowe and Dana Caragiulo at Corbis, for help with images and permissions.

Zhiyan Wu (Maggie) would like to express her sincere thanks to Dr. Jeannie Forbes, Mr. Jiang Wu, and Dr. Lei Guo for graciously assenting to be interviewed. Also thanks to her family for their support.

Janet Borgerson would like to thank Sir Steve Smith and the University of Exeter, UK, for providing the research environment in which much of this work developed.

Jonathan Schroeder wishes to express his thanks to Jamie Winebrake, Pat Scanlon, and Lorraine Justice for support and encouragement, to Cassandra Shellman for administrative support, to Teresa Kellett for technical assistance, and to the William A. Kern Endowment at Rochester Institute of Technology for resources necessary for completion of this book.

Shanghai and Rochester, April 2013

Introduction

Chinese branding in the global marketplace

From Chinese Brand Culture to Global Brands uses a Chinese perspective to examine the capacity of Chinese brand culture to serve as a complement to existing models of brand globalization. Moving away from the trend to study the managerial aspects of Western brand building in Chinese contexts, we examine how Chinese branding efforts express significant aspects of their own brand culture.

We investigate conceptual and strategic relationships between brands and culture, and reflect the concerns of Chinese companies interested in developing global brands. In so doing, we explore the possibilities and processes of constructing global Chinese brands, which include calling attention to the growing significance of the Chinese diaspora.

Towards this aim, we have conducted in-depth studies in multiple locations, drawing upon several years' worth of interviews with consumers, employees, managers, and executives. In taking a cultural approach to branding, we focus on the circulation of cultural meanings, objects, and identities across time, space, and cultures. This enables in-depth examination of participant experiences gathered through interviews and observation, and offers wider implications for the understanding of Chinese brand culture.

From managerial insights to Chinese brand case studies

Our investigation originated in a series of interviews with Chinese managers. Insights from these discussions on the benefits of being a producer rather than being an assembler, as well as producing new design, brands, or *art*, rather than *goods*, pointed out the relevance of these distinctions for the future of Chinese global brands and suggested initial directions for our research. We began by contacting major Chinese brand holders and global marketers in Wenzhou and Hangzhou. We also conducted exploratory interviews with Chinese managers working in the UK. We focused on two important questions: Did these Chinese companies wish to develop global brands? And what were their opinions of Chinese brand globalization?

When we began the project in the UK, a Chinese manager suggested that we attend the International Trade Exhibition in Birmingham, a major trade show where companies from around the world exhibited bathroom and kitchen housewares and related appliances. We were able to interview additional participants at this location.

Our preliminary respondents were brand managers and Chief Executive Officers (CEOs) – seven were Chinese and one was Italian. Of the Chinese interviewees, two worked in the apparel industry, with companies based in Wenzhou; two in an automobile company located in Hangzhou; and three in the kitchen and bathroom appliance industry, with companies located in Shanghai, Gangzhou, and JiangSu. Later, the first author conducted face-to-face interviews with brand managers and CEOs in Wenzhou, Hangzhou, Shanghai, and Gangzhou, among the most developed cities in China, gaining further access to business networks with nodes in different contexts, Chinese and Western.

We also gathered information through observation, and by further analysis of interviews, journals, and branding materials. Indeed, we mined multiple resources, and scanned through tangible and intangible cultural products, such as brochures, flyers, business cards, newsletters, newspapers, and online materials, which produced a wealth of information. We followed four key websites and several additional media resources to study Chinese brands in the global context. These locations and sources were particularly significant, as these portals have pioneered the release of news and commentary on globally relevant Chinese brands. In studying the websites and other media, we employed methods of visual analysis to capture and understand the roles of meaning, pattern, and experience in strategic communication (Collier, 2001; Schroeder, 2006). Whereas the websites provided essential source material for up-to-date information on Chinese brand development, participation in events such as the international trade exhibition offered the opportunity to view Chinese brand development in a Western context.

Several moments from the early stages of our investigations stand out. In attempting to address Europe's concerns over the upsurge of Chinese products and competition in the textile industry, Bo Xilai, the former Minister of Commerce of the People's Republic of China, said: "Because of the low profit margins of Chinese textile products, China needs to export 800 million shirts in order to buy one Airbus A380!" (China Daily, 2005). Recognizing trade-offs between producing cheap products and exporting global brands, or focusing on domestic, rather than international markets, indicates a key concern when thinking about the potential and possibilities of building Chinese brands.

Despite its hyperbolic tone, this comment accurately represents the general concerns in China surrounding the low profit margin of Chinese export products. At the Third Global Textile Business Forum in 2006, Bo Xilai illustrated his point with figures. At that time, the average profit margin of Chinese textile exporters amounted to a mere 3 to 5 percent, and only 10 percent export their own brands, as most Chinese exports serve original equipment manufacturers or original design manufacturers (Azhari, 2008). Average export profits have been estimated as even lower, at 1.8 percent, according to *The People's Daily*, 2010. These paltry profit figures may be contrasted with the fact that 80 percent of prominent Western (mostly European) luxury brands (textile, clothing, and fashion goods) are located in the Chinese market, with China accounting for $9.4 billion of their annual revenue in 2009 (Gale and Kaur, 2004; KPMG, 2007). However elementary, these comparisons nonetheless serve to demonstrate two important features of the Chinese brand market – that the profit margin of China's exported products and commodities is often low, and that Chinese export brands continue to languish far behind prominent global brands.

Each year, the Interbrand branding group ranks the top global brands, and publishes the list online. Interbrand's findings on the globalizing of Chinese brands reveal a bleak picture and isolate factors preventing Chinese brand development on a global scale (e.g., Interbrand, 2011). For example, Chinese brand globalization has yet to grasp the needs and desires of foreign consumers, and many Chinese firms remain deficient in global marketing expertise and adequate communication skills, and consequently suffer from a low reputation. All in all, China seems to lack competitive advantage for building global brands.

In a well-known declaration, Shelly Lazarus, chairman of Ogilvy & Mather Worldwide advertising agency, put a fine point on these issues, exclaiming "so far China has no brands in any real sense" (quoted in Wang, 2008, p. 145). It was no coincidence that Lazarus attributed China's lack of authentic brands to Chinese brand builders' lack of stamina in sustainably developing long-term intellectual and emotional bonds between brands and consumers abroad. In a widely circulated article published in *Business Week*, Lazarus further argued that Chinese brands like Lenovo and Haier only offer safety to consumers, rather than moving beyond trust and developing strong emotional connections with consumers (Peterson, 2004). These thoughts are echoed by brand strategist Vincent Grimaldi, writing for the influential branding blog Brand Channel: "What is generally missing from Chinese brands is twofold: emotional dimensions and brand management" (Grimaldi, 2006). As one commenter on the controversy observed, "Shelly Lazarus brought the Chinese dream of making their brands Olympian down to earth. Thus far, the Big Two [Haier and Lenovo] have been preoccupied with the making and branding of corporate culture at the expense of brand culture" (Wang, 2008, p. 146). In this book, we aim to take a deep look at brand culture as a way to understand a set of successful Chinese related brands.

A potentially valuable antidote to Lazarus's critique emerged in a novel remark offered by our Italian respondent during his interview at the International Trade Exhibition in Birmingham. His comment highlighted the value of cultural specificity. He suggested that investing Chinese products with Chinese culture was among the most feasible ways to define and distinguish Chinese brands. He was not alone in sharing this perspective. At Wenzhou City, China, CEOs of two prominent Chinese brands, with aims to make their brands global, voiced their appreciation of internationally successful pop star Jay Chou's use of Chinese aesthetic values in his music, and suggested that he was well on his way to creating a distinctive and potentially global brand. One CEO pointed to the potential impact of the 2008 Beijing

Olympics on enhancing the image of Chinese brands and products in the global context. Another subscriber to this view, a brand manager in the Geely automobile manufacturing group – whose portfolio includes Volvo – posited the benefits of exploring ways to use historical Chinese culture as a global branding strategy.

Getting started: The emergence of three case studies

While attending the International Trade Exhibition for Kitchens, Bathrooms and Appliances in Birmingham, we found that all the Chinese exhibition stands were arranged at the farthest end of the exhibition hall, and that the only exhibitors forbidden to take photos of the Western firms' display areas were Chinese. Moreover, the decoration, layout, and general ambient appeal of the Western brand displays were far superior to those in the Chinese display areas. When asked for an explanation of these circumstances, one exhibitor, a manager of a Chinese housewares and appliance company in Shanghai, responded with the following:

> Of course, the arrangement is unfair, but we are used to it. They do not allow us [Chinese exhibitors] to take photos! I know they worry that we will copy their new designs. If this exhibition were held in Shanghai, our stands would be more beautiful and larger than theirs. You know, here, we are far away, so we are limited by how many products we can bring.

He relayed one particular incident that seems to sum up several key issues in Chinese branding. On the morning of March 4 2008, a representative of Kohler, a leading global brand, stormed over to the Chinese brand's display to complain. He said that the multi-functional computerized shower cabin exhibited by the company was a counterfeit of a Kohler original. The Chinese manager was asked to remove it immediately. Later, in private, he revealed: "Actually this product is genuine [Kohler]. It is the latest style and I have bought it for this exhibition. It is very easy to reproduce!" Another manager of a Chinese kitchenware and bathroom appliance company in Changzhou, China, also at the show, confirmed this claim: "it is not difficult to produce these kinds of products. You know, the parts are all available in the Chinese market. We just buy it and assemble it. So we can produce every product the clients require!" he declared proudly, embracing an ethic that has dominated China's industrial rise.

However, an exhibitor from a well-known Chinese corporation in Guangzhou, China, disagreed with these two managers' claims. He said:

> That day isn't far when these companies will be shut down, if they continue to copy the others. They are not producers, but assemblers. Profit margins of the Chinese manufacturing industry are decreasing rapidly in recent years. They will be closed down if they don't care to develop their own designs. This is my third visit, and after visiting their stands [he points to the Western stands], I have to say: we are producing goods while they are producing art. For example, I was attracted by Axiom, the premium worktop and accessories range with honed and etched textures. Their stand is really like a kitchen art gallery. I love their slogan, "kitchen studios."

His admiration for "art" revolves around key features of contemporary branding, which has moved away from merely identifying products toward building strong connections and creative co-operations with consumers.

A sales manager from a well-known Italian housewares and appliance corporation agreed with this sentiment, and added:

> Chinese companies should recognize that design is the way companies improve their competitiveness. They should invest more time and money in design and R&D. After I look around, there is a big surprise. Some Chinese stool designs look like Chinese traditional porcelain in different colors, such as blue and white. It is brilliant!

These stories, gathered from Chinese and Italian managers, highlight the low stature of Chinese products from the vantage points of the Western managers, and the lack of care and creative investment often given by Chinese producers in the design of their products. The Italian manager's proposition that styling Chinese housewares with traditional, culturally specific motifs is a potentially appealing way to make Chinese commodities more distinctive and attractive in global markets provides at least one solution to this predicament. Making Chinese products specifically Chinese-styled should, he seemed to imply, become a priority for Chinese producers.

Over a period of five years, from 2007 to 2012, we tracked several websites, including globrand.com, brandcn.com, and interbrand.com, that publish information on Chinese branding and export. Global Brand Network, along with Join the Portal, were key media sources that showcased the views of thousands of leading industry experts from marketing, management, strategy, and supply chain management, as well as those of independent entrepreneurs, on issues related to Chinese and foreign branding. Brandcn.com, the official website of Brand China Industrial Alliance, is one of the most important Chinese brand communication platforms for experts, brand owners, academicians, and brand managers in China and abroad. Interbrand.com, a leading world brand consultancy, specializes in a large number of brand services and activities, including brand analytics, brand engagement, brand strategy, brand valuation, and corporate identity.

Most of the reports we followed regularly indicated the existence of problems in Chinese branding, and showed concern over the relatively low standing of Chinese brand development among world brand builders, professionals, governments, and other related authorities. For example, Interbrand/Business Week's findings from yearly online surveys of global consumers and brand professionals on "Chinese brand impression" consistently revealed the negative repute of Chinese brands and products in international markets.

Branding and fashion: Some initial insights

The garment industry makes up one of the largest players in China's industrialization. In the course of our initial interviews, in Wenzhou city, Zhejiang province, we interviewed two brand managers, who we will call 'Mr. W' and 'Mr. P', attached to prominent Chinese brand apparel companies, and asked their opinions on Chinese brand globalization. These interviews were conducted in person.

Mr. W: We have been the men's suit supplier of Marks & Spencer [a large UK department store chain] for several years. You know, the profit is diminishing annually, though our products' quality has improved and is competitive worldwide. Our brands, like Baoxiniao, are well known in China and in other Asian countries, but we want to reach more countries, such as the UK and the US. But we really know little about this. [He paused before continuing.]

Interviewer: Do you have any detailed plans or ideas about it?

Mr. W: Actually, I think my company could look for high-standard retailers like Marks & Spencer and Walmart to carry our brand in Western markets. We discussed this possibility with Marks & Spencer, but nothing came of it. Actually, we know little about high-level Western markets. We want to change the bad image of Chinese products and brands in Western consumers' eyes.

At this point in the interview, the conversation was interrupted by a phone call. It was his young daughter. He answered the phone, and had an animated conversation. After almost ten minutes, he continued.

Mr. W: Sorry. My daughter asked me to pay for a Jay Chou concert ticket – 880 Yuan [about $130]! I really do not know why young kids love him! Do you like him too?

Interviewer: Yes! I love him too. I am going to attend this concert too!

Mr. W: Oh! How delighted I would be if my brand were as famous as Jay Chou! I heard that Jay Chou is popular not only in China but overseas as well.

According to this thoughtful CEO, his company wants to develop into a global brand, but without a positive image, innovative design ideas, and the support of successful international retailers, they are frustrated. However, he inadvertently demonstrated an awareness of what a successful brand might be by identifying Jay Chou, loved by multitudes of people willing to spend large amounts of money to consume his products. A second manager added a few words to this discussion:

Mr. P: I think the main problem in our brand development is the lack of professional experts. There are professionals who work for global markets. If we had them, they would bring their professional skills and knowledge to our process of brand development. Further, at the government level, I think the Chinese government should enhance the export of Chinese culture through movies, songs, art, and traditional events.

Interviewer: Could you explain this in greater detail?

Mr. P: For example, South Korea is one of the world's top ten cultural exporters. The Korean government made a great effort to export Korean culture through the 1988 Seoul Olympic Games and the 2002 Seoul World Cup. After that, exports of Korean TV dramas, movies, and pop music songs burgeoned in the past decade and forged the emergence of a Korean wave. Simultaneously, Korean brands like Samsung, LG and Hyundai-Kia emerged as strong brands in global markets.

Interviewer: Do you mean Korean cultural exports enabled the rise of Korean global brands such as Samsung, LG and Hyundai-Kia?

Mr. P: Yes! I think so. When foreign audiences watch Korean dramas, they gradually learn about Korean culture and appreciate Korean values. This enhances the positive images of Korean brands and increases their openness to consuming Korean products.

Interviewer: In your opinion, should the government hold more exhibitions and international events?

Mr. P: Yes! Of course! Although the Chinese government did a great effort in hosting the 2008 Beijing Olympics, it did little to boost the export of Chinese movies and music. Jay Chou is popular in Asia, and the Chinese government should offer some support to make him more popular in the West, or support more singers like Jay Chou.

This interview revealed a common handicap among Chinese producers and marketers, namely their lack of professional skills and expert knowledge in developing global brands. Mr. P asserted that the export of Chinese culture was likely to help the global brand development of Chinese products, and expressed hopes that the Chinese government would do its part to help out. Mr. W's conversation about musician Jay Chou demonstrated the degree to which Jay Chou represents – from the perspective of Chinese consumers and producers – a successful Chinese brand.

Inspired by our informants, our first case study examines Jay Chou, and investigates his international success through the lens of *brand culture*: a synthesis of consumer culture theory and strategic brand management. The in-depth investigation involved observing on site at Jay Chou's concerts, visiting websites, browsing various types of related media, and conducting

Figure 0.1   **Jay Chou performing in Shanghai**
© Imaginechina/Corbis

interviews. For many non-Chinese readers, Jay Chou may not seem like a global brand – he is mainly popular and known in China, Taiwan, and within the global Chinese diaspora. In 2011, however, he launched his Hollywood career by appearing in *The Green Hornet*, stepping into the legendary shoes of Bruce Lee in the role of Kato, the masked superhero's faithful side-kick. We consider Jay Chou as an established Asian brand now emerging globally, with the immense Chinese diaspora playing powerful roles in carrying his brand forward.

The 2008 Beijing Olympics have been described as "the largest international event in Chinese modern history, becoming an unprecedented showcase for presenting the image of modern China at its best to the world" (Qing et al., 2010, p. 1432). The opportunity to develop the 2008 Beijing Olympics Opening Ceremony as a second case study arose when the first author volunteered at the Olympics. The importance of this topic was highlighted in the interview with one of the garment industry CEOs, who suggested that the potential impact of the Olympics offered a clear picture of what such international events can do for a country's global image, including that of its commercial products. China aggressively used the 2008 Olympics to brand itself. In particular, the Opening Ceremony, staged by renowned film director Zhang Yimou, can be considered one of the largest and most expensive branding events ever.

In discussing the "rebranding" of China the Olympics afforded, one commentator stated:

> hosting the Olympics offered a golden opportunity to reshape China's national image. [...] Out of the Beijing Olympics, with many plumes of smoke and multiple flashes of fireworks, China has relaunched itself as a determined, united, powerful, wealthy, culturally rich nation singing harmoniously as one (Brady, 2009: pp. 8, 24).

Various observations made before, during, and after the Opening Ceremony, in conjunction with website visits, examination of relevant media materials, interviews with brand managers, visitors, and consumers, as well as visual analysis of the event, offer compelling clues, not only to understanding this phenomenal branding effort, but also to the resources available from Chinese aesthetics and historical culture, including recent historical culture.

Figure 0.2 **The Beijing 2008 Opening Ceremony in Bird's Nest Stadium**

© Erich Schlegel/Dallas Morning News/Corbis

In an interview shortly after the Beijing Olympics, we talked with the CEO of a prominent automobile manufacturer, together with the brand manager for the firm. Their insights raised a crucial question:

> I think this Opening Ceremony is a good example for our brand owners to note carefully. It blends the past with modern technologies. As for the international branding of our brand, we used elements of the Chinese past to market our brands overseas. For example, we named one of our sports cars China Dragon. In China, the dragon's symbolic meanings are myriad, and most of them are positive. This car also contains some facial makeup elements drawn from the Beijing Opera in the design of its hood. But the question remains, how does one make these kinds of products and branding activities popular? (Hangzhou)

The brand manager added: "We used some elements of facial mask-like makeup drawn from the Chinese Opera in the design of 'China Dragon,' though our colleagues find this somewhat unfashionable."

Their comments suggest they are looking for successful ways to invest their products with historical Chinese features, specifically how to refashion historical features into appealing product traits, a relatively straightforward, but unsophisticated use of cultural resources. Following upon these remarks, we posted an English and Chinese notice on an individual, pre-existing MSN account (97 Chinese and foreign friends) asking "how to make products with historical Chinese cultural elements fashionable in the global markets (please use an example)." We also emailed this question to over 100 managers and marketers, in China and abroad, and received responses from 69. Shanghai Tang, a fashion brand, garnered the most mentions. On its website, Shanghai Tang bills itself as "the first and leading luxury brand emerging from China" (shanghaitang.com). As its brand represented a distinctively Chinese brand with global ambitions, it made an ideal company for investigating cultural aspects of Chinese global brand development. Thus, Shanghai Tang emerged as our third case study.

Figure 0.3 **Model Lin Chi-ling in a Shanghai Tang fashion show**
© Imaginechina/Corbis

Emerging global brands

Our initial investigations indicated that Chinese brand global-ization included the following problems: familiar images of low price and low quality; lack of international marketing skills upon which to draw; and a poor understanding of the needs of foreign consumers. Interviews with these CEOs of well-known Chinese brands revealed gaps in their brands' globalization resulting from poor knowledge of global marketing, branding, and export culture, combined with the negative image of Chinese products across the globe. However, interviewees implied that entertainer Jay Chou provided a model of successful Chinese brand development, and that the Beijing Olympics proved similar events in the future could enhance the image of Chinese brands worldwide. Further, our informants at the International Trade Exhibition in Birmingham pointed out that the poor repute of Chinese brands might be improved by applying new paradigms, particularly drawing on Chinese styling and design innovation to improve and distinguish contemporary Chinese products.

Our selection of Jay Chou, the 2008 Beijing Olympics Opening Ceremony, and Shanghai Tang, an inspiring global fashion brand with aesthetic roots in Chinese historical culture, as illustrative cases is fully consistent with this unwritten and unspoken consensus around exploiting Chinese cultural specificity toward the global development of Chinese brands.

Although these three cases may seem "under the radar," we believe that, together, they provide unique insights into the relation between brands and Chinese culture, and offer intriguing possibilities for thinking about global Chinese brands. So, rather than canvass the usual suspects, such as Haier and Lenovo, we set off to investigate an unconventional trio of case studies. We acknowledge that they represent different realms of branding: Jay Chou is a celebrity brand, we frame the Beijing Olympics Opening Ceremony as a branding event, and Shanghai Tang represents a more traditional luxury fashion brand. Each draws upon Chinese cultural resources in its efforts, and each reveals similar aspects of the circulation of brands and cultures.

Collectively, these three cases offer a lens through which to study Chinese brand development in the global marketplace. Drawing on these examples sheds light on the ways in which brands and culture co-create and inform each other in global brand culture. Furthermore, we use these insights to argue for the development of Chinese brand culture into a strategic brand resource. This is not a simple matter of drawing upon a shared set of characteristics in all cases; rather, Chinese brand culture reveals itself as a subtle and complex resource with a diversity of applications, impacts, and impressions.

How this book is organized

This book explores Chinese brand culture in its capacity as a complex of cultural forms, and analyzes how brand actors construct brands and cultures around them. The introduction discusses notions of culture and branding as points of departure, focusing on the Chinese context. The chapter also outlines the research methods and rationale for the case studies in the book.

Chapter 1 sets the stage for the three case study chapters by providing a conceptual review of key concepts, including global branding, fashion systems, and historical culture. A brand culture perspective is introduced as a framework for considering the possibilities of thinking about Chinese global brands. In contrast to research on the ways in which Chinese consumers interpret Western brands via "revival and reconstruction" of Chinese history, we explore attempts to create Chinese global brands through investment of Chinese historical culture in aesthetic expressions that reach out to global audiences. This may involve what has been called forging "imaginings of the nation-state" evoked in other recent research (e.g., Cayla and Eckhardt, 2008; Dong and Tian, 2009; Zhao and Belk, 2008).

Chapter 2 highlights how a successful Chinese music artist, Jay Chou, developed into a global brand. The study of Jay Chou sheds light on the potential for building a Chinese global brand that draws upon Chinese historical and cultural resources combined with global music fashion systems. We examine the strategic linking of consumer research and artistic and historical conventions of aural and visual representation, such as poetry, martial arts, and music, and argue that this network provides a useful model of brand development for Chinese brand builders.

Chapter 3 deploys the example of the 2008 Beijing Olympics Opening Ceremony to underscore how the Beijing Olympics facilitated the growth of China as an international brand through a culturally specific model. This case study looks at historical and mythical Chinese culture in the context of branding. We position the Opening Ceremony as a cultural and aesthetic resource co-produced by government, business, and cultural producers, for shaping China's global brand. The Opening Ceremony demonstrates the convergence of the production and consumption of modern images and historical identity within global brand cultures. We offer international perspectives and accounts of

Imagined China pertaining to the Opening Ceremony. We factor in myth markets created by mergers between historical Chinese culture and global fashion systems, and finally consider how the construction of the "new China" identity throws light on cultural identity anxiety.

Chapter 4 explores how Shanghai Tang, an aspiring global fashion brand, currently controlled by the Swiss luxury corporation Richemont, uses cultural resources to reconfigure historical and traditional Chinese culture into a distinctly Chinese brand identity. Consequently, the notion of "Chinese" with respect to Shanghai Tang has come to represent a culture transcending local and regional boundaries. From a consumer perspective, we engage issues of brand culture and meaning, as well as the symbolic consumption of historical codes, fashion, and brands to shed light on the Shanghai Tang story. We also approach the global high-end luxury position of Shanghai Tang's "Chineseness" from a managerial perspective, and consider the myth of Imagined China as a global brand through the filter of Shanghai Tang.

Chapter 5 expands upon insights from the three cases and elaborates on how an ethnic diaspora market responds to a global branding approach. We address how the Imagined China myth has reconstructed the identity of modern Chinese lifestyle, and explore the selective use of historical Chinese culture toward the creation of the myth of modern China. Invoking aesthetic insights from previous chapters, we propose the circulation and co-creation of brands and cultures in order to articulate a Chinese-styled global branding model. Reflection upon the three case studies reveals processes that generate brand meaning and value in different contexts. The notion of "Chinese" emerges as both culture proper and cultural form. Furthermore, the case studies suggest that brands boasting myths of Imagined China can, by harnessing the very same myths that brought them success in local contexts, also circulate successfully across the globe. The chapter concludes with an argument for the reconceptualization of Chinese branding by bringing the investment of circulating cultures and brands into brand development. For those interested in more details of the study, further information on our research methods is presented in the Appendix. There, we delve deeper into the conceptual background necessary to understand our case studies.

Brand culture provides clues to the ways in which aesthetic values and historical culture inform, and offer possibilities for, a global reception of branded products and services. This is crucial in moving Chinese brands from a focus on commodities toward the development of global brands. These opportunities are offered by an ever-evolving brand culture, or more specifically the co-creation and circulation of brands and cultures.

The label "Made in China" has communicated cheapness and dubious quality for decades. That is about to change. Jeff Swystun, Global Director for Brand Channel, has extensively analyzed Chinese brands. His conclusion: "Chinese companies are struggling with what it means to be modern Chinese in the global market and what attributes of China and Chinese character help differentiate their brands" (2006). This, too, is about to change.

1 Global Branding, Fashion Systems, and Historical Culture

Global brand culture includes "the contention that culture and history can provide a necessary contextualizing counterpoint to managerial and information processing views of global branding's interaction with consumer society" (Schroeder, 2007, p. 351). In other words, international marketing managers need to pay more attention to both the cultural and historical context of brands and branding practices across the globe. In light of the fact that global brand culture derives in part from the impact of society and history on consumer culture, one could argue that the understanding of global branding would only benefit from perspectives that integrate managerial, social, and cultural perspectives. Consumer researchers Julien Cayla and Giana Eckhardt have shown how the Asian world can be understood via brands that reanimate and repackage historical culture to reveal a more modern and multicultural Asia (2008). From this perspective, brands can be treated as cultural forms by researchers. This chapter explores the cultural role of brands and aspects of brand culture in the global marketplace. The following sections enumerate managerial and cultural perspectives, global branding, brand culture, historical culture, and fashion systems.

Exploring brands in their cultural context

Culture is often perceived as a resource upon which branding processes and practices can draw, but less acknowledged are the ways in which branding processes and practices – and brands themselves – co-create culture. Indeed, brands are ubiquitous in everyday life, and they engage multiple actors in processes and practices that produce cultural meanings. Various aspects of the media, such as television programming, online content, magazines, movies, and books, as well as other stakeholders, such as labor unions, retailers, sports, brand professionals, and brand researchers participate in brand myths, brand meaning, and branding activities – from product placement and endorsement to social media target marketing. While companies painstakingly employ time-tested strategic branding techniques, for example in generating brand myths, consumers of all varieties invest brands with particular meanings by consuming them in socially negotiated ways. As brand researcher Susan Fournier has argued, brands can act as companions that co-create and contribute to life experiences (1998).

At a basic level, a brand is a mark that communicates a proprietary ownership of something that others might wish to possess and from which they are specifically excluded, but also an invitation to, or recognition of, inclusion through a sharing in the value of the mark. This tension between exclusion and inclusion, outsider and insider, fuels a movement basic to human needs, wants, and desires. Co-constructed by various brand actors, brand meanings are closely determined by relationships and context. In keeping with this paradigm, brand culture shifts and changes through repeated interactions between various actors across time and space.

These conceptual connections notwithstanding, most studies on international marketing and consumer culture have paid scant attention to precisely how brand development adapts to market conditions and contributes to public discourse, and thus much research lacks focus on the cultural analysis of brand development. In contrast, this book investigates the possibilities and processes of developing global brands via a cultural approach. In the same vein, the cultural analysis of brands attends to brand "actors" and the various discourses that pertain to the cultural meanings of brands (Bengtsson and Östberg, 2006; Holt, 2004). In his model of cultural branding, brand researcher Douglas Holt draws upon consumer perspectives from varied cultural contexts and joins historical and cultural analysis to reveal patterns of brand success, as well as the problems faced by brands (Holt, 2002, 2004). A key example of a cultural approach to brands examined the Starbucks brand myth to show how brands can take on ideological and political roles that influence an entire industry (Thompson and Arsel, 2004). The cultural approach towards brand development highlights the cultural richness of brand meanings and brand myths, thereby revealing the diversity of brand culture.

Arguably complex and difficult to define, culture might be understood as "the way of life of a group," and meanings that arise as part of this way of life, including "the transmission, communication and alteration of those meanings, and the circuits of power by which the meanings are valorised or derogated" (Kendall and Wickham, 2001, p. 14). In this definition, culture encompasses meanings embodied by symbols with "an historically transmitted structure" and "a system of inherited conceptions expressed in symbolic forms" that allow communication, development, and perpetuation of knowledge and relevant attitudes "toward life" (Geertz, 1973, p. 89). Because human activity alters these symbolic meanings, meanings are necessarily susceptible to both change and stasis. Consequently, culture is "continually produced and reproduced by means of which the human subject modifies his physical environment and bends nature to his will" (Berger, 1990, p. 6). In other words, culture is a process by which "people try to make sense of their own lives and sense of the behavior of other people with whom they have to deal" (Spindler et al., 1990, p. 2). Not least, culture refers to products that exist in material cultural forms, but also as artefacts in their capacity as texts with symbolic content. These artefacts include brands and branding processes.

In the cultural analysis of brands, brands are treated as symbolic forms enabling companies to compete gainfully, and enabling consumers to achieve optimal identity projection. Ostensibly, in an attempt to satisfy consumers, brand-owning firms create and execute systematic strategies aiming to convince consumers that brand consumption adds value to life, such that brand implementation has turned into a distinctive cultural form, which to all intents and purposes encapsulates brand builders' worldviews (Cayla and Arnould, 2008). Branding activities engage brand myths that are meant to graft brand builders' worldviews onto consumers' unmet desires and needs, recognizing that in some cases consumers are brand builders.

In brand development, consumers become key brand actors and assume co-creative roles. In other words, a company's capacity for creating brand meanings enjoys only limited success, because the world in which it functions is dominated by the power of consumers who, in turn, engage brand meanings in ways that serve their own identity projections. The ways in which different groups of consumers develop meanings around brands vary, and these meanings have the potential to differ from what sponsoring firms may have intended in branding activities (e.g., Kates, 2004; Kozinets, 2001; Muñiz and O'Guinn, 2001).

Although cultural resources provide potentially productive areas for pursuing brand development, many marketing scholars have yet to take notice of historical culture's important role in brand development research. Nevertheless, one ground-breaking paper from consumer researchers Eric Arnould and Craig Thompson went further, and called for more non-Western studies to address gaps emerging from local differences and contingencies of global consumer culture (2005). Taking up their challenge, this book focuses on the Chinese context, deploying a cultural approach and examining particular narratives and potential pathways regarding ways in which Chinese brands globalize. We draw on existing notions of *cultural branding*, *brand culture*, and *brand actors'* roles in brand development in order to mobilize these specifically in terms of cultural forms. In so doing, this work seeks to emphasize the potential of brand culture in the global marketplace.

The focus on China acknowledges its steady rise as a global economic power, with the cultural, economic, and ideological role of brands sure only to increase. As one economic analyst predicts:

> One inevitable trend in the coming decades – now that rising costs and the end of easy money are forcing Chinese companies to become long term strategic thinkers and look for new revenue models – is that more Chinese companies will go abroad. Western consumers had better get used to seeing Chinese brands, not just the "Made in China" stickers, on the shelves of America's retailers. Likewise, Western brands will have to start fending off competition from new emerging Chinese brands that will disrupt the world's markets and the global pecking order, much as Japanese firms did in the 1980s (Rein, 2012, p. 12).

More specifically, China is gaining momentum in the fashion industries, which exert a powerful influence on many other sectors:

Fifty years ago, Italy benefitted from market growth centered in the United States, while today Shanghai benefits from growth centered in Asia. The sheer size of the numbers associated with China's projected growth guarantees the arrival of Shanghai as a world-class center of fashion because fashion follows money (Mead, 2011, p. 563).

Thus, our three cases, emerging from the world of entertainment, sports, and fashion, provide a useful lens to view the continuing development of global Chinese brands.

Managerial perspectives on global branding

Key topics in the international marketing literature include global branding, global brand standardization and adaptation of brand names and brand strategies, and managerial perspectives on global branding. It has been three decades since pioneering marketing guru Ted Levitt isolated the notion of the globalization of markets (1983). Yet, the concept of "global brand" remains ambiguous, as demonstrated by discrepancies that exist between literature definitions and popular managerial rankings of global brands (e.g., Dimofte, Johansson, and Ronkainen, 2008; Quelch, 1999; Roth, 1995; Whitelock and Fastoso, 2007).

Our understanding of the term global brand derives from a position where multiple perspectives – including the marketing standardization and consumer perspective approaches – dovetail. Differences of opinion notwithstanding, common wisdom holds that global branding refers to global branding decisions and that these decisions apply around the world. Furthermore, the brand – as a concept, a cultural object, and a managerial tool – has shifted in its meaning and execution from merely adding name recognition and value to existing products and services (Askegaard, 2006). In recent years, the concept of global branding has exceeded the traditional implications of trademark to encompass complex decisions that affect the development of a brand on a global scale (e.g., Bently, Davis, and Ginsburg, 2008).

Elementary branding strategy assumes that global branding decisions should align with a number of other elements, including the brand's core essence, the brand personality and positioning, and the brand's execution, which may include media and advertising. Global branding therefore refers to a complex process of reinforcing and aligning multiple elements at an international level.

From the marketing standardization perspective, a key objective of brand development is maximizing economic profits, achievable by standardizing the brand globally and cutting the concomitant costs of marketing, research and development, sourcing, and manufacturing (Craig and Douglas, 2000; Özsomer and Altaras, 2008; Yip, 1995). Standardization, which involves developing a distinctive brand identity and reproducing this identity across differing cultural, historical and structural terrains, is a cost-effective means to target and fulfill those consumer demands generally shared by affluent and youth markets across the world (e.g., Borgerson et al., 2009; Griffiths, 2013; Hassan, Craft and Kortam, 2003; Kjeldgaard and Askegaard, 2006; Quelch, 2007).

Although scholars typically agree on which features make a brand global – the use of the same name worldwide and similar positioning strategies and marketing mixes in target markets – there exist some disagreements about the lengths to which a brand must go before it can be christened "global" (Özsomer and Altaras, 2008). Some studies maintain that absolute, undiluted standardization of brand strategy and marketing mix is essential (Levitt, 1983). Nevertheless, a majority of marketing experts argue that absolute standardization remains impossible to put into practice, as firms that own global brands often vary in the levels of globalization they aim to achieve and pursue. Specifically, the strategic thinking behind brands varies, and resulting decisions may affect how global brands ultimately develop (Aaker and Joachimsthaler, 1999; Hsieh, 2002; Johansson and Ronkainen, 2005; Kapferer, 2012; Schuiling and Kapferer, 2004). In defining global brands, however, many look to the degree to which brands depend on standardized marketing strategies and programs across the global markets.

For their part, research firms measure global brands and their values on the basis of economic benefits. For example, Interbrand/Business Week, one such research institution gaining a sizeable reputation, issues annual awards, such as Best Global Brands and Best Chinese Brands, enabling the measurement of global brands using both financial and reputational indicators. Interbrand's selection algorithms dictate that a global brand must derive at least one-third of its sales from foreign markets, be well recognized by individuals who may or may not be purchasing consumers, and engage highly recognizable marketing resources and publicly identified financial data. In this reckoning, global brand values are measured by sales volume, market leadership, sustainability, and global reach (Interbrand, 2012).

A consumer perspective defines global brands in terms of the degree to which consumers perceive the brand as being global when it reaches foreign markets (Özsomer and Altaras, 2008). In other words, the global status of brands is constituted by their multi-market reach defined by "at least a minimum level of awareness, recognition and sales all over the world" (Quelch, 2007, p. 560). Despite its well-rounded approach, research engaging a consumer perspective does not generally focus on multiple brand actors in the definition of a global brand. In our view, a global brand is one interpreted by brand actors worldwide, including managerial workers, consumers, and the media. Accordingly, global branding refers to brand actors' discourses on a global scale. These discourses include advertisements, trade fairs, brand communities, consumers' meanings, fan blogs, official brand websites, investment analyses, and media commentaries.

Global brand standardization/adaptation

In marketing scholarship, many of the main issues of international branding have developed via a debate regarding standardization versus adaptation of global branding by exploiting global branding opportunities in local markets. The debate concentrates on the standardization/adaptation of brand names and brand strategies at the international level, though more recent discussions include investigating the link between brand name standardization and profitability in the international branding practices of US companies (Alashban et al., 2002). The standardization of products, packaging, and communications at an international level has also been explored (Holt, Quelch, and Taylor, 2004). Other relevant concerns include the adaptation to local contexts of advertising strategy and brand execution elements in ways that continue to retain their international marketing mix content and remain aligned with brand characteristics (de Chernatony, Halliburton and Bernath, 1995; Kates and Goh, 2003). What is left to be done is to examine brand image strategies from alternative perspectives. Towards this end, we offer an analysis that examines brand images from the perspective of cultural brand actors.

Many consumer-focused studies of global branding have highlighted the interactions between brand globalness and localness. The relevant consumer segments provide the basis for constructing positioning strategies and valuing the depth versus the breadth of the effectiveness of brand image strategies (Roth, 1992). However, consumer preferences for global brands are often based on the questionable assumption that global brands offer not only prestige but also a quality that exceeds that of local brands (Steenkamp, Batra, and Alden, 2003). Indeed, local brands and their features have been compared with those of global brands, and while local brands enjoy a distinct advantage over global brands with regard to brand awareness and trust, there often exists little or no difference in quality and/or prestige between them (Schuiling and Kapferer, 2004). These insights encourage further investigations into the ways in which specific differences between local and global brands are perceived by consumers, and how brands create value and influence consumer choice. Armed with a cultural approach, this book enters the fray in an attempt to examine brand globalization through the discourses brand actors create around global brands.

The managerial perspective of global branding in the Chinese context

The Chinese translation of global brands and the ways in which global brands have standardized and adapted to China has been of great interest (Aaker and Williams, 1998; Greyser, 2008; Lu, 2008; Melewar et al., 2004; Wang, 2008; Zhang and Schmitt, 2001). Brand name standardization/adaptation strategies employed by Fortune 500 consumer goods companies in China and Hong Kong reveal how global brands successfully avoid unfortunate brand name errors and invest their brand names with distinctive features – cultural symbols, additional product benefits, and positive cultural associations – when entering the Chinese market (Francis, Lam, and Walls, 2002). Consumer researchers Xin Zhao and Russell Belk investigated Chinese consumer perceptions of global brands and the appeal – and foreignness – of television and print advertisements for global brands (2008). Their findings revealed two different reactions among Chinese consumers. The group that aspires to international cosmopolitanism and its imagined prestige (in Chinese, *mianzi*) identifies with global advertisements. The other group, which is driven by nationalistic feelings and the desire to maintain local prestige, identifies with the representation of Chinese values (e.g., Tian and Dong, 2011). We build upon existing studies of consumer perception of global brands and branding by expanding the range of brand actors to include not only consumers, but also global managerial workers and the media, in investigating how their stories of brands contribute to a more comprehensive definition of global brands and branding.

Brand culture and the cultural approach to global branding

Brand culture goes further than recognizing the roles that culture, in various guises, may play in branding processes. Indeed, brand culture comprehends the ways in which brands and branding participate in processes of co-creating culture. As cultural forms, brands evolve in accordance with changes in the historical, geographical, and social context. In their overview of brand culture, Jonathan Schroeder and Miriam Salzer-Mörling write that "if brands exist as cultural, ideological, and political objects, then brand researchers require tools developed to understand culture, politics, and ideology, in conjunction with more typical branding concepts, such as equity, strategy, and value" (2006, p. 4). From this perspective, cultural, ideological, and political environments influence the process of building brands, brand meanings, and values. Along these lines, brand culture can be recognized within "the cultural codes of brands – history, images, myths, art, and theatre – that influence brand meaning and value in the marketplace" (Schroeder, 2009, p. 124). Brands, understood as cultural forms, reflect people's ideologies, their lifestyles, and their cultural values.

Table 1.1 Aspects of brand culture

Brand identity	The strategic heart of the brand – what the brand manager imagines the brand to be. This concept contributes to models of brand equity, strategic brand management, brand leadership, and living the brand programs.
Brand image	Brands are psychological – brand image is in the minds of the customer, in the actual marketplace. This concept forms the basis for understanding brand community, online brand forums, and market segmentation models.
Brand culture	Refers to the cultural dimensions or codes of brands – history, images, myths, art, science – that influence brand meaning and value in the marketplace.

Source: Adapted from Schroeder, 2009

Various brand actors, such as brand owners, consumers, media, brand communities, and other stakeholders, participate in determining processes of brand development, brand meaning, and brand value (e.g. Kornberger, 2010; Schultz and Hatch, 2006). Branding also provides a way of recounting the evolution of brands and narrating the consumer's world. Echoing Schroeder, some scholars suggest that, "Different types of brands and ways of managing and consuming brands have also emerged in different places, which we call brand cultures" (Cayla and Arnould, 2008, p. 101). In this sense, branding processes and brands are said to reflect, and react and respond to, different locations and contexts – the loam from which branding emerges – producing different kinds of brands and modes of branding, as well as differing ways of consuming brands. Notions of brand culture go further, relating to diverse scenarios of cultural entities, not least of which are new co-creations between branding and cultural forms.

From these perspectives, branding no longer merely represents manipulative and hegemonic corporate intentions. Global brand strategists who advocate marketing standardization miss the point by viewing culture from the outside, a variable that marketers can adapt, or neglect, at their discretion. A brand culture approach reveals that branding practices perform as, and engage with, other cultural forms, such as, music, movies, sports, fashion, and historical narratives. Thus, brand culture sheds light on the diverse ways in which aspects of culture inform and interact with global branding, such as how the Marlboro brand strongly links itself to people's impressions of what constitutes the American West; but also bringing insight to Japanese global brands that do little to express "Japanese lifestyle" (Iwabuchi, 2006).

Successful iconic American brands, suffused with culturally charged myths, provide a kind of resolution to social and cultural contradictions (Holt, 2004). Chinese brand success in Eastern Europe has been explained as satisfying the need for safety and authenticity in these regions (Coulter, Price, and Feick, 2003; Manning and Uplisashvili, 2007). In other words, an analysis of brand meaning derives not only from networks of users, producers, and other brand builders, but also from local and global events such as definitive moments in a nation's history, consumer boycotts, and anti-globalization movements (Gerth, 2003; Holt, 2002; Klein, Ettenson, and Morris, 1998; Schroeder, 2009). Furthermore, as can be seen in Western brands' impact on global culture, global branding practices influence local culture (Dong and Tian, 2009). Brands, brand meanings, and brand values can be understood as cultural, political, and ideological forms, and brand researchers and others are encouraged to develop new brand culture approaches.

The use of historical culture and mythmaking in global brand development

Historical culture provides a rich foundation for branding processes and practices; and deploying history and heritage in brand development hardly requires a leap of faith given how deeply and extensively the past infiltrates everyday life. We have, as one writer put it, more or less emerged from our antecedents (Lowenthal, 1985). For example, two concepts – craft in Europe and marketing skill in the US – have been evoked to describe the importance of history and heritage in luxury brand development (Kapferer, 2006). Although the impact of history and the past assumes many different forms, looking at cultural and historical codes of strong brands can provide particularly useful insights into branding practices (Holt, 2004). If historical awareness is a central feature of brand development, it is equally important to recognize how the past is implicitly filtered through the present (Lowenthal, 1985). Our compulsions to select and reject certain aspects of the past are heavily determined by our present-day proclivities – and our approach to branding and brand development is deeply indebted to this particular understanding of the past and the present as being mutually inclusive.

Human experience is inundated with relics and residues, pervasive histories and memories, and this includes retro-styling in numerous product categories, such as coffee makers, radios, and watches (Brown, 1999). Retro retail stores ensure the past is never far behind. Retroscapes, such as living history museums, retro-themed shopping malls, and entire geographic locations, such as Hawaii, create instant blasts into various pasts (e.g., Borgerson and Schroeder, 2003; Boyer, 1992; Brown, 1999; Brown, Hirschman, and Maclaran, 2000; Costa and Bamossy, 1995; Maclaran and Stevens, 1998). The past two decades, in particular, reveal evidence of a growing tendency of brand strategists to mine the past through such means as retro-design, retro-aesthetics, and heritage marketing hybrids (e.g., Brown, 2001; Brown, Hirschman, and Maclaran, 2000). In some cases it seems that the presentation and consumption of the past in marketing is part and parcel of the postmodern condition, in which boundaries in time and space, between past, present, and future, are blurred (Brown, 1995). The appeal of the retro has also been understood in terms of secularization (Belk, Wallendorf, and Sherry, 1989; O'Guinn and Belk, 1989).

The investment of historical culture into branding campaigns can invoke nostalgia and feelings of being reconnected with an authentic past, and tap latent religious affinities (Askegaard and Kjeldgaard, 2007; Belk, Wallendorf, and Sherry, 1989; Holbrook, 1994; Holbrook and Schindler, 1996; Stern, 1992). Some brand managers consider authenticity equivalent to a notion of brand essence – the distillation of what the brand stands for and promises to offer the consumer (Brown, Kozinets, and Sherry, 2003). The consumer's search for authenticity, however, is such a deeply ingrained desire that its study constitutes a central pursuit in contemporary marketing research. Whereas from a brand culture perspective, notions such as "essence" and "authentic" are contested – their apparent meanings subject to rethinking and contextualizing – the ways in which brands aim to achieve such goals remain significant.

The sacred space of brand myth

One of the foundations of consumer culture concerns distinctions between the *sacred* and the *profane* (Douglas and Isherwood, 1982). In our focus on brand culture, we begin with the sacred in brand development, particularly as the sacred evokes other places, other times, and in that way often has connections to historical, cultural, and aesthetic traditions. The sacred has been described as an ideology focused on natural imagery, communalism, manual labor, the rural, interpersonal cooperation, and the consumption of simple, self-produced, or naturally derived products and services (Hirschman, 1991). In this sense, we can witness sacredness at work in brands.

The properties of sacredness primarily reside in the tendency to present the sacred as something of an entirely different order, sometimes evoking negative responses toward the sacred. Consumer researcher Russell Belk and his colleagues have proposed, "the sacred involves magic, shamanism, animism, and totemism in some societies. Such societies often accord sacred status to components of the natural environment that are revered, feared, worshipped, and treated with the utmost respect" (1989, p. 2). In other words, elements related to religion, and historical and traditional cultural belief systems, offer a reservoir of sacred source material. The sacred is powerful, and can affect people, times, places, experiences, and things it touches. The sacred can inspire reverence, awe, commitment, sacrifice, and mercurial extremes, such as ecstasy, peak experience, flow, and liminality. Moreover, the sacred has the potential to flatten social distinctions and enables participants to gain release from social straightjackets through fantasy (Belk, Wallendorf, and Sherry, 1989).

Making the sacred specific can occur via representation by means of an object; via emergence from ritual rules guiding the ordinary person's behavior; and via development from repetition of myth, which possesses occult features defying logical comprehension. In contemporary religious practices, the sacred also refers specifically to "certain gods, shrines, clothing, days, relics, and songs" (Belk, Wallendorf, and Sherry, 1989, p. 2). A potential vision of materiality emerges here – of human subjects and sacred objects and images in a co-creative relationship – and suggests intersections of consumers, consumption objects and experiences, and consumer culture.

The quality of sacredness serves to define the most notable and identifiable features of religion (Eliade, 1959). In contrast, the secular refers to those things lacking in religious significance. Religion is not merely related to a notion of god, or a sacred person, often found at the center of a religious doctrine; sacredness here relates to "the idea of the sacred in general" (Marcel Mauss, in Ferrarotti, 2007, p. 182). Religion encompasses ancestral or cultural traditions, and their historical and mythological texts, which are invested with varying degrees of personal and religious faith (Savage, 2008). Religion constitutes a distinctive and extraordinary realm of experience, replete with sacred features (Pargament, Magyar-Russell, and Murray-Swank, 2005). The secular can sometimes become intertwined with the sacred following some manner of transformation, such as contamination, or a mixing and blurring of the two realms. Secular objects can gather or lose sacredness depending on the nature of their journeys through time and space (Belk, Wallendorf, and Sherry, 1989). In this way, the historical past and its objects can gain a sacred quality, being consumed through specific channels in the present. The converse also holds true – that sacred things can lose their sacredness.

Places can also become sacred. A sacred place includes notions of space and time, geography and temporality: sacred places can be located variously on a map, a timeline, or a temporal circle (Ostwalt, 2003). It must at the very least be "uncrowded" if not empty in order to allow for the projection of fantasy and the evolution of myth. A sacred place thus serves "as a void into which myth comes into being" (Oswalt, 2003, p. 79). Along these lines, one could argue that history and the spaces it connotes constitute a kind of sacred place, because history can be considered both cyclical and temporally definite. It is as replete with characters and things as it is devoid of specifics that enable us to walk through it on a sure footing. History is, in fact, the perfect sacred place, that void, or cultural black hole, within which the projection of fantasies and myths first evolves.

Myths in global brand development

Historical culture often plays an important role in developing mythic brands. As such, brands draw upon stories of history and its heroes, and reflect cultural contradictions and conflicts

(Maclaran, Otnes, and Fischer, 2007; Schroeder, 2009). Brand myths, in particular, emerge from networks of stories about legendary persons, heroic individuals, and personified ideas that circulate and re-adapt to changing mores (Holt, 2004). All of these historical stories, part fiction and part fact, provide raw material for the development of brand myths.

Consider the British Royal Family as a long-standing, mythic global brand. This storied and popular "brand" for example draws power and resonance from the legend of King Arthur, by which Diana becomes the "fairy-tale princess" or "People's Princess" and Queen Elizabeth I is the "Great White Goddess" (Maclaran, Otnes, and Fischer, 2007). Even the fabled stories of King George VI's and Queen Elizabeth's walks through London after the blitz of the Second World War to raise money for the war effort are equal part myth and fact. The British monarchy functions like a brand in strategically maintaining "continuity (maintaining heritage and symbolism); visibility (having a meaningful and prominent public profile); strategy (anticipating and enacting change); sensitivity (rapid response to crises); respectability (retaining public favor) and empathy (acknowledging that brand ownership resides with the public)" (Balmer, 2009, p. 639). Indeed, many lauded historical events and individuals can be understood through the lens of brands and branding practices.

Mythmaking thrives on contradictions that emerge between what people think of the world and the facts of concrete reality. According to Holt, iconic brands must first be conceived with classic mythic features that address social concerns. Iconic brands tend to succeed when they adequately capture social contradictions and provide empathetic interpretations of prevalent social ideologies. Holt further suggests that a myth market is tantamount to a national conversation in which various contenders exemplifying a particular view of national ideology compete to offer the most persuasive myth through their cultural products. To succeed in such a market, brand myths must resonate with consumer desire. From here, Holt goes on to argue that a cultural branding approach can "identify the most valuable type of myth for the brand to perform at a particular historical juncture, and then provide specific direction to creative partners on how to compose the myth" (2004, p. 218). He draws on the model of American cultural branding to show how brand myths re-invent themselves by stretching and shifting focus to suit changing times. Carefully targeting appropriate myths not only engages the "knowledge of the country's key existing and emerging myth markets," but also becomes a means to subsequently claim political and cultural authority over these myths (Holt, 2004, p. 218).

An identity myth develops from a multi-level process beginning with a synopsis. A synopsis of the myth "describes the identity anxieties the myth should address and the way in which the myth will resolve these anxieties" (Holt, 2004, p. 218). An identity myth also should acknowledge "the populist world in which the myth will be located, and the strategy for the brand to develop an authentic voice within this world," and, finally, develop "the brand's charismatic aesthetic, namely, an original communication code that is organic to the populist world" (Holt, 2004, p. 219). Once the right myth market is targeted, and the brand is utilized by consumers to satisfy their identity desires, the market myth will require further development, including reinvention, in order to maintain its original relevance. Coke, for example, tapped varying cultural strains during different historical periods, such as American patriotism during the Second World War, suburban nuclear paranoia in the 1960s, and racial tension in the 1970s (Holt, 2004).

The significance of bringing culture to bear on brands and branding lies in its capacity to help brand managers as well as brand researchers acknowledge the formulation of cultural meanings by various actors – whether positive, negative, or neutral. Consumer movements, somewhat surprisingly, can become powerful catalysts in the development of brand myths. Anti-brand movements fighting for greater transparency can force companies to refresh their branding paradigms. Still, consumers are "revolutionary only insofar as they assist entrepreneurial firms to tear down the old branding paradigm and create opportunities for companies that understand emerging new principles" (Holt, 2002, p. 89).

The marketplace has been a mythic and symbolic reservoir to develop narratives of identities for various brand authors (Elliott and Wattanasuwan, 1998). Brands in their capacity as cultural forms in marketing research can illuminate the cultural dynamics of consumption and the formulation of cultural meanings, such as the cultural narratives and myths that various actors adopt in everyday life (e.g., Holt, 2002;

Klein, 1999). For example, the Starbucks effect not only accelerated the anti-global brand movement in the United States but also forwarded a different myth – that of the independent coffeehouse as an intimate space that supports private enterprise (Thompson and Arsel, 2004).

Global brands can embody global myths. Brand mythology may move beyond national cultures and boundaries and become part of global mythology and global branding practices, which, in turn, influence how brands develop (Askegaard, 2006; Cayla and Arnould, 2008; Strizhakova, Coulter, and Price, 2008). Further, brand myth markets extend national boundaries and participate in global commercial "ideoscapes" (Appadurai, 1990; Arnould and Tissier-Desbordes, 2005; Askegaard, 2006). For example, the product category of extra virgin olive oil successfully draws upon mythic images of "the Mediterranean Diet" and the Mediterranean region's delicious and "real" gustatory discourses to capture a regional self-understanding of extra virgin as both modern and authentic (Meneley, 2007). Similarly, Georgian beer draws upon mythic images of Caucasian peoples and Soviet-era "productionism" to frame Georgians as both European and rooted in a particular region (Manning and Uplisashvili, 2007).

It has been argued that in the United States and some former Eastern Bloc countries, consuming globally branded goods to communicate personal identity becomes a means to participate in the global myth of modern world citizenship (Strizhakova, Coulter, and Price, 2008). This argument responds to the contention that a key metaphor of global brands involves modern identity, and moreover, identity construction via consumer practices (Askegaard, 2006). Others have described brands as metaphors that authenticate the modern, global, and self-actualizing consumer (Cayla and Arnould, 2008). In the process of self-actualization, consumers often have unstable desires and values that do not bridge the gap between perception and reality. These gaps are central in the commercial success of brand myths in contemporary markets (Holt and Cameron, 2010). The gaps also provide the requisite spaces for the creation of fantasy, nostalgia, and sacred emotion via the representation of history and cultural legend.

Brand identity and consumer identity

Brand identity plays an important role in the branding market-place, and has been an essential concept in strategic brand research since brand guru Wally Olins' differentiation of brand identity from corporate identity (1989). Brand identity can be understood as a means to construct and strengthen corporate representation via brand names, logos, symbols, characters, spokespersons, and slogans. Brand identity refers to the specific vantage point from which brand builders intend consumers to perceive their brands, their company, and their brand-related products and services. Brand identity is not simply the name of a brand or its external visual appearance; brands embody cultural values (Csaba and Bengtsson, 2006). To more fully comprehend and address a cultural approach to brand identity, we consider important issues from brand management literature, contemporary social theory, and cultural studies.

Using a managerial perspective, brand identity has been conceptualized as a comprehensive entity that filters different qualities of brands – a brand identity prism (Kapferer, 2012). Brand researcher Jean-Noël Kapferer's influential model of brand identity reflects six components: the physical facets of the brand; the relationship between the brand and its consumers; the consumers from the perspective of brand builders; brand personality; culture (values); and consumer conceptions of what the brand means (Kapferer, 2012). Kapferer argues that several facets of the brand identity prism are "interrelated," and that "the content of one facet echoes that of another," and in so doing, constructs "a well-structured entity" (2012, p. 187). This well-structured entity is often identified and targeted by brand managers in developing a strong brand. This notion of brand identity favors the significance of senders (brand builders) over consumers, and also employs the brand strategist's view, confirming that though the brand manager's dominant role in the construction of brand identity creates strong brand exclusion, it does not weaken the consumer's relevance and value systems (Kapferer, 2012). According to him, brand strategists might draw upon consumer values, but ultimately interpret brand identity in ways that represent the organization's strategy.

Another approach conceives of a brand's core identity as generating distinct associations in the minds of consumers

(Aaker, 1996). From this perspective, for consumers, brand identity hovers between core identity and extended identity – or the brand as product, organization, person, and symbol. Core identity stands for a timeless and central essence of the brand, which in turn derives from the organization's cardinal beliefs and core competencies involving the brand. A notion of brand essence further develops this system: "a single thought that captures the soul of the brand" (Aaker and Joachimsthaler, 2009, p. 45). Brand essence is a versatile identity bank of sorts from which various identities can be mined, combined, and re-invested with new meanings through brand communication, though always in keeping with the essence of brand identity.

In addition to brand essence, brands can be conceptualized as part of an identity system (de Chernatony and Dall'Olmo Riley, 1998). Here, brand identity operates as a carrier that a brand deploys to disseminate its individuality and distinctions across different groups of consumers. Multi-faceted brand identity derives from a company's vision, culture, positioning, personality, relationships, and self-presentation. A brand employs the company as a center where brand strategists gather various interpretations from different groups within the company (de Chernatony, 2001). The interpretations, according to this perspective, would include interpretations of the company's vision and culture; the people behind the brand; the positioning strategy; company personality, which conveys certain functional and emotional attributes; internal and external relationships with consumers and stakeholders; and finally ways of integrating these various facts in creating a comprehensive identity that enables consumers and stakeholders to easily grasp and digest the essence of the brand.

In a nutshell, brand strategists emphasize ways of inspiring corporate employees to commit themselves to the values the brand promotes, reinforce them, and adapt them to the needs of customers and stakeholders (e.g., Borgerson et al., 2009). It is from these combined, complex efforts that the essence of the brand emerges (de Chernatony, 2001). This approach tends to under-emphasize the co-creation aspects of brands, in which both consumers and producers contribute to brand meaning and value, as well as the brand culture approach, wherein culture represents an explicit third dimension of brand development.

Thus, we are reminded that models of brand identity represent only one aspect of understanding brand development. The next step involves translating brand identity and communicating brand essence, separating out core and extended identity into various forms, and thereafter disseminating a brand message in ways that both stimulate consumers and resonate with brand identity (Csaba and Bengtsson, 2006).

In contemporary culture, consumption can be seen as increasingly meaning oriented, transcending merely functional attributes. Consumers often think of brands as symbolic resources for the construction and maintenance of identity (Elliott and Wattanasuwan, 1998). In simple terms, the consumer builds an identity beyond symbolic tangible objects and uses brands to convey cultural, personal, and social meanings. In social and cultural theories, this kind of consumer has been described as "the performing self" (Featherstone, 1991, p. 187), or working on "a narrative of self-identity" (Thompson, 1995, p. 210). From this perspective, consumer identities are reflective and dynamic. They are both changeable and essential, and are often understood through the notion of *identification*, which is constituted through narratives of the self or collective selfhood in acts of identification (Giddens, 1991; Hall, 1996). Identities are formulated through association with others or something outside the self and articulated through relations with particular people, places, and material goods (Du Gay, 1996). Identities comprise multiple, conflicting, and contested aspects and represent many cultural attributes at work, such as the struggle for social status (e.g., Miller et al., 1998).

Theories of consumer culture tend to question the dominance of brand identity – the corporate ideal for the brand – in the consumer's construction of identity, suggesting that consumers are, in fact, more than well equipped to manipulate brand identity to articulate their own intended identities. For example, consumer researchers Richard Elliott and Krit Wattanasuwan argue that the consumer's self-identity constructed through brands does not always – and predictably – affect brand identity (1998). They show how contemporary consumers use brands as measures of virtue that convey consistency of meaning, and how brands act as cultural resources, protecting consumers against loss of individuality, discontinuity, and social decomposition.

Managers and consumers thus use brand identity not merely to establish and communicate fundamental cultural categories, such as social status, gender, and age, but also to protect themselves behind the shield of brand consistency and dependability from identity breakdown and fragmentation (Elliott and Wattanasuwan, 1998; Thompson, 1995). Brand identity is therefore defined in terms of cultural form by managers, and subsequently decoded by consumers deploying it as social and personal identity. In this book, we draw upon theories of brand identity supplemented and enhanced by brand culture approaches to understand multiple perspectives and actors in brand development. We discuss an important aspect of brand identity in use, that is, the ways in which managerial workers and consumers engage brands in their capacity as symbolic resources.

Brand image and the imagined community

Traditionally, brand identity and its attendant values are thought to be communicated to the consumer through strategic brand communication. Communication presents a brand identity, which comes to life as a brand image in the mind of the consumer, enabling the consumer to evaluate the virtue of purchasing the promoted products or services. Ideally, brand identity should be reflected in the consumer's brand image. Brand identity and brand image play almost equally important roles in the work of brand managers and in the choices consumers make. Part of the challenge, however, is that different cultural backgrounds and experiences lay the foundations for different, and sometimes oppositional, brand images. Brand actors imagine different communities of brands and discuss brands along varying lines of thought, and draw different conclusions.

In sociologist Benedict Anderson's view, imagined community refers to a nation, or a community, that is politically constructed and socially imagined by individuals who perceive themselves as belonging to a certain group (2006). Imagined communities come in different shapes and sizes, and perform different functions. A nation is a culturally imagined community, and consists of "historical ethno-symbolism," which refers to "historical clusters, or heritages, of myths, memories, values and symbols for cultural community formation" (Leifer, 2000, p. 12).

Some scholars of branding practice have indicated the fragility of an imagined community limited by national boundaries. Cayla and Eckhardt, for example, pointed to strategic solutions employed in Asian branding. They discovered that Asian brand managers tend to highlight universal practices of globalization that simulate "a generic, hyper-urban, and multicultural experience [...] infused with diverse cultural referents, and therefore contribute to the creation of an imagined Asia as urban, modern, and multicultural" (Cayla and Eckhardt, 2008, p. 216). In other words, the "imagined Asia" as a global brand is characterized by modern, metropolitan, and multicultural forms. For instance, both Singapore-based retail brand 77th Street and Hong Kong-based fashion brand Giordano emphasize Asian branding and Asia.

In the Chinese context, the concept of an Imagined China evokes diverse meanings depending on who is doing the imagining. Different brand actors imagine differently. We propose that an Imagined China, while it connotes a certain cultural homogeneity, also has the potential to cross national boundaries and express a unique imaginary with potentially global relevance.

Brand culture in the Chinese context

As we have argued, brand culture is not simply a matter of drawing upon cultural resources within the branding process. Rather, brands participate in, and co-create, culture. In the Chinese context, one aspect of brand culture often centers on the representation of historical Chinese cultural resources, including representations of Chinese religion, history, tradition, and cultural myths. The three most predominant philosophical and religious systems of Taoism, Confucianism, and Buddhism have left their footprints everywhere in the Chinese landscape (Hucker, 1995). These systems have exerted a tremendous impact on Chinese ideology, and have provided ethical guidelines for the proper behavior of individuals for more than 2000 years (Thompson, 1996).

Taoism, which sought to promote the inner peace of individuals and harmony with surroundings, is characterized by the

Three Jewels of Tao – compassion, moderation, and humility (Palls, 2008). A primary belief is that every element has positive and negative energy (yin or yang, the two poles of primordial energy), which encourages the balance of life (Bidgoli, 2010). The principles of Tao influenced Chinese alchemy, astrology, cuisine, martial arts, traditional medicine, feng shui, and various styles of qigong breath training disciplines (Palls, 2008).

Confucianism, based on the teachings and writings of the philosophers Confucius and Mencius, is an ethical system that sought to cultivate good behavior in individuals. In it, "filial piety" and "gentleness and sincerity" are considered among the greatest of virtues. Whereas "filial piety" must be shown toward the old, the living, and the dead, including ancestors, and probably explains the widespread trope of nostalgia in Chinese cultural practices, "gentleness and sincerity" have been particularly influential in Chinese aesthetics (Dawson, 2003).

Based on evidence in the Dunhuang manuscripts, discovered in China in the early 20th century, Chinese Buddhism arrived from India with monks traveling on the Silk Road during the Han Dynasty (220 BCE–200 CE). The importance of Buddhism can be gauged by the status of the great teacher Xuan Zang's pilgrimage to India and his return to China armed with the tenets of Buddhism, which remains the single greatest event in Chinese cultural history (Nan, 1998). Chinese Buddhism advocates faith (Whitfield, 2004). Some have suggested "polemical and political attacks from hostile Chinese quarters forced Buddhists to respond with apologia and ultimately reshape Buddhism into something the Chinese would find not only inoffensive, but attractive" (Craig, 1998, p. 81). This explains Buddhism's adaptation to existing Chinese religions, such as Taoism, and the advocacy of tolerance (Nan, 1998). Given the importance of historical cultures in Chinese history, one could argue for their introduction into brand development as a cogent means to build strong brands. That is to say, bringing the sacred to branding activities by investing brand development with aspects of Chinese Confucianism, Taoism, and Buddhism has the potential to refresh and reinvent patterns and styles of consumption.

The creation of regional Asian brands and the construction of a transnational imagined Asia could function as the way to build Asian brands and shape a transnational imagined community in the increasingly culturally globalized world (Cayla and Eckhardt, 2008). Four processes make Asian brand culture notable in this culture-centered world: 1) synchronicity and the construction of cultural proximity; 2) *de-territorialization*, the unmooring of brands from specific places; 3) the construction of a multicultural collage; and 4) the creation of a mosaic Asian culture (Cayla and Eckhardt, 2008). However, how to de-territorialize and unmoor brands from the Chinese context in order to express a mosaic Asian branding culture remains a key question for Chinese brand builders. A number of brand strategists in China and abroad have suggested that investing branding with the Chinese past is the proper way to facilitate the introduction of Chinese brands into a diverse Asian brand culture.

Retrospective branding, or investing branding with the past, enjoys a long history in China. Research into the history of Chinese branding has shown that although place names stamped on wares to mark their origin were common in China during the Han Dynasty (220 BCE–200 CE), and the first documented sophisticated brand in the world was in the Song Dynasty period (960–1127), brands in imperial China have generally not developed solely as commercial instruments (Eckhardt and Bengtsson, 2007). Rather, they have served a variety of social purposes ranging from signifying affiliation with the Imperial Palace to demonstrating the worth of a family name (Hamilton and Lai, 1989). However, some expressly commercial brands have emerged since the Qing Dynasty. For example, White Rabbit (a needle brand) and Tong Ren Tang (a traditional Chinese medicine brand that continues to thrive today) provide evidence of distinctive symbolic brands. White Rabbit refers to a well-known Chinese legend, *Chang'e benyue* (Chang'e's ascent to the moon). *Tong ren tang* means "to help people for good public order," which follows in the footsteps of the revered tradition in the Chinese medical industry, and exploits the character of *ren* in Confucianism that means humaneness or gentleness (Cochran, 2006). Both these symbolic brands thus reinforce connections to the past.

Chinese aesthetics are influenced by Taoism, Confucianism, and Buddhism, which share common ground in the concept of harmony in nature (Ferroa, 2003). In Chinese ideology, nature, which is aligned with notions of self-creativity, includes heaven, earth, and the human world. All interact with one other harmoniously (Greenberg, 2007), because "the world is one continuous field of *qi* (literally the breath of life), with each phenomenon not a separate thing but a temporary form within it, like a whirlpool in a stream" (Barnhill, 2005, p. 1). Chinese arts, "rather than the shallow description of surface reality [are] the evocation of the spirit of phenomena" (Barnhill, 2005, p. 16). When the artist has seized the subtle *qi*, his or her work will vividly present the spirit of *qi*. In this way, the artist joins in the creation of nature. Anyone desiring the ability to capture *qi* must assiduously follow these principles. The practice of attainment comprises ridding oneself of the illusion of a separate self and urging oneself to succeed. It also involves focusing on the subject until direct communion is achieved (Barnhill, 2005). Consequently, the key concern in historical Chinese aesthetics consisted in achieving balance between the self and nature, or between the inner and the outer (Dale, 2004). Emotions grew from interactions with environments, and nature was conceived as "an ongoing dynamic of stimulus and response among all things," encompassing human activities (Barnhill, 2005, p. 16).

In early accounts of poetics such as the "Great Preface" to the *Book of Song* (*Shi jing*; 1st century BCE), for example, poetry was considered to be a voicing of responses. There was a strong correlation between the outer "scene" (*jing*) and inner feelings or emotional response (*qing*). A great poet was able to harmoniously blend the two (Barnhill, 2005). In painting, qualities that distinguished the painter involved self-cultivation and self-expression (Craig, 1998, p. 68). Because nature includes humans, human culture corresponds with nature, an understanding that is emphasized in *The Literary Mind and the Carving of Dragons*, a foundational text of Chinese aesthetic criticism (Barnhill, 2005).

It was this correlation that led to the development of the Chinese *wen*, which means both literature and culture. The *wen* of humans is an expression of human culture, especially Chinese traditional literature and art. Accordingly, words written by a poet are equivalent to the tracks a bird makes in sand. The notion of *wen* gradually evolved, becoming "a semantically multivalent term" that now refers to "physical markings, patterns on coloured woven silk and painted designs of carriages as well as writing, literature and culture" (Craig, 1998, p. 69).

Consequently, in Chinese aesthetics, culture is natural, though this naturalness can be achieved only if the doer behaves in accordance with nature's patterns, spontaneously, and in keeping with his or her real inner nature, rather than following the ego's desires (Barnhill, 2005). Accordingly, Chinese aesthetic appreciation focuses mainly on harmony and *wen*, both of which are experiential and essentially "moving."

Despite the importance of the aforementioned concepts in Chinese historical culture, there has been little research conducted on how to employ them toward the global development of Chinese brands. Historical culture, which includes imagined communities, aesthetic principles, and sacred concepts, can play a key role in the development of global brands, because history offers a kind of *tabula rasa* for people to imagine and reimagine, and myth offers them the means of exploring and imagining cultural identities, including brand identities.

Global vs. local

A key issue within global branding concerns global versus local strategy and thinking. Social theorist Jonathan Friedman has indicated "the production of local difference on a global scale" (1995, p. 135), specifically advancing concerns about the status of the local within the global. In particular, Friedman is concerned with whether the production of local culture is actually a newly radical transformation, and whether a new cultural world order is moving toward creolized commodification crossing national borders. He asks questions regarding "how these objectified and politicized phenomena" relate "to everyday social practice in a place" (Friedman, 1995, p. 135). Friedman ultimately deals with how deeply objectified and politicized issues actually relate to daily social activities; whether they enjoy an exclusive position in lived identity; whether models of habitual living conserve the global, and whether or not everyday identity draws on the public rhetoric of group identity. How do objectified and politicized issues translate in a small, stable localized social group? In other words, Friedman's production of local difference on a global scale refers to the sustaining of local cultural exclusivity but in keeping with the pace of up-to-date global production.

Consumer researcher Güliz Ger argues that local companies or governments could strengthen the perceived, appreciated, and available cultural resources for "outlocal" global competition in the global brand development process. She contends that time and energy are needed to discover latent local resources before their value can be appreciated. She claims that local governments need to develop foresight and use innovative thinking; deploy appropriate strategies; exploit available skills; further refine existing expertise; and build supportive political environments in order for local companies to be able to out-localize (Ger, 1999). In so doing, local cultural recourses can become alternatives in global markets. In specific terms, local firms could begin to design products to satisfy consumer needs in local conditions similar to their own – that is, with economic or social cousins in different parts of the world (Ger, 1999).

Ger's local to global branding approach is not without certain implications. First, the consolidation of locally perceived cultural capital in the production of branded culture oriented products for alternative, foreign markets is worthwhile only if the potential volume of those foreign markets exceeds the needs of local markets. For example, although the taste and demand for Vietnamese restaurants, Reggae music, Egyptian novels, Chinese films, Indian clothes, and Afghan jewelry in the US and Europe are growing, the desired volume cannot compete with the vastly more ingrained preferences of American and European consumers for things like bread, beer, and wine. Second, stressing local cultural capital to produce user-centered, low-price products and services to meet the needs of similar markets elsewhere might be a losing battle, as alternative markets are really a euphemism for low-income foreign markets, the profit margins of which are generally low – a fact that compels local firms to resort to a low price strategy. The current unhappy predicament of Chinese exporters provides ample evidence of the negative impact of such strategies on company profits.

Consumer researchers Søren Askegaard and Dannie Kjeldgaard advocate using "reputational capital" and product place imagery to make local products global through local branding activities. By their account, reputed local resources are the basis of the high quality of local products. They have the capacity to invest their products with the high quality that derives from the responsible production ideology of sustainable small-scale production (Askegaard and Kjeldgaard, 2007). In short, reputed local capital has the potential to create iconic-authentic or quasi-authentic value, which, in itself, can discharge its own variety of social and/or utilitarian function. These two approaches are linked, in that both draw attention to the latent value of local cultural "authenticity" in the creation of distinction leading to greater consumption.

For their part, Cayla and Eckhardt look at how certain brand managers attempt to spin new webs of interconnectedness by establishing a transnational imagined Asia. These brand managers focus on the common experience of globalization and diverse cultural referents of local differences to stimulate an all-encompassing, urban, and multicultural experience. In their development, Asia – and Asian – communicate a global brand that is modern, urban, and multicultural. Their brand globalization model uses global systems to combine ubiquitous instances of local difference towards a new image of Asia. In the Cayla and Eckhardt model, modern and urban features frame the Asian past (2008).

In China, the emergence of Chinese brand culture, invested with historical Chinese culture, expresses what has been called "the production of local difference on a global scale" (Friedman, 1990, 1995). But what does this say about the position of Chinese brand culture in a global context? Chinese cultural branding is something new and still transforming. Despite growing exports, increasing appreciation of Chinese currency, and the rise of consumerism in contemporary Chinese society, the number of Chinese brands included in top global brands lists remains low, perhaps indicating that Chinese global branding still has a way to go. Regardless, China has a long and weighty history, which is to say that Chinese brand culture will almost inevitably creolize and transnationalize.

On the one hand, history is often conservative, and popular models of lived identity typically preserve Chinese habits and mores. On the other hand, Chinese brand culture also relates to modern realities that absorb and co-opt group identities which borrow from larger global identities. Although Chinese brand culture derives from a stable and continuous regime of local meanings grounded in local social groups, it also draws upon international ideologies and meanings. In keeping with Friedman's theories of local culture in the global marketplace, the development of a distinctly Chinese brand culture is an achievable goal. Historical culture and social contradictions can become the basis on which to develop new commercial myths.

Fashion and fashion systems in the development of global consumer culture

Fashion forms a strong basis not only behind the origins of global consumer culture, but also behind contemporary diffusions of consumer culture around the world. According to sociologist Chandra Mukerji, consumer goods bear symbolic and cultural meanings throughout the processes of production and consumption (1983). Diversified commercial mythmaking strategies produce new commercial myths and new cultural forms with the construction of new popular memories and counter-memories (e.g., Thompson and Tian, 2008). Concepts and theories from fashion and fashion systems offer insight into the aesthetics, culture, and values of (local) brand globalization.

Because fashion has many connotations and definitions, fashion culture has received various levels of attention from scholars in diverse academic disciplines such as cultural studies, management, and psychology (e.g., Barnard, 2002; Bruzzi and Gibson, 2000; Davis, 1992; Moore and Birtwistle, 2004). Fashion invokes a wide range of branding issues: the visions of charismatic designers, notions of luxury, icons of attraction, and concepts of consumer taste, appearance, and identity.

Fashion fulfills two distinct psychological needs: social identification and distinction (Gronow, 1997). From this perspective, fashion should be a means of both distinguishing oneself from others and adapting oneself to social needs. Cultural historian Regina Lee Blaszczyk categorizes fashion into four M's: *mode*, or how to dress; *manners*, or how to express oneself; *mores*, or how to live; and *markets*, or how to gain demographic and psychological definition (2007). The process of making decisions for social identification and distinction through fashion, or through other cultural forms, creates a context for what has been called "sign domination," emphasis on social structure, and "sign experimentation," relying on consumer agency, that is, active participation in envisioning brand images (Murray, 2002).

Fashion is a process in at least two senses: "it is a market-driven cycle of consumer desire and demand; and it is a modern mechanism for the fabrication of the self. It is in this respect that fashion operates as a fulcrum for negotiating the meeting of internal and external worlds" (Evans and Breward, 2005, p. 2). Fashion, in its capacity as a social phenomenon that has influenced various fields, including clothing, design, music, and sports, can be understood as a kind of symbolic mode of production and consumption, what sociologist Yuniya Kawamura describes as an "institutionally constructed and culturally diffused" feature (2005, p. 44).

Fashion scholars have examined the social nature of fashion from a cultural viewpoint, highlighting the people, the networks, and the institutions that constitute the fashion system (Crane, 2000; Kawamura, 2004). For example, an influential four-fold description of fashion systems uses fashion's interactions with individuals and society, and its linkage of macro and micro continuums (Cholachatpinyo et al., 2002). At a *macro-subjective* level, fashion is an existential global phenomenon that reflects economics cycles, lifestyle trends, and social needs. Second, in a *macro-objective* realm, fashion trends become tangible concepts that symbolize the lifestyles of individuals and organizations, including fashion investors, designers, manufacturers, and marketing people. Third, at a *micro-objective* level, individuals interact with fashion in the marketplace, selecting the products of fashion in order to develop their looks and fit into certain contexts. Fourth, in a *micro-subjective* field, individuals cultivate certain looks in order to fulfill their social and cultural aspirations. In all the above accounts, fashion constitutes creativity and innovation, and represents the spirit of the time, or *zeitgeist*, reflecting existential social concerns and psychological needs (Blaszczyk, 2007; Cholachatpinyo et al., 2002; Evans and Breward, 2005).

The fashion system, in turn, involves all the people, networks and institutions involved in the creation, transformation, and recreation of symbolic meanings of cultural objects over time (e.g., Barthes, 1990; Kaiser, 1996; Solomon et al., 2006). Cultural objects, of course, include branded products. In this sense, fashion operates as a social and symbolic system that involves people, networks, and institutions, all of which, through production and consumption, convey certain meanings and embody brand value. Meaning flows through branded products that circulate as consumer goods bought and sold by individuals in various rituals and social activities (McCracken, 1986; Thompson and Haytko, 1997). Therefore, the concept fashion systems refers to the comprehensive material and commercial discourse in which fashion products are produced, marketed, consumed, manipulated, appreciated, and discussed by makers, marketers, buyers, and observers.

Fashion discourse, symbolic production, and consumption of fashion goods

Fashion touches all cultural forms, and music, art, movies, museums, public events, and clothing have been investigated from managerial and cultural perspectives. A consumer perspective, however, produces a number of debates about fashion and branding. The idea that consumers explore their identities through fashion has been extensively explored for at least 20 years. Fashion theorist Fred Davis, for instance, articulates how fashion and clothing express consumer identity, which might include certainty and ambivalence through social status, gender, and sexuality (1992). Fashion researchers Louise Crewe and Alison Goodrum studied how British designer Paul Smith stimulates consumer imaginations and generates consumer desires via his successful – and global – lifestyle brand (2000). Brand researcher Bruno Remaury has written that "fashion is based on creating a need where, in reality, there is none. Fashion is a factory that manufactures desire" (quoted in Tungate, 2008, p. 8). Indeed, some critics have argued that fashion discourse seldom empowers a consumer point of view, that fashion research typically favors the dominant ideologies of fashion creators and marketers, and that consumer perception gets shunted off into a narrow, homogeneous category.

In an effort to correct this bias, some scholars have begun applying folk theories to open up the understanding of fashion systems (Thompson and Haytko, 1997). Specifically, folk theory enables discussions about the nature of self and society, and provides room for consumers to freely describe their perceptions and experiences of fashion. Such research produces productive insights that counter prevalent notions of fashion systems from the producer and marketer's vantage point. They reveal how consumers adjust to and modify fashion systems to match their everyday environment. In other words, consumers are able to reinterpret fashion by countervailing dominant fashion meanings and intentions. This insight forms the heart of the consumer perspective, illuminating how cultural and consumer processes intersect.

Fashion and myth-making

The myth of the American South helps explain the cultural production process:

> When different commercial mythmakers draw from a cultural mythology, they are also vying for identity value through the strategic and ideological framing of popular memories. Commercial mythmakers' strategic transfigurations of popular memory are structured by an awareness of the counter-memories that are invoked by competing representations that circulate in the mass-mediated myth market. Their diversified strategies to manage these competitive quandaries, in turn, generate new commercial myths and new configurations of popular memories and counter-memories that are projected forward toward changing cultural and marketplace conditions (Thompson and Tian, 2008, p. 611).

In other words, commercial mythmaking strategies generate new cultural forms through many organizations, which join in the symbolic production of cultural objects within a single "universe of belief" (Bourdieu, 1993, p. 15). These institutions often disseminate symbolic meanings to the public through the media, namely through the internet, newspapers, magazines, television, and social media. In the fashion arena, institutions articulate fashion in different ways, such as high fashion and popular, everyday fashion.

Fashion artefacts that inspire belief in the symbolic value of fashion are considered to be high fashion among elite consumers, at times equivalent to the status of high art in intellectual circles. These artefacts contribute to the "ideology of creation," and consolidate the magical aura of high fashion even among non-consumers of high fashion (Bourdieu, 1993). Cultural theorist Angela McRobbie maintains that French and European fashion is interpreted by "the rigidity and elitism of the fine art world" (1998, p. 36). From a critical perspective, fashion belongs to the realm of "specialists in symbolic production" or "elitism" (Featherstone, 1991). In other ways, however, "fashion is a 'popular thing'" (McRobbie, 1998, p. 8). The popular and the elite form two parts of the full scope of contemporary fashion.

The process of symbolic production depends on two basic factors – the display of the symbol and people with the appropriate mentality that will capture it (e.g., Hirschman and Holbrook, 1982; Ligas and Cotte, 1999). Product and brand symbolism literature provides certain insights into the consumption process that consumers use to satisfy certain psychological needs and desires (Escalas, 2004). Branded clothing and popular music, for example, which function largely through visual and aural presence, are said to suggest that people consuming these products are satisfied and concerned with surface appeal. They seek these products because they seek no more than what the surface provides, and for what it suggests about them to observers.

The symbolic quality of branded clothing often materializes through styles, brands, retailer outlets, uniforms, and through membership of particular subcultures (Banister and Hogg, 2006). Music draws upon similar symbolic resources, including what the words sound like against the musical background. Management researcher Yen Tran indicates that "the value which these industries bring about does not go directly to the fashion product, but it enhances the recognition and attraction of the products. In fashion, branding plays a crucial role in driving consumers to keep purchasing" (2008, p. 127). In other words, branding facilitates the expression of fashion and the enhancement of brand value. Journalist Mark Tungate has shown that fashion functions through various independent and intersecting channels, such as advertising, store design, fashion blogging, and celebrity photo shoots in popular magazines, all of which collectively mobilize the symbolic value of fashion and brand image in branded products (2008).

Symbolic consumption refers not simply to consuming fashion items, but also to social practices, such as purchasing newspapers and magazines, visiting museums, watching films, and preparing and eating food (e.g., Hines and Bruce, 2006). All these activities express symbolic meanings that help consumers express their identities in positive and negative fashion, that is who they are and what they stand for, as much as who they are not and what they reject. Products sell and brands resonate when consumers begin to perceive compatibility between symbolic meanings and values and their personal identities.

Notions of brand symbolism develop through interaction with people and groups, through connections made through them, and through interaction with stereotypical images of brands disseminated by groups and learned through hearsay (Erickson, 1996). It is common for consumer judgments about brands to depend inordinately on opinions aired by typical consumers of those brands and products (Hines and Bruce, 2006). Accordingly, Kawamura's description of "consuming fashion as symbolic strategy" contains three components – public consumption, communication, and image (2005, p. 94). In her reading, symbolic meanings and values are visible and noticeable to the consumers of brand products, and these same meanings and values are subsequently conveyed in an equally visible fashion to others, though all consumers are unlikely to swallow brand meanings in the same way and with equal ease.

An influential review of consumer culture research indicated that previous studies of symbolic consumption mainly "draw from semiotic and literary critical theories to analyze the symbolic meanings, cultural ideals, and ideological inducements encoded in popular culture texts and the rhetorical tactics that are used to make these ideological appeals compelling" (Arnould and Thompson, 2005, p. 875). Studies or symbolic consumption mainly focused on "sign domination" and "sign experimentation" (Murray, 2002). As portrayed by consumer researcher Jeff Murray, sign domination tends to engage a structuralist perspective on meaning creation, whereas sign experimentation recalls a psychological point of view that focuses on consumers' creative potential.

Fashion discourses also involve an interpretation of historical themes and contemporary social concerns, often via fashion images. Many global fashion images embrace metaphorical references, which are effectively condensed and constructed from current social concerns or historical themes. Fashion theorist Caroline Evans argues that various historical cultures have been distinctively referenced in fashion products, such as the citation of the Renaissance and Baroque periods in modern fashion (2000). These periods have become emblems via their relocation or dislocation and through appearance as abbreviated images. However, modern fashion images with historical references are subject to the contemporary perspectives of their makers and users, who tend to retrace links and rethink history through selective subjective lenses. Evans suggests that fashion images with historical references illuminate the present with refined images combining complex and contradictory meanings.

Social theorist Walter Benjamin has termed such images "dialectical images" (1999). Ostensibly referencing the past, dialectical images do so selectively, and often in contradiction to their sources. A dialectical image is not grounded in simple comparisons between the past and the present. Rather, it produces new meanings that may conflict radically with prevailing historic meanings (Buck-Morss, 1991). In Benjamin's notion of history, present vision destroys the past to reconstruct it. This process creates a dialectical image. Good or bad, global fashion systems thus create a multitude of distinctive and novel brand images that use a historical touch to address social desires and anxieties. Although various consumer research studies have addressed the significance of fashion within culture generally, it now remains for a comparable body of knowledge to develop regarding similar processes at work in the Chinese context. Global consumer culture has close links with the fashion system, which can be understood through a discussion of the origins and development of global consumer culture.

Global consumer culture and fashion systems

Much has been written about the origins and development of global consumer culture, and about its role in the history of the modern West. After anthropologist Grant McCracken's influential book *Culture and Consumption* (1998a), the most provocative arguments occur in consumer culture studies of the Ottoman Empire in the late 16th and 17th centuries, in the 15th through 18th centuries in England and in 19th-century France (Karababa and Ger, 2011; McKendrick, 1982; Mukerji, 1983; Williams 1982). These studies show that consumer culture in England, France, and the Ottoman Empire underwent changes in tastes, preferences, and buying habits that were as revolutionary as those of the modern world. The consumer revolution has produced a fundamental shift in Western concepts of time, space, society, the individual, the family, and the state. Such changes have introduced new categories of goods, new patterns and sites of purchase, new marketing techniques, new ideas about possessions and materialism, new diffusion patterns, symbols, and patterns of decision making, as well as changed points of reference and class mobility. The aforementioned studies of the history of consumption have not only explored these changes and analyzed their meaning, but have also shown that consumer culture and various fashion systems have collectively contributed to the rise of the modern West.

China has also contributed to the formation of global consumer culture through such products as chinaware, silk, furniture, and tea. Since the Song Dynasty (960–1127 CE), Chinese pottery replete with text and symbolic images has enjoyed wide consumption (Wang, 2008; Zuo, 1999). More widely, "China has pioneered a rich, consumption-focused material culture since the Song Dynasty" (Eckhardt and Bengtsson, 2010, p. 212). Already in late imperial China (1368–1911), consumerist society was well established, and Chinese imperial consumer culture subsequently reached its peak in the Ming Dynasty (1426–1566). During this time, people's drive to consume was fueled by the desire to achieve and maintain status (Hamilton and Lai, 1989).

For example, the symbolic function of *Gongpin*, which encompassed items as diverse as clothes, shoes, combs, medicines, and food, was so high that it was considered suitable tribute to and by emperors (Yang, 1987). The dispatch of such items to relatives and friends by emperors represented the privileges of high-status office. Beyond the elite imperial and aristocratic realms, Chinese products also reached world markets. During the imperial period Chinese businesses traded extensively with Western countries, exchanging tea, chinaware, and silk clothing for Western goods and other trading favors, and it was through such long-term historical trading patterns that Chinese products gained a foothold in the culture of global consumption.

Global consumer culture in the Chinese context

Whether they are dominated by signs or subject to experimentation, meanings are constantly moving through different spaces and across different fields of brand actors. Regarding China, brand research often concentrates on how Western brands influence Chinese consumers and producers, and develop in the Chinese market. For example, consumer studies have investigated the appeal of Western advertisements for Chinese consumers and the government (Tse, Belk, and Zhou, 1989; Zhao and Belk, 2008; Zhou and Belk, 2004), how Chinese consumers consume Western brands (Dong and Tian, 2009; Hooper, 2000; KPMG, 2007; Wang, 2000, 2008), and how Chinese consumers consume gifts in the gift-giving process (Joy, 2001). China is the most populous market in the world, and companies attach great importance to its enormous, yet untapped, commercial potential reflected in the size of its advertising industry, which, by all accounts, is the world's fastest growing example (Wang, 2008). China is now inundated with foreign and local goods, images, advertising, and consumption ideas (Bergstrom, 2012; Davis, 2000; Lu and He, 2003; Wang, 2008; Yang, 2002).

Many scholars have analyzed the appeal of Western advertising in China, adaptation by foreign advertisers to the Chinese context, and the benefits that could be reaped by global brands using local names in advertising along with the disadvantages of using non-Chinese names in advertising by local brands (e.g., Cheng, 1997; Cheng and Schweitzer, 1996; Cheng and Chan, 2009; Cui, 1997; Gram, 2007; Lei, 2000; Liu, 2001; Qiu, 2003; Tai, 1997; Wan, 2001; Weng, 2002; Wu, 2001; Ye, 2003; Yin, 1999; Zhang, 2001; Zhang, 2003).

Recent research has shown that foreign brands are increasingly less appealing to Chinese consumers as compared with the growing appeal of Chinese brands and prices. For example, in examining how Chinese consumers read global and local television and print advertising, consumer researchers Zhou and Belk discovered two very different responses. One group's preference for global cosmopolitanism was reflected in its desire for *mianzi* (prestige face). The other group, driven by nationalist desires, preferred advertising stimulated by recognizably Chinese values (Zhou and Belk, 2004). Individualism and collectivism constitute another important area of study in global consumer research pertinent to China. Marketing researchers Jennifer Aaker's and Patti Williams's research has shown that the collectivism-oriented Chinese ideology resulted in Chinese consumers paying less attention to the individualism-themed American advertisements (1998). In a study of foreign brand advertising in China, advertising researcher Jiafei Yin discovered that more than three-quarters of them favored combining the global with the local (1999).

Although these findings reveal a local and national emphasis in Chinese consumer culture, there also exists a growing strain of hybridization that is already affecting Chinese consumption practices. For example, anthropologists Annamma Joy and John Sherry, in describing art as "a knowledge-based cultural product," suggest that hybridization underlies the emergence of knowledge in China. Hybridization conveys "the transformative engagement of the artist and the art world through outside (primarily Western) influences. It also underscores "the present- and future-oriented process of invention through complex cultural borrowing from abroad" (Joy and Sherry, 2004, p. 310). Influenced by Hollywood's model, the state of the Chinese film industry from the mid- to the late 1990s has undergone "institutional restructuring, reprising Hollywood's model of vertical and horizontal integration as well as the industry's concomitant, commercially-oriented film trends" (Zhu, 2002, p. 187).

In other words, the marketization and decentralization of the film industry directly impact the growth of entertainment. Greater imports of Hollywood popular culture into cinemas as compared with the earlier emphasis on propaganda, the market orientation of erstwhile anarchic writers like Wang Shuo, the taming of Fifth Generation film makers, and the gradual commercialization of Sixth Generation film makers, all these changes clearly indicate that global brand culture, heavily defined by Western culture, is on its way to conquering Chinese consumption patterns.

Recent research on contemporary Chinese society has increasingly paid attention to Chinese brand development and its relationship to Western branding models (e.g., Bergstrom, 2012; Rein, 2012; Temporal, 2001, 2006; Wang, 2008). Many researchers use a managerial approach in advocating the application of Western branding models and frameworks in Asian markets. Cayla and Arnould, however, argue against this. They claim that Western branding models and principles may not work effectively due to vast cultural differences between Western and non-Western contexts, and instead point out the utility and effectiveness of a cultural approach (Cayla and Arnould, 2008).

This book steps in to contribute a research-based examination of Chinese brand development using a brand culture approach. The next three chapters present in-depth looks at our case studies – Jay Chou, the Beijing Olympics Opening Ceremony, and Shanghai Tang – which offer useful insights into how global branding, fashion systems, and historical culture come together.

2   Jay Chou, Pop Star: Chinese Aesthetics and Contemporary Trends

Oh! How delighted I would be if my brand were as famous as Jay Chou! I heard that Jay Chou is popular not only in China but overseas as well.
Mr. W, garment industry manager, Shanghai

Zhou Jielun, more famously known as Jay Chou, is the most popular Chinese music artist of the past decade. Credited with inventing a new pop genre, *Zhongguo feng* (中国风) music, Chou enjoys record sales, a massive fan base, and packed concerts. Despite rampant piracy in China, which typically causes a 90 to 95 percent decrease in the sales volume of the Chinese recording industry (Fung, 2008), each of his records has exceeded 2 million in sales (baidu.com, 2010). It is difficult to measure the exact number of Chou fans, but Chou has been named the most popular music idol among Chinese aged 9–14 across at least five urban centres (baidu. com, 2010). In 2006, he was the number one favourite star among people aged 8–25 across seven East Asian and Southeast Asian countries (baidu.com, 2010). He has also been noted as a top Asian celebrity endorser for sports marketing (Liao, Chen, and Hsu, 2009).

Chou has performed numerous concerts across more than 30 Chinese cities, as well as making appearances throughout Asia, the US, Canada, and Australia. He was the first singer to mount a show at Shanghai Stadium, which accommodates an audience of 80,000. Tickets sold out in a matter of days. According to a 2010 report on jay-chou.net, Chou has once more been crowned the top moneymaking singer in Taiwan with an annual income of NTD852 million (about $28 million). These figures reflect revenue earned from 31 shows in a world concert tour, 20 paid performances, and numerous endorsement deals – all in one very good year (baidu.com, 2010).

A number of factors, from aesthetic to economic, allow researchers to fully examine precisely how a brand, in this case Jay Chou, generates an entire market – endorsements, sponsored events, and advertising contracts that market products specifically through music, art, and personality (Schroeder, 2007). In Chou's case, support from the Chinese government has been crucial. His work cites historical sources so strategically that many consider the sum total of his career so far to be no less than a one-man popular renaissance of Chinese traditional culture, one that adequately suits dominant political ideology and its goals. A good example of the strength of Jay Chou's political endorsement is his frequent appearance singing Chinese-themed and styled music for the New Year's Gala on CCTV (China Central Television), the outlet for China's Central Propaganda Department.

Specifically, Chou's Chinese-styled music showcases *Zhongguo feng* (China Wind), a new genre of Chinese music fusing traditional Chinese instruments and musical styles with Western rhythm and blues and rock that reached a peak in Chou. In Chou, *Zhongguo feng* transcends simple musical stylings to encompass lyrics and content. Chou's lyrics are pointedly cultural, imagistic, and emotionally poignant. They emulate well-known forms from ancient Chinese poetry, incorporating history, folklore, and common social and political themes, such as war, violence, and drug abuse. In his concerts, state-of-the-art technology produces a spectacular stage design. Chou, dressed in trendy Western clothing and singing his distinctive fusion music, creates an unforgettable image of modern China.

Chou adapts well to differing cultural contexts. At a 2007 show in Los Angeles, Chou dressed in a shiny American-style waistcoat while performing his songs "Faraway" and "Nun-Chuks," each brimming with Chinese cultural references. Chou's public image comprises this mold of hybrid Chinese, where Western individuality meets Chinese filial piety, which Chou avows is "the most important thing" in his life (Zhou, 2010). Though he is reported to be a hardworking perfectionist

Figure 2.1   **Jay Chou in Shanghai on the eve of a world tour**
© Imaginechina/Corbis

and self-directed music artist, Chou describes himself as a
shy young man who feels no shame admitting he is actually
"a mama's boy" (Zhou, 2010).

How did Jay Chou, a singer of modest background, and
barely any connections to speak of, become a hugely successful
Chinese star with a sizeable global reach? What cultural strategies did the managerial team behind Chou deploy to propel him
onto an international stage despite the political, economic, and
cultural constraints of the Chinese market? In the context of
global branding, Jay Chou sheds light on some of the mechanisms required to build distinctive Chinese global brands.

Branding and aesthetics

Consumer culture theory "has its historical roots in calls for
consumer researchers to broaden their focus to investigate
the neglected experiential, social, and cultural dimensions of
consumption in context" (Arnould and Thompson, 2005,
p. 869). Such a position encourages exploration of consumption's
aesthetic concerns, particularly as positive images of brands and

emotional feelings of consumers towards brands engage varying aesthetic properties.

Aesthetics has been defined as "the study of the feelings, concepts, and judgments arising from our appreciation of the arts or of the wider class of objects considered moving, or beautiful, or sublime" (Blackburn, 2005, p. 8). Philosopher George Dickie refines the notion of the beautiful object to include not merely its properties, but also the subjective experience of beauty (1997). The sublime, on the other hand, refers to an experience that is "great, fearful, noble, calculated to arouse sentiments of pride and majesty, as well as awe and some-times terror" (Blackburn, 2005, p. 354). Aesthetics concerns the experience of objects, which are invested with elements of beauty, and which sometimes move us in emotion or spirit. Although these definitions and discussions emerge amid apparently Western notions of aesthetics and emotions, they nevertheless provide compelling insights into the Jay Chou brand.

Brands can be considered through an aesthetic approach in that the consumption of brands produces powerful cognitive responses that harness sensory and affective feelings. Naturally, there are different kinds of consumption for different kinds of objects, and different varieties of aesthetic responses to the same object. Moreover, there are cultural products for which an aesthetic function is primary: for example, classical music, poetry, and high arts, are labelled aesthetic products, as their consumption is experiential, often "moving," and involves the consideration of beauty (Charters, 2006). An appreciation of aesthetics in everyday life ranges "along a continuum between simple hedonic pleasure and profound" feeling and does not always require consuming art (Holbrook and Zirlin, 1985, p. 3). Aesthetic issues can equally apply to products with a high aesthetic component such as mainstream film, music, photog-raphy, or basic consumer goods such as personal electronics, soft drinks, and tennis shoes (Holbrook, 1999; Holbrook and Schindler, 1989; Schroeder, 2002; Venkatesh and Meamber, 2008).

In accordance with the power of aesthetics in everyday life, branding has recourse to a variety of processes and practices, including, but not limited to, design, styling, and visual aesthet-ics. Furthermore, branding aesthetics also refers to the existing value of products even before the application of additional aesthetic manipulation through spatial design and modes of communication. Brand aesthetics may be "created through primary attributes (such as color, shape, material, and symbols) that collectively constitute styles and themes" (Schmitt and Simonson, 1997, p. 65). These directly contribute to brand identity and brand image.

Brand image is a psychological concept. It can be understood as a symbolic notion developing in the minds of consumers, composed of information and expectations related to a product or service (e.g., Borgerson et al., 2009). A good expression of brand image is one that emerges through a cluster of attributes and associations that consumers connect to the brand name. These evoked associations can be categorized as "hard" or "soft" emotional attributes (Biel, 1991). Within this framework, hard attributes include the specific perception of material or functional attributes, such as speed, premium price, user friendliness, length of time in business, or the number of flights per day. Soft attributes refer to emotional feelings, such as excitement, trustworthiness, fun, dullness, masculinity, or innovation (Biel, 1991). Apple, for example, may evoke youthful ingenuity, while IBM may evoke efficiency. Prudential might be associated with stability, while Allstate might be consistent with care (Biel, 1991). As such, the softer features of a brand's image, such as brand personality, often suggest differentiated, enduring, and meaningful attributes to consumers. Hard attributes, on the other hand, are readily associated with the brand's visual representation.

Brand image, as it exists in the consumer's mind, is defined in terms of a brand-related network. It involves details of brands that consumers contemplate, and how they ultimately perceive and mentally organize all texts associated with that brand (de Mooij, 2009). In this way, the blurring of boundaries between the customer's self-image and the company's brand image becomes a key motivational element in consumer culture (McLoughlin and Aaker, 2010). For example, the use of snapshots or "snapshot-like" imagery has been seen as an important strategic branding resource, in that consumers often perceive snapshot-like images as authentic factors even for casual brands, revealing a blurring of the notion of a personal and a strategic image (Schroeder, 2012). When applied to branding processes and practices, the notion of aesthetics can be deployed to enable consumers to recognize sensory perceptions that are tantamount to aesthetic experiences.

Jay Chou, Chinese music, and marketing

Jay Chou has managed to create himself in the image of a successful brand with an exceptional music style; however, the tensions between music and business have not been kind to other artists with similar aspirations. Some Chinese researchers, cultural critics, and consumers state that the arts should not become more commercial than they have already done (Cui and Zhou, 2001). Music, they claim, should be separated from commerce, and "good" art does not call for marketing, it should sell on the basis of quality alone. Cui Jian, the founder of Chinese rock music, for instance, was vehemently against the commercialization of art and music. He insists that commerce makes art and music vulgar, and instead advocates more "authentic" music production (Cui and Zhou, 2001).

Despite its naysayers, the Chinese music market has grown significantly since the early 1990s, its commercial boom neatly coinciding with the recent history of economic liberalization in China (Kloet, 2010). Many Chinese music artists support commercialization. They claim that commercial mechanisms are inherent in the music and art market due to branding's prominent role in cultural practices (e.g., Borgerson and Schroeder 2003; Bradshaw, McDonagh, and Marshall, 2006; Joy and Sherry, 2003; Maclaran, Saren, and Stern, 2009; Schroeder and Borgerson, 2002). Their view expresses the idea that successful music artists who manage to record, perform, and sell widely are a kind of twin engine, equal parts knowledge and branding, a consummate entity combining art and image making (Schroeder, 2005).

Jay Chou's large fan base displays some proof that most Chinese consumers approve of commercialization, and suggests that holding back on marketing and branding is a sure-fire means to limiting an artist's career. Modestly run marketing campaigns often do not work in a world where individuals are accustomed to consuming cultural forms through commercial networks defined by marketing. In other words, marketing itself functions as a cultural code that is read by consumers. In Chou's case, the marketing codes and his foundation in Chinese-styled music combine. Marketing that grasps such cultural codes extends its reach, because it is these cultural codes, and not just the intentions of marketers or brand managers, that sustain meaning and co-create value (Schroeder and Salzer-Mörling, 2006). In the following, we explore how cultural codes steer and help construct the brand meanings of Jay Chou.

The Imagined China as modern-cultured Chinese features

The Imagined China manifest in Jay Chou's music, lyrics, and branding activities has a distinct style reflecting realities of contemporary China infused with tradition and modernness. The following sections present this imagined China complete with traditional and modern features defined by myth and history, and fueled by global fashion mechanisms.

Art has been described as "a knowledge-based cultural product;" art in the context of the People's Republic of China is a hybrid entity (Joy and Sherry, 2004). Its hybridization conveys "the transformative engagement of the artist and the art world through outside (primarily Western) influences," and "the present- and future-oriented process of invention through complex cultural borrowing from abroad" (Joy and Sherry, 2004, p. 310). How Jay Chou exemplifies this definition of hybridization will be discussed below.

Jay Chou grounds his work in contemporary social contradictions and concrete realities; he expresses both traditional and fashionable brand culture through his songs, concerts, and activities. This is something brand strategists, advertisers, tourism promoters, and marketing agents actively promote to ensure his work reverberates more deeply across his fan base. Of course, Chou's handlers are not unique in their deployment of this strategy. Marketers frequently make recourse to images expressing social anxieties to make stories reverberate, a tactic intended to give the impression of social relevance, and facilitate the formation of groups and group images in which people can claim membership (Holt, 2004; Thompson and Tian, 2008). Jay Chou's example demonstrates that the creation of group membership is key in brand development; and the group image that his case expresses is patently that of the Imagined China. Chou develops a potent brand culture via an innovative blending of historical culture and contemporary trends.

The Imagined China via the representation of historical Chinese culture and sacred meaning

The representation of historical culture in brand identity creates a natural magnet for emotional responses, including feelings of reverence and pride in consumers. Although the stimulus itself might not be sacred, feelings evoked by historical representation could be understood as sacred emotion. Whereas sacred meanings develop from religious associations, sacredness is also dependent on spatial and temporal context, and secular consumption provides one such context (Belk, Wallendorf, and Sherry, 1989). In Jay Chou's case, some of our interviewees suggested that Chou develops sacred or sacred-like meanings by absorbing historical Chinese culture into his work. He weaves

Figure 2.2   **Jay Chou rehearsing for the Beijing CCTV Spring Festival Gala**

© Feng Weifeng/Xinhua Press/Corbis

in Chinese classical instruments and traditional music styles. During an interview with a young Chinese Chou fan, for example, she said, "Jay's work is very sacred to me. His works and performances vividly and creatively reproduce Chinese historical culture, such as martial arts and traditional Chinese poems. A lot of young people find this very holy."

In her narrative, "sacred" seems to refer to feelings of veneration, which typically pertain to divinity or divine things, or, in this case, to historical culture. Chou's work frequently cites martial artists and Chinese poetry, entities that are widely venerated in Chinese culture. For instance, one of Jay Chou's songs entitled "Fearless," or "*Huo Yuan Jia*" in Chinese, immediately evokes reverence. Huo Yuanjia was a real-life hero, a martial artist whose name became synonymous with patriotism after his widely chronicled feats employing the Huo family style martial art, *Mizongquan*, or "Hidden Trace Boxing," in attacks on foreign invaders at the turn of the 20th century. Huo Yuanjia thus became associated with the protection of Chinese sovereignty at a time when China was corroded by colonization and foreign concessions. This eponymous song is basically a patriotic tearjerker that invokes feats of the swashbuckling national hero, and consequently pride in Chinese sovereignty. The chain of associations extends even further. Huo Yuanjia serves as a mnemonic device for a range of historical Chinese practices and belief systems beginning with martial arts and ending in religion and philosophy.

In Chinese martial arts, the value of bodies and weapons includes and transcends utilitarian concerns such as self-defence. Martial arts represent various ideologies, such as the cultivation of health and the search for virtue. No doubt they are an aesthetic of bodily control and physical skill, but they also refer to the aesthetics of mind, or *qi*, or vital energy, as the inner *gong* (Xu, 1999). *Qi* is also important in Chinese belief systems, such as Confucianism, Taoism, and Chanzong, which advocate the cultivation of body and mind through *qi* (Xu, 1999). *Qi* nurtures virtuous behavior in Confucian rituals and Taoists' mythic knowledge about "spiritual transcendence and immortality." *Qi* encompasses bodily movement and quiet sitting meditation to achieve union with the occult and the all-permeating Tao, which is a means to liberate the ego-centered self and Chan Buddhism's "dharma body" (Xu, 1999, p. 967). *Qi* requires dedication and stamina. Its practice evokes esteem and admiration. Citation of it, practices aligned with it, and historical individuals associated with it, in a pop song by a good-looking superstar in trendy clothing is consequently a recipe for the instant creation of awe, and perhaps even envy, which is perhaps what the young fan was referring to in stating that Jay Chou's work was very sacred to her.

Historical musical instruments, their sounds, the associations and images they immediately invoke, and historical poetry, are also central to Chou's work. In China, court musicians typically performed classical poems and prose during ritual celebrations. Solo instruments in small ensembles of plucked and bowed stringed instruments, such as the *pipa guzheng*, the *guqin*, and the *erhu*, combined with flutes, cymbals, gongs, and drums, were used in traditional holiday celebrations (Lee and Shen, 1999). In his song "Fearless," Chou employs Chinese drums and cymbals to express the strength and determination of the hero Huo Yuanjia. But he also uses the *erhu*, the *dizi*, and the *pipa* while singing parts of the song in a thin, falsetto voice, all of which collectively express sadness at the hero's assassination by Japanese attackers. Thus, the song becomes a cleverly choreographed chronicle of history manipulated by acoustic stimuli that generate nostalgia and feelings of loss that transcend time and place. This, in effect, is also the Imagined China at full steam and in full color, an abstract and concrete world of the past and present fused into an indivisible entity.

A hybrid image: The Imagined China via the representation of historical Chinese culture and fashion discourses

De-localization, or glocalization, caused by global forces and the mobility of populations leads to the cultural form of "hybridization" through television, the internet, advertising, trade, and travel (Pieterse, 1995). With respect to China, Chinese entrepreneurs gained access to Western ideas, forms, and discourses through the filter of the Chinese intelligentsia, members of which maneuvered localization, in that they freely added Chinese ideas, forms, and discourses to Western imports, concrete and abstract, with little or no regard for contradiction.

This process led to the development of hybrid representations of what it meant to be "Chinese" (Cochran, 2006).

Jay Chou exemplifies this kind of hybridization propelled by global fashion systems. He is modern, traditional, historically rooted, and internationally bound. His hybrid brand image combines traditional culture and global fashion trends. Brand images are nourished by consumer emotions, such as excitement, trustworthiness, fun, boredom, and innovation (Biel, 1991). Jay Chou's brand image is no different.

The sacred feature of Jay Chou's hybrid image

Beyond classical Chinese references, Jay Chou is a master of borrowing and re-imagining popular culture. Specifically, his mechanism relates to *wulitou* subculture (nonsensical humor), which was popular in the 1980s and 1990s (Davis, 2004). Like tropes of humor and comedy elsewhere, *wulitou* subculture is distinguished by the flattening of social boundaries through fantasy. If Chou's landscape is that hybrid of old and new, contemporary and future, its population is joined by a common trope of nonsensical, light-hearted humor, which provides release from normative social roles and the impression of equal status.

Chou's song "Nun-Chuks" provides a good example of this process at work. The song uses Chinese-styled compositions including the powerful, explosive sound of a traditional drum, the graceful, relaxing sound of the piano, and the refreshing catharsis provided by the sorrowful sound of the *erhu*, a traditional Chinese instrument. Collectively, this instrumental backdrop elicits reminiscences and nostalgia. Strategically included martial arts expressions in the lyrics instantly produce the impression of stoicism. We hear such symbolic phrases as "practicing the Iron Palm," "playing with the Tang family spear," "the *qi* flows," running "with sandbags tied to one's ankles," and "walking on walls" (JayChouStudio.com, 2010a). These citations are responsible for the distinctive expressiveness and imagist richness of Jay Chou's songs. These carefully combined musical gestures and themes, which enable identification with nun-chuks's heroes and heroines, facilitate familiarity with listeners' inner feelings, or re-acquaintance with previously suppressed emotions.

Furthermore, in the "Nun-Chuks" music video (available for viewing on YouTube), seemingly surreal visual expressions unify classical themes, such as martial arts, and modern vulgar street violence, which elicits humor. Chou raps the song, but instead of mimicking US "street culture" moves as so many global rappers do, he employs martial arts moves, whipping nun-chuks over and around his body to the music. In this way, he seems to integrate an imported musical form – US rap – with an ancient cultural art. To some extent, these paradoxical meetings are historically accurate, and capture the thrilling subculture of *wulitou*, the seemingly irreverent expressions of which contribute to the creation of an atmosphere of absurd nonsensical humor (Davis, 2004).

Clever and opportune, the employment of *wulitou* appeals to young audiences and reminds older ones of their youth, with evocative images of schooldays. For the first author, the song evokes an experience from her youth, when on being bullied by older students while on her way to school, she confronted the situation by imagining herself as the son of a martial artist on his way to Shaolin Temple or Wu Dang Mountain to learn martial arts to fight violence. Likewise, young people influenced by traditional Chinese culture are likely to associate the historical aspects of Chou's songs with some part of their youth. Moreover, on a general level, the songs' themes evoke heroism, which most people are likely to enjoy. Against the backdrop of urban violence and crime, many of Chou's songs offer a fantasy world of heroes and heroines fighting for justice, following a virtuous path, and conquering evil, all through the system of pop music, bright lights, great costumes, and a general sense of levity and fun.

Chou might have captured the pulse of young people through *wulitou*, but he is not without introspective features that appeal to broader audiences. His song "Chrysanthemum Terrace" draws upon elements of Chinese vocal music, which has traditionally been sung in a thin, non-resonant voice or in falsetto, typically with a solo accompaniment of the *guzheng* and the *erhu* (traditional stringed instruments). Like many of his songs, "Chrysanthemum Terrace" treats audiences to a slice of older Chinese music aesthetics (Kartomi, 1990). Lyrics from classical Chinese poems also make such songs notably nostalgic in feeling. They describe how an ancient Chinese general and his wife desperately long for each other while the general is away at war. Their mutual passion, though strong, is expressed through restrained and mournful feelings, which indirectly touch upon the foulness of war through vivid expressions such as "The crescent moon hangs in the past [...] pale with sickness" (JayChouStudio.com, 2010b).

The lyrics are filled with numerous classical expressions, such as "Distant dreams [...] rise like incense," in which metaphor generates an open-ended image (JayChouStudio.com, 2010b). The distant dream could be the general's war ambition, though endless war also makes glory in war a distant dream, a castle in the air. Or, it could be the couple's reunion, or peace.

If some expressions, such as "Chrysanthemums fall [...] weeping to the ground" or a smile emerging on "a yellowing scroll," indulge in generalities, the song title and repeated reference to the title flower produce a very specific image. In ancient China, chrysanthemums represented loneliness and unhappy things. Even today, they evoke melancholy (Reckert, 1993). The lines quoted above use the common rhetorical device of *synaesthesia* from Chinese poetics (Harrison, 2001). This manifests in the "yellow" of the chrysanthemums and the "yellowish" smile of the woman, suggesting that the wife's bright and warm smile is turning yellowish from absence and longing, which, in turn, evokes the image of the husband at war.

The songs' lyrics and their musical devices thus collectively create a sensorium of history and times past that nonetheless evoke familiar feelings. The Chinese styling of these songs, through references to history, traditional motifs, and poetic symbols and their emotive landscapes, set against traditional acoustic scenarios, is designed to attract listeners but also to maintain a historical distance from the present. This distance is key, in that it alone sustains the particular relationship between the song and the listener – that of veneration and awe.

The fashionable features of Jay Chou's hybrid brand image

Jay Chou's music is indebted to the past, though it lives very much in the present. He knows his audience and responds to their needs. The emotional feeling of Jay Chou's music is also fashionable. It rides on Western rhythms. The hybrid styling became so distinctive that it has its own name. Chou Style describes Jay Chou's trademark cross-cultural migrations, into history, across the globe, into art, myth, and philosophy. Chou Style also refers to his uninhibited traversing of musical genres, such as R&B, hip-hop, rock, blues, Western classical music, and country.

Some of Chou's biggest hits draw on hip-hop conventions and aesthetics. Hip-hop is hybrid: "Hip Hop assembled energetic music, passionate graffiti artists, acrobatic dancers, and skilled wordsmiths into a unified aesthetic, each in its own way representing passion for life and a commitment to individual and collective expression" (Price, 2006, p. 41). Jay Chou is also a practitioner of unified aesthetics. Many of Chou's songs are written in the pentatonic (five-note) scale with bright color, energetic movements, and dramatic effects that set his work apart from the typical preference in contemporary pop music for the diatonic (seven-note) scale. In his famous song "Blue-and-White Porcelain," for instance, Chou combines the *guzheng*, a traditional Chinese instrument, and the Western acoustic guitar, using the pentatonic scale to make the sound passionate.

Chou also incorporates a diverse array of world music elements into his music, such as Spanish guitar in "Red Imitation" (*"Hong Mofang"* in Chinese), American techno/electronica in "Herbalist's Manual" (*"Ben Cao Gang Mu"*), Western classical music undertones in "Reverse Scales" (*"Ni Lin"*), and Bossa nova in "Rosemary" (*"Midei Xiang"*). He also cleverly westernizes the song titles, and, on many occasions, his lyrics contain classic Western storylines, a decision that seems to have paid off. In another interview, a 36-year-old male Chou fan said:

> I have to say, I really like the names of his songs and albums! He names a lot of Western places, activities, and heroes and heroines. They sound interesting, maybe very imaginative. For example, I always think of power when I listen to "Bull Fight" [one of Chou's songs]. Spain has a long history of them. They say that bullfighting is a form of worship and sacrifice in ancient Spanish rituals.

This fan's description indicates that the title "Bull Fight" functions like a mnemonic invoking European culture, history, and aesthetics. Indeed, bullfighting embraces contradictory aesthetics – the wildness of a cruel cultural practice living on in civilized life. Bullfighting is a violent, cruel, and bloody game played between man and beast. Philosopher Alain Renaut states that "Bull fighting symbolizes man's combat with nature – a nature that is constantly threatening to engulf him from without and from within while he attempts to breaks away from it countering violence and aggressively with reason and calculation" (quoted in Ferry, 2004, p. 152). In this description, bullfighting represents man "breaking away" from a natural state in contrast to the animal staying imprisoned. This contrast underwrites the foundation of modern humanism, and bullfighting is one of the most tangible, visible examples of the humanistic idea par excellence (Ferry, 2004). In scarcely 20 minutes, man gains control of the beast. He manages to slow, channel, direct, and attract the bull. He plays with the bull's savage force, which becomes subject to the will of man, and thereby elicits emotion from the spectator. The submission of brute nature, or violence, to man's will, the victory of freedom over nature, makes for a heady mix of feeling and spectacle. It also underlines that man conquers nature through intellect. As they watch, the spectators enjoy fine food, wine, and cigars. The game is a consummate performance of the elegantly and successfully executed maneuvers of modern life (Renaut, in Ferry, 2004).

The sacred in culture refers to the attribution of the divine to things produced and consumed by people (Belk, Wallendorf, and Sherry *et al.*, 1989). In Spain, bullfighting has an atavistic, or primitive, function, newly translated into a spectator sport in keeping with modernforms of ritualized social worship common in sport culture (Ellingham and Fisher, 2004). Bullfighting evokes a sense of empathy with how primitive ancestors confronted nature, and becomes a means to commemorate this distant past. Although it is not atavism at work in Chou's work, there is a profound sense of connection with the past and a desire to hold onto it in various ways. Holding onto the past also appears in other songs. "Rosemary," for instance, represents love and remembrance (Huston, 2006; Webster, 2008). "Ninja" commemorates the art of stealth and invisibility as practiced in feudal Japan (Draeger, 1992). "Red Imitation," which is about the legendary cabaret Moulin Rouge in Montmartre, Paris, traces conspiracy, madness, and the decay of the Belle Epoque (Mirambeau, 2004).

Songs that blend Asian and Western styling are particularly admired and equated with Chou's fashionable sensibility. According to another of our informants, a 24-year-old medical professional from Shanghai, Chou's "songs sound good, pretty good! [There] is a Western taste [*yangqi* in Chinese] running through all his work, such as 'William's Castle,' 'Fantasy,' 'Red Imitation,' and so on." She adds:

> Some of his lyrics are really, really funny and odd! [She laughs]. For example, like this one [she points to the lyrics of "William's Castle" in her hand] – the black cat's smile likes crying; the pig elegantly speaking French; when smiling is like crying, you can imagine how hard it is; then when I read the pig elegantly speaking French, a pig wears a black suit with a bow tie, you can imagine how funny it is! [She continues laughing]

To Chou fans, the unrestrained, vigorous, and sometimes satirical style of his music makes him an artist brimming with talent, an impression illustrated by this description of the lyrics in "William's Castle."

To careful listeners, Chou's work also contains elements of parody and pastiche. Chou's work appears both modern and fashionable, though equally proficient in evoking agreeable doses of sentimentality and nostalgia. Replete with Chinese and Western icons, and styles that cross cultural boundaries and express musical versatility, Jay Chou represents what modern China is and can become. His uniqueness, nonetheless anchored in Chinese history and tradition, has the distinct advantage of representing cultural fact and cultural potential.

The Imagined China and the representation of historical Chinese culture

Brands can globalize by developing brand mythology, which derives from creating myth markets around the world (Cayla and Arnould, 2008). Myth markets, in turn, derive from grasping social contradictions (Holt, 2004), or apprehending mythic stories, including historical figures and events. In Jay Chou's case, his music expresses social concerns and meets social needs, such as the desire to be heard and comprehended. Specifically,

Chou's lyrics express the complex and paradoxical nature of contemporary generations, which consume brands to distinguish their identities, yet continue to seek the approval of society, parents, and other respected figures. This is because, on the one hand, they have to deal with social relationships with colleagues, bosses, clients, parents, classmates, and teachers. On the other hand, they crave a psychological space where they can escape societal control and express inner anxiety and anger. Many of Chou's lyrics address these issues, including street and school violence, drug abuse, war, love, and longing. For example, "Rice Fields" confronts the loss of rural countryside to urbanization.

Fashion emerges from and changes due to cultural forces, technological innovation, economic cycles, holidays, and many other factors (Cholachatpinyo et al., 2002). It is expressed in ambiguous and ambivalent ways to meet social needs, and represents the spirit of the time. Jay Chou's work appeals precisely because its themes address social issues arising from social and political contexts. More specifically, Jay Chou's work provides a psychological space for his audiences to release their anxieties through his Chinese-styled compositions, traditional plaintive numbers, poetic lyrics, and traditional martial arts themes spiced with Western elements. For example, the lyrics and music video of 2003's "Second Class of Year 3" represent the enormous pressures people face in today's educational environment, with endless examinations, competition, comparison, and expectations (Fung, 2008). "In the Name of the Father" reflects how people's stubbornness and refusal to abide by rules results in rejection and isolation. It also shows that what they truly desire is not a direct resistance, but rather the forgiveness of their parents. This reveals people's hidden desires to maintain relationships with parents, colleagues, and bosses, and to develop intimacy in friendships. Consumption of popular products, such as Jay Chou's work, is a way for people to mobilize their peer network – a phenomenon also seen in the West (Skelton and Valentine, 1997).

Jay Chou not only brings martial arts into his songs, but he also takes a critical view of the past by showing that martial arts should not be used for street violence, or, for that matter, for any kind of violence. The lyrics of 2001's "Nun-Chuks," for instance, provide correctives. They express Chinese tradition and values including conscientiousness, tolerance, and reserve, for example when he sings, "The virtuous one has no enemies." Thus despite the martial arts trope, these songs ultimately represent rebellion against war and violence.

The vast popularity of Chou's work can be attributed to a variety of factors, not least of which is the media, including the state-owned TV and media companies that generally play an essential role in generating and circulating fashion (Blaszczyk, 2007). Beyond appearing on state TV, Chou has also been a long-standing endorser of the state's commercial ventures, such as M-Zone, a mobile youth marketing program run by the state-owned China Mobile Company. "It's My Site; It's My Command" (*Wo De Dipan, Wo Zuo Zhu*), which is the company's tag line, was marketed by Chou, whose fan base was naturally a primary target (Fung, 2008). Chou's impact on marketing under the aegis of state media, which hold the bulk of the market share, thus extended to a new generation of people who are willing to spend money on text messaging and other special features such as Mobile QQ (a mobile messaging service) to maintain their network (Fung, 2008). These ventures marketed more than just access to media – they also marketed the official spokesperson, Jay Chou.

Hybridization in Chou is a comprehensive phenomenon, in sync with the idea that global branding calls for the participation of differentiated local cultures (Kjeldgaard, Csaba, and Ger, 2006). For example, in "East Wind" ("*Dong Feng Po*"), he performed a typical Chinese melody in rhythm and blues style with Chinese traditional instruments and in the poem style of the Song Dynasty. The song's lyrics subtly express sorrow and solitariness in a way similar to traditional Chinese poetry (Fung, 2008).

The symbols of Chou's music are thus anchored in sentiment, which creates a sense of community by crystallizing imaginary identities into a sentimental adventure (McClary and Walser, 1990). Still, sentiment does not operate merely through feeling but is also grounded in social, economic, and cultural contexts, which Chou seems to have grasped well. Chou has exploited these contexts fully. He has used state mechanisms, rejuvenated Chinese history, roused patriotic feeling, paid homage to Chinese art and traditional culture, and harnessed global fashion systems to create a hugely successful brand.

The Imagined China, brand actors, and Jay Chou's global hybrid image

Jay Chou has worked extensively with international movie stars and directors who enjoy international exposure. In 2006, he collaborated with Jet Li, the international marital artist and movie star, composing and performing the theme song for *Fearless*, an internationally released film. Later that year, Chou worked with Zhang Yimou, the creative director of the 2008 Beijing Olympics Opening and Closing Ceremonies. Chou has also worked with veterans Chow Yun-Fat and Gong Li in the film *Curse of the Golden Flower*, once again singing the film's theme song. That film marked Chou's North American acting debut and brought him international exposure. Both *Fearless* and *Curse of the Golden Flower* featured Chinese historical figures, involved Chinese martial arts, and depended on the pop appeal of Chinese fusion music, in another example of Chou's preference for projects that present modern China through a hybrid aesthetic.

Other expressly Western ventures have also added to Chou's considerable résumé. In 2010, he teamed up with Seth Rogen, the Canadian actor, comedian, and film producer, and Christoph Waltz, an Austrian-German actor, in a new Hollywood version of *The Green Hornet*, directed by maverick French author and music video director, Michel Gondry. The film was released in North America, Australia, and the UK in January 2011, and globally shortly thereafter, eventually grossing over $227 million. In this film, Chou reprised the role of Kato, previously played in the well-loved 1960s US television series by the legendary martial artist, erstwhile philosopher, and actor Bruce Lee. Thirty years after his untimely death in 1973, Lee continues to be perceived as a cultural icon across the world, and particularly in China for his portrayal of nationalistic and righteous characters.

Playing a role that someone like Bruce Lee made famous is a challenging job for any actor. Thus Chou's task was tremendous; but his own musical career, based on hybridization, cultural fusion, and the globalization of Chinese cultural traits, helped to ensure that he had no trouble filling Lee's shoes. Chou's well-known modesty served him well in this regard. Chou promised that although it would be "an overwhelming experience to take on a role made famous by Bruce Lee," he would not try to be Bruce Lee's Kato (Moy, 2009).

The construct of the Imagined China resides in every aspect of Chou's musical branding. From his lyrics and endorsements to his choice of musical instruments, styles, and cultural and historical citations, Chou has insightfully fused myriad worlds to create a globally successful brand anchored in the construct of the Imagined China.

Although the concept of imagined community has been used in various instances of historical nation building, nation is only one instance of imagined community. Barker goes further when he defines imagined community in terms of forms of collective identity: "Just as national identity takes the form of identification with representations of the nation, so can ethnic groups, feminists, classes, new social movements and other communities of action and identity be understood as imagined" (Barker, 2004, p. 99). The imagined community also includes "the process of social modernity – secular rationalism, a calendrical perception of time, capitalist-driven technological development, mass literacy and mass communications, political democratization, the modern nation-state" (Tomlinson, 2001, p. 83). Jay Chou's interpretations of the Imagined China demonstrate similar processes of social modernity in the Chinese context. Music, fashion, media, film, and advertising, have collectively forged this imaginary in which the community is both modern and culturally Chinese.

Jay Chou: Strategic use of Chinese culture

Looking at the mechanisms driving Jay Chou's success sheds light on at least some scenarios behind the underprivileged position of Chinese export brands in the global market. Specifically, the strategic use of Chinese culture and ideology seems to be a key factor lacking in the brand development of Chinese brands. Chinese brand builders have a lot to learn from Chou's development of a distinctly Chinese-styled aesthetic, which draws from history, religion, philosophy, and folk traditions but also redefines them through global fashion resources that respond to consumer needs and aspirations. His embracing of global Chinese consumer culture shows the success of a Chinese branding strategy that is grounded in history and culture and in contemporary life and technology. This represents an attractive mix of cultural myths, historical figures, and contemporary trends filtered through a Chinese perspective of the world. More broadly, "Jay Chou's music production has wittingly strategized to construct images and products that can be both locally and nationally assimilated into Chinese culture and nationally accepted as a 'prototype' product – a product whose political standard has been authoritatively acknowledged by the state" (Fung, 2008, p. 69). Here lies Chou's success, and here might also lie the success of Chinese brand builders.

Most contemporary Chinese music artists recognize the need to rejuvenate and refresh their branding strategy. Many have taken steps toward this end. This is all to say that Jay Chou is no exception to the rule of thumb dictating the general tendency to rapidly commercialize and live with the times. But Chou's results have been exceptionally successful. He is a star beyond all pop music stars in China.

Moreover, he might be the most commercially successful Chinese pop star to express a reverent interest in the past. His music expands what it means to return to the past for inspiration. He has found an attractive mix of fashionable nationalism and culturally sensitive cosmopolitanism. This recipe applies to all his products, from his recorded music and concerts to his endorsements and films. Unlike other Chinese pop stars, Jay Chou has managed to redefine the myth of the imagined community through the lens of a China that is young, growing, and fashionable, and yet still rooted in its ancient, venerable past. As much as this recipe re-imagines China, it also reiterates that Chou and his music are effectively a potent and compelling icon of the Imagined China. In Chapter 3, we take a close look at another global branding effort that drew from historical culture and captured the world's attention: the Beijing Olympics Opening Ceremony.

3 The 2008 Beijing Olympics Opening Ceremony: Branding China for the World

You know, this ceremony shows many mysterious Chinese cultures and inspires me to buy more of its products and brands. Two weeks after this Opening Ceremony, I bought a Haier washing machine, a well-known Chinese brand. Furthermore, I told my friends how fantastic the Beijing Olympics Opening Ceremony was and encouraged them to watch it. After that most of my friends agreed with what I said and were interested in Chinese culture, products, and brands, such as planning to visit China, and buying Fuwa [the 2008 Beijing Olympics mascots, literally "good luck dolls"].
Miss J, from Hong Kong, living in the UK

Arguably, China itself emerged as the most evident and notable brand of the 2008 Beijing Olympic Games. The magnificent staging of the XXIX Olympiad effectively and efficiently employed the Olympics to enhance "the country's visibility and the salience of its marketplace on the world stage" (Greyser, 2008, p. 1). Of course, sporting events and competition were the focus of the 2008 Beijing Olympics, but viewers, participants, and commentators also sought a window on contemporary China, hidden from many behind the veil of the past.

Many past Olympics, such as the 1964 Tokyo Olympics, the 1988 Seoul Olympics, and the 2000 Sydney Olympics, have boosted the hosting nation's stature (Liang, 2011). However, the 2008 Beijing Olympics is generally considered to have been the most expensive in history, at an estimated cost of over $42 billion, and played a key role in branding China to the world (Fowler and Meichtry, 2008). As one article put it: "the 2008 Beijing Olympic Games can be considered a tool in the soft power and international communication strategy that China has been pioneering in recent years" (Chen, Colapinto, and Luo, 2012, p. 188.)

The Beijing Olympics also functioned as an institutionalized fashion system that generated its own marketplace replete with branded products. The fashion world participated, displaying new trends via Chinese Olympics-themed fashion shows, Olympics themed advertisements in fashion magazines, Olympics themed clothing, and related entertainment paraphernalia. Hollywood took notice, too. The American Film Institute named the television coverage of the Opening Ceremony as one of the year's highlights: "The Opening Ceremony, directed and staged by acclaimed Chinese filmmaker Zhang Yimou, marked the most significant live event of the year" (Kiday, 2008, p. 1).

This chapter explores how the 2008 Beijing Olympics facilitated the growing use of China's historical culture as a resource for global branding, by focusing on the elaborate, theatrical, and phenomenally costly Beijing Olympics Opening Ceremony. A cultural theme was intentionally – and strategically – built into the staging of the Games:

> For the Beijing 2008 Olympics, a key policy recommendation from the People's University concluded, "On this basis, we cautiously propose that in the construction of China's national image, we should hold the line on 'cultural China,' and the concept of 'cultural China' should not only be the core theme in the dialogue between China and the international community in Olympic discourse, but also it should be added into the long term strategic plan for the national image afterwards (Brownell, 2009, p. 1).

We see the Opening Ceremony as an expression of China's aspirations – a cultural, consumer, and strategic branding event that showcases a sophisticated, yet earnest and nostalgic, effort to position China as a modern economic, political, and cultural power with a long historical and cultural legacy.

The Olympic Games can be thought of as an iconic brand, built upon the worldwide appeal of phenomenal athletic performance; and the cycle of the Summer and Winter Games builds anticipation and enhances the rarity of the competitions. In addition, Olympic events have frequently served as vehicles to express world unity, national pride, economic progress, and shared values regarding hard work, ambition, and commitment to success (Greyser, 2008). The US television network NBC paid nearly $900 million for broadcast rights to the 2008 Olympic Games, and on an average, had 30 million viewers glued to their screens each night across the US. Millions more watched the events on NBC cable channels. Thirty million unique users visited NBC's Olympics website and 6.3 million shared videos from the coverage streamed on the site (Carter and Sandomir, 2008). The 2008 Beijing Olympics was in effect China's "coming out party" (Greyser, 2008, p. 1), and the Opening Ceremony constituted a hybrid cultural, fashion, and sports product showcasing China. For Beijing, hosting the Olympics marks an important event in its biography (Coles, Knowles and Newbury, 2012).

The 2008 Beijing Olympics Opening Ceremony had many target markets, such as Chinese watching it on TV at home, Olympic guests, spectators, and a global audience. Only parts of the Ceremony were broadcast on global television, and different

Figure 3.1   **Beijing Olympics Opening Ceremony**
© Sampics/Corbis

audiences were shown quite different views. Thus, the Opening Ceremony necessarily resulted in different coverage depending on who and where you were.

We examine the Opening Ceremony to explore ways in which the Olympic context engaged culturally specific, yet internationally familiar, fashion mechanisms to contribute to the international branding of China and an emerging Chinese myth market. As well, we challenge the popular notion of the Beijing Olympics Opening Ceremony as a singularly positive communication of Chinese national pride. Brand meanings can be negative, positive, or neutral, and those emerging from the Opening Ceremony, created by the various discourses, are no different.

In this case study, Imagined China refers to global audience discourses about China in relation to the Beijing Olympics Opening Ceremony. The term Imagined China derives from the concept of "imagined community," in which a nation is a community that is socially constructed and imagined by those who perceive themselves as part of that group (Anderson, 2006). Our research draws upon Anderson's theory of imagined community, adapted for marketing and consumer culture studies to conceptualize the Imagined China as a means to interpret China as a global brand (Cayla and Eckhardt, 2008; Tian and Dong, 2011).

Looking at the Opening Ceremony in the context of China's global image and examining aspects of international responses from a cultural and social perspective, we aim to reveal how viewers, organizing staff, and the media, working in conjunction with the Beijing Olympics Opening Ceremony, developed the concept of Imagined China into a global brand, and in turn suggested how Imagined China might be understood in the future by global consumers, politicians, academics, and managers in China and abroad (Latham, 2009).

Global brand mythologies: Developing a new identity

The 2008 Beijing Olympics Opening Ceremony was a spectacular event that generated attention and controversy throughout the world. For many, the presentation was magnificent entertainment offering a tantalizing glimpse of a mysterious country. As one commentator stated:

The opening event in Bird's Nest Stadium for the 2008 Summer Olympics in Beijing stunned the world with its scale, precision, sound, and beauty. The intricate costumes, drumming patterns, displays of technology, and sheer mass of performers showed China at its finest hour. More than 2000 musicians pounded drums simultaneously. The number of performers at the opening event, 14,000, was greater than the number of athletes in all the subsequent sports competitions put together: 11,000. The originality and huge scale of the opening performance were undeniably powerful. For viewers in the West, the ceremony inspired both excitement and fear, leaving them to wonder what was taking place in this new China (Justice, 2012, p. 1).

For others, it represented crass propaganda in a global power battle, an exercise in "glossy image making" (Coles, Knowles, and Newbury, 2012, p. 117; see also Brady, 2009; Latham, 2009).

Indeed, the Beijing Olympics Opening Ceremony gave rise to multiple categories of consumer interpretations. For example, one category comprises viewers whose perspectives are defined less by politics than by culture. These include Chinese people and some non-Chinese participants. A second type of consumer interpretation emerges globally from a vantage point impacted by notions of history and politics. This category includes those enmeshed in Western narratives that seek to sustain China's image as a non-democratic and backward society lacking in human rights (e.g., Kidd, 2011).

In China, and to some external observers, the Opening Ceremony represented a concerted effort to position China as a global brand. Writing just before the 2008 Games, Chinese cultural theorist Jing Wang predicted:

It will be correct to think that the Beijing Olympics is the torch that will light the biggest bonfire for the Chinese; the field is already primed for a convergence of all the forces crucial to the debut of a "New China" on the Olympian stage (2008, p. 289).

This New China draws upon ancient cultural history and deeply ingrained Chinese myths.

Global brand mythologies depend on targeting global cultural myths (Cayla and Arnould, 2008). Brand researcher Holt's view of the strength of American branding and consumer researchers Cayla and Arnould's notion of culturally developed global branding suggest a re-examination of the ways in which the Opening Ceremony's development of Imagined China targeted myth markets by rejuvenating Chinese history and myth in a cycle of global fashion resources.

Global brand mythologies develop when the mythic landscape is absorbed into the global brand landscape. In this landscape, branded products represent identity myths in ways that seemingly unite global consumers ranging across diverse contexts. A global myth thus reveals differing relations to cultural anchors. Its myth status applies to cultures both within and outside its origins. Coca-Cola, for instance, enjoys a mythic status both within the US and beyond, which is to say for all its mythic associations elsewhere in the world, it is no less, and perhaps even all the more, mythic in the US. Coca-Cola represents unity, cultural strength, and refreshing taste everywhere. A Chinese global myth could function no differently. It should be as mythic in China as it might be elsewhere in the world. This kind of myth can create a successful market when its narratives involve not only the past and the distant past, namely the origins of things, but also social realities regarding the gap between what is and what can be (Holt, 2004; Segal, 2004). It must be retrospective and forward looking. It must live simultaneously in the past, the present, and the future.

Authenticity, nostalgia, and hyperreality

Marketing scholars have a long history of examining the role of authenticity in consumption (e.g., Arnould and Price, 2000; Arsel and Thompson, 2011; Beverland and Farrelly, 2010; Brown, Hirschman, and Maclaran, 2000; Elliott and Davies, 2006). It has also been argued that referring to aspects of historical culture in branding campaigns can evoke authentic and nostalgic emotions (Brown, Kozinets, and Sherry, 2003; Holbrook, 1994; Holbrook and Schindler, 1996; Stern, 1992). Drawing these relationships out further, nostalgia has been described as an authentic aesthetic response to the evocation of the past (Jameson, 1991). Proposing two types of authenticity in marketing practices, consumer researchers Kent Grayson and

Radan Martinec identify what they called *indexical authenticity* and *iconic authenticity* (2004). Indexical authenticity refers to an object that has a factual and spatio-temporal link to history, while iconic authenticity refers to an object that is similar to the original physicality by recourse to reproduction or quasi-authenticity (Bruner, 1994; Crang, 1996; Grayson and Schulman, 2000).

The representation of Imagined China in the Beijing Olympics Opening Ceremony was an evocation of the past par excellence, provoking feelings of longing and belonging for many, in response to the presentation of thousands of years of accumulated history and cultural pride. Such reactions to the Opening Ceremony reflect the success of an Imagined China myth, particularly in bringing forth an authentic China by means of sophisticated technology. For example, Miss J, one of our informants, said:

> It grew dark in the stadium. I could only see red drumsticks. Then I heard the sounds of the drum [*fou*, the ancient percussion instrument of China] beating – like "rat-a-tat thump." Then, suddenly there were many drum beaters on the stage! My friends and I were deeply struck by what we saw. We tried to keep our eyes on everything! What a vivid imagination he [director Zhang Yimou] has. It [the *fou*] is very much like the real thing.

The success of the Opening Ceremony was implicitly dependent on the masterly production of authenticity through modern technology, and Miss J's use of words such as "imagination," "real" and "vivid" marks the *fou* performance's evocation of authenticity.

The *fou* is a Chinese percussion instrument with a 3000-year history. The phrase "beating fou" (*ji fou* in Chinese) appears in the Lian Po and Lin Xiangru sections from the *Records of the Grand Historian* by Sima Qian in the Han Dynasty. The distinctiveness of the *fou* goes hand in hand with an idiomatic phrase sung in tandem with the beating of the drum, *Ji fou er ge*, which refers to having fun, and expresses notions of friendliness and happiness that define public participation in China.

The *fou*'s grand appearance during the Opening Ceremony is an excellent example of what some scholars have called fantasy consumption and contains aspects of pastiche or hyperreality through which varied times and spaces, pasts and futures, overlap, their boundaries blurring in a melding of new, innovative sets of meanings (e.g., Brown, Hirschman, and Maclaran, 2000; Grayson and Martinec, 2004). Although the *fou* performance pays homage to the past, it does so with a twist. Traditionally, *fou* beating, which accompanied death ceremonies among ordinary people, is associated with folk life and its mourning practices.

However, in the Opening Ceremony *fou* playing occurred in tandem with the playing of the *ding*, a traditional three-legged Chinese cooking vessel, an instrument that signifies elite power. In this rendition, the folk and the elite join hands. The sound of mourning joins the sound of triumph and power. In this new context, both the *fou* and the *ding* emerge reconfigured through the other's presence, consequently renewing the notion of authenticity, and Imagined China. This particular rejuvenation of historical Chinese culture enacted by calling upon iconic authenticity in the Opening Ceremony evokes powerful sentiments, in part because its images of the past are quasi-authentic, or what have been called dialectical images (Benjamin, 1999; Pensky, 2004).

Figure 3.2   **Drum (*fou*) Beaters – Beijing Olympics Opening Ceremony**

© Paul J Sutton/PCN /PCN/Corbis

Fashion theorist Caroline Evans has suggested that Benjamin's conception of dialectical images applies to fashion. This is because fashion contains "examples of how the traces of the past can be woven into the fabric of a new story to illuminate the present" (Evans, 2000, p. 108). In this way, yesterday's emblems become tomorrow's commodities.

A good illustration of this mechanism at work in the Opening Ceremony is found in the official emblem "Chinese Seal, Dancing Beijing." The emblem represents a dancing, sporty figure, suggesting the wriggling movements of a dragon, the icon of Chinese civilization. The formal qualities of the image resemble the stamp of an official seal, another powerful symbol of Chinese culture. So we are presented with a contemporary dancing, sporty figure ensconced in the past, or the past and the present contained in one indivisible entity. This new version of the past stimulates nostalgia and evokes pleasure: the past appeals because it is no longer distant but here, now, and new. The contemporary version of the past serves various functions, such as invoking nationalistic and cultural pride, but also responding to cultural and social dissatisfaction in the present. The new version of the past offers resolutions to an uncertain or unhappy present. Some interview narratives illustrate this point:

> They gave a very good performance. I am very, very proud of them [Zhang's teams]. This show makes me miss everyone and everything about my hometown. I haven't been there for fifty years. My favorites were the old Silk Road performance and the Chinese Opera performance. I strongly feel that I had better visit the Mainland [China] as soon as possible" (informant from Taiwan; speaking in Chinese by telephone).

This informant's nostalgia for his hometown was evoked by idealized and romantic representations of the Silk Road in the Opening Ceremony. Nostalgia becomes a particularly strong feeling within contexts that might have involved desertion, illness or death (Holden and Ruppel, 2003). He is an ex-military officer from the Kuomintang who left for Taiwan in 1949 with Chiang Kai-shek, the founding president of Taiwan. His narrative suggests that older people yearn for certain aspects of the past that can never be made whole. Leaving one's hometown under duress of war or threat of incarceration serves as a foundation for nostalgia. In Chinese terms, nostalgia mines a range of traditional values, such as respecting the old and the hometown, one's country and one's locale, as captured by the Chinese proverb "the leaves that fall into the root of the tree" (*luo ye gui gen*), which describes the old returning to their origins.

Nostalgia constitutes selling points in many cultural products, such as period films, retro and vintage clothing, vinyl records, old-fashioned recipes, and revivals in architecture, fashion, and visual art (Borgerson and Schroeder, 2003). Nostalgia transcends yearning for lost childhoods and scenes of early life, and embraces imagined pasts never experienced by its devotees or, for that matter, by anyone. A massive audience remains for nostalgia, a rare device whereby consumption of the past enables individuals to self-reflect without the taint of narcissism.

A fashionable identity

Sometimes, fashion provides a mechanism to address cultural contradictions under the guise of interrogating the subjective experience of modern life (Evans and Breward, 2005). Like other aspects of fashion systems, sporting events, such as the Olympics, can take up social concerns. In conjunction with the notion that certain myths and the markets for these myths derive from existing social concerns and contradictions, one could argue in turn that fashion's resolution of these contradictions, however abstract, helps develop the myth market. The Beijing Olympics, for instance, transmuted the common concern for harmony among nations into the five circles of the Olympic spirit, which were represented in a new way for the Opening Ceremony. As Wang Ning, the deputy director of the Opening & Closing Ceremonies Department of the Beijing Olympics Opening Ceremony Organizing Committee, pronounced on Beijing2008.cn:

> For the first time, the shape of the Olympic Rings will be formed in the sky; in addition to that, Olympic symbols and elements will be part of fireworks designs with an aim to promote Olympic ideals. To reflect the "Green Olympics" concept, some of the fireworks will use less smoking powder to minimize smoke and dust pollution" (Beijing2008.cn, 2008a, p. 1).

In Wang's account, the sky-flying Beijing Olympic Rings and fireworks modeled after Olympic symbols and elements collectively represent peaceful co-existence and the Olympics ideal of "Faster, Higher, Stronger." This motto, from the Olympic Charter, expresses a philosophy extolling virtues such as harmony, strength of body, will, and spirit, all of which restore dignity to human life (Corral et al., 2010). Wang's comments suggest that the Opening Ceremony's rendition of the Olympic spirit is an aesthetic response to contemporary strife, violence, disease, and discrimination, and an attempt to educate people to embrace "non-discrimination, peace, and the psycho-physical improvement of the human being" (Corral et al., 2010, p. 4). In this sense, the Olympics Opening Ceremony can be understood through notions of myth and the market for these myths.

Chinese identity anxiety

Myths must express concrete connections with contemporary values and contexts in order to communicate well and capture the imagination. Constructing an identity myth is complex. Constructing identity myths for brands requires at least five phases: 1) preparing a synopsis of identity anxieties, 2) stating the means by which resolutions will occur, 3) acknowledging the contextual statistics of the locale in which the myth will be located, 4) outlining tactics used in developing an authentic voice for the myth, or brand, and 5) developing a code of communication, or an original aesthetic, which is organically linked to the world (Holt, 2004, pp. 218–19).

Chinese identity anxiety derives from a number of concerns, not least of which is the lingering image of a backward and poor China. Some respondents have indicated that the Beijing Olympics, especially the Opening Ceremony, shook off this old perception of China. For example, Mr. F from Shenzhen, China, said:

> In the eyes of some Western people, China is poor, backward, and uncivilized, and does not merit a big event such as the Olympics. But China does not merely make things. It also does things very well, such as the Opening Ceremony. It has helped to correct the image of China that people had before this ceremony.

Mr. F believes that anxiety around the old Imagined China identity is biased, outdated, and even malicious – based on images that may derive from the history of China's humiliation by Japan and various stages of Western imperialism (e.g., Fairbank and Goldman, 2006). Specifically, these views derive from victimization accounts referring to *luohou aida* – "the backward will be beaten" (Gries, 2005, pp. 50–1; see also Dong and Tian, 2009). More recently, China's embarrassments can be seen to have shifted from the realm of politics to the domain of economics, often focused on market production and accusations of producing cheap and inferior quality goods for export (e.g., Rein, 2012).

Western political critics often link China's backwardness after 1949 to the absence of democracy, a political context from which China attempts to draw attention by referring to its history of humiliation at the hands of the West (Yahuda, 2000). Critics argue that the term "backward China" refers less to economic issues than to political ideology, and that no amount of Olympics "fakery" and propaganda can take away from the fact that the country's media and political freedoms continue to be undermined by the absence of democratic process. For example, outspoken writer Trench Martin-Liao, the former director of the Washington, DC-based Logia Research Foundation, was openly critical about the China Olympics. In an opinion piece in the *New York Daily News*, published during the 2008 Beijing Games, she wrote:

> Behind the grand and scripted stage of these Summer Games – so carefully planned for the cameras by a Chinese government eager for its close-up – is a very different, far uglier backstage. It is rife with pollution, corruption, poverty, bureaucracy and repression. The people of China know that world. They know it intimately. The government of China knows that world too, and tries with all its might to whitewash it out of existence. And here's the sad, funny part. The people are not only used to the deception; they are, by and large, okay with it. In Beijing now, the air is cleaner, the traffic is lighter, the city is beautifully decorated with flowers, and all the nasty beggars and migrant workers have disappeared. So too have the protesters. If you catch a few out of the corner of your eye, just wait – they'll disappear soon enough. Is it live or is it Memorex? The cute little girl in the red dress who sang at the opening

ceremony was only a puppet. The real one was hidden away some-
where because of her "uneven teeth" and poor appearance, all for
the sake of "national interest." You see, China could lose face if
such an unattractive kid sang "Hymn to the Motherland" in front
of all its international friends. Well, at least the glittering chain
of brilliant fireworks that lit the sky from Tiananmen Square to
the Bird's Nest showed how glorious the great nation of China is.
What? Those were fake, too? [...] I suppose whoever revealed this
news will be lucky enough not to join the 44 Chinese journalists
imprisoned by the government, accused of revealing state secrets
and disrupting social order (Martin-Liao, 2008).

Martin-Liao is obviously angry at the lack of democracy in
China. But she, too, has an agenda. She was born in Nanjing,
China, graduated from Taiwan National University, and served
as editor-in-chief for a biographical series on Chinese political
prisoners.

Martin-Liao makes some important points, however. The
Beijing Olympics' record of facilitating economic and social
development remains mixed, and it has also been criticized
for its impact on Beijing and its citizens, before, during, and
after the Games (e.g., Broudehoux, 2007; Shin, 2012; Song
and Buchanan, 2012). Deng Xiaoping's *gaige kaifang* (reform
and opening-up) spurred Chinese economic development and
created a wealthy leisure class. Some people argue that the Deng
era has witnessed a profound shift, from ideological politics
to commerce and patriotism. Emphasis on reform and freer
markets has enabled China to focus on at least one of the two
goals, modernization and democratization, set out in the May
Fourth Movement of 1919. However, achieving modernization,
or "Mr. Science," has only highlighted the continued absence of
political reform, or "Mr. Democracy," terms coined by a founder
of the Movement (see Gu, 2001). This is also an implication
of Martin-Liao's critique, that although the Beijing Olympics
might have made life look pretty in China, political restrictions
continue to hamper the country's development into a truly
modern nation.

Martin-Liao refers specifically to restrictions on media coverage during the Beijing Olympics to illustrate an unpleasant
side of Chinese politics, including the possibility of imprison-
ment for those "accused of revealing state secrets and disrupting

social order." Her comments match other reports of restrictions on what was worth covering and what was worth covering up (e.g., Latham, 2011). Many have claimed that media reporters were instructed to follow official statements and stay silent about pro-Tibet protests and other civil unrest that took place during the Beijing Olympic Games (see Stelter, 2008). On that score, Martin-Liao continues:

> The government makes the myths, and the people eat them up. In China, it seems, it has always been this way. For example: No one died at Tiananmen Square in 1989, except for one brave People's Liberation Army soldier who was killed by the violent mob. The evil foreigners only want to tell us fairy tales in order to split our beloved motherland. Our school textbooks said so. Truth? What does it matter? The 21st century belongs to the Chinese. China will be big and strong. Untroubled by ugly reality. Look forward. Be optimistic. Put on a great show (Martin-Liao, 2008).

These concerns, in effect, constitute the broad strokes of Chinese identity anxiety. As much as its pre-1949 past informs China's image, it remains largely defined by its more recent history of absent democracy and cheap and inferior mass production.

Identity anxiety and brand development

A key step in strong brand development is the creation of an identity myth, which in turn addresses common social anxieties (Holt, 2004). In a sense then, denying these anxieties only delays the possibilities of developing identity myths that can enter into the myth market of global brands. Participant impressions of the Beijing Olympics and its Opening Ceremony suggest that the event helped shape a modern cultural identity for China by addressing various issues pertaining to Chinese identity anxieties – including poverty, an image of backwardness, and a limited democratic movement. Identity often develops discursively across various social and historical dynamics, concerning as well narratives of the self or collective selfhood in multiple, conflicting ways, which also affect identity formation (e.g.,

Giddens, 1991; Hall, 1996; Luedicke, Thompson, and Giesler, 2010). This section traces the formation of various Chinese identities through the narrative discourse surrounding the Beijing Olympics Opening Ceremony.

Some informants discussed the formation of identity through the representation of historical culture in the Opening Ceremony. For them, China emerged as a new and different historical community through the performances of the Opening Ceremony. For example, Mr. Q from Greece said:

> The Beijing Olympics Opening Ceremony helps China build its identity, a long history with modernity. The first thing to attract my attention in this event was the historical culture, such as the four great innovations of ancient China [paper-making, printing, gunpowder, and the compass] and the old Silk Road. Then the use of high technology performs these historical elements.

Miss X from Shanghai, echoed these comments:

> This ceremony cleverly portrays five thousand years of unique Chinese history by tracing remarkable achievements in art, music, and science in such shows as the Silk Road, movable-type printing, and the compass. These achievements are truly different from those of other countries.

In Miss X's narrative, the historical aspects of Chinese culture serve to differentiate China from other countries, and help define its identity.

Identity is discursively constituted through narratives of the self or collective selfhood in acts of identification (e.g., Giddens, 1991; Hall, 1996). In this light, the China of the Opening Ceremony can be identified by four great innovations that took place in ancient times: paper-making, printing, gunpowder, and the compass, in conjunction with the achievements of the old Silk Road. These features of Chinese history not only appealed to Miss X but clearly represent for many people the pinnacle of Chinese achievement; hence their inclusion in the Opening Ceremony. At the same time, the construction of identity takes place through contrasts and difference. Identity formation is contingent upon that from which the self differs, and is constructed in relation to others or to something outside the self. Miss X's comments reflect this point. China showcased its unique features in the Opening Ceremony, based on the notion that difference highlights and creates identity.

Identity develops through relations with people, places, and material goods. It is polyvalent, conflicting, and contested because there are various cultural attributes at work in identity formation, such as the struggle for social position, and the processes this entails. One of the reasons people yearn for the past is because identity thrives on the past – the act of recollecting and identifying the past provides meaning and purpose to life (Lowenthal, 1985). Our informants suggested that the ceremony demonstrated China's sincerity, romance, friendliness, and innovation. Mr. S from Beijing stated:

> The drum beaters then began a thunderous welcoming ceremony, chanting the Confucian saying "Friends have come from afar, how happy we are!" Then an image with the text in Liu-style calligraphy appears around the stadium – at that time, it seems as if I am in a Chinese art gallery or museum. This idiom shows the friendliness and hospitality of Chinese people, and indicates the sincerity of the city!

Mr. S's narrative of the Beijing Olympics Opening Ceremony indicates that China's identity is constructed through various cultural forms, such as the Confucian saying he mentions, Liu-styled calligraphy, and the *fou* drum. Mr. S's appreciation of Chinese identity as represented in the ceremony might sound simplistic, but it parallels familiar processes of identity construction in the sense that many cultural attributes play a role. In this case, particular attributes encourage the perception of Chinese culture, including the drum beating as an indispensable part of Chinese welcoming ceremonies, the chanted Confucian saying, "Friends have come from afar, how happy we are!" and the visual representation of this saying circling the stadium, transforming the environment and creating an enhanced aesthetic atmosphere, much like being in an art museum.

Imaging the new Apsaras of a modern China

Asian brands have been shown to help demonstrate the modernity of Asian cultures (Cayla and Eckhardt, 2008). In keeping with this understanding, the Opening Ceremony did not merely represent China's historical culture, it also showed viewers modern Chinese life, where advanced technology thrives in a nation with long-standing traditions. Imagined China emerged from responses to the Opening Ceremony, reflecting aims for achieving "New Beijing, Great Olympics." The Organizing Committee stated that Green Olympics, High-tech Olympics, and Humanistic Olympics were the major themes of the Beijing Games. As China scholar Gary Xu proposed, the Humanistic Olympics theme, in particular, provided China with an opportunity to reimagine the value system of Chinese culture and project a new image of a China shaped by internationalism and enduring cultural harmony (Xu, 2006).

The Beijing Olympics Opening Ceremony's combination of outstanding performers and spectacular lighting showcased the marriage of cultural achievement with modern technology (Dyer, 2009, p. 13). This union, so to speak, was a point of pride among those responsible for the show. Zhang Yimou, creator of the opening and closing ceremonies, for instance, acknowledged his accomplishment in bringing traditional Chinese culture to the world in the latest multimedia forms. In conversations, Zhang referred to advanced technology, stressing that he was able to demonstrate resoluteness in harnessing this resource to reveal the new modern China. Such a high-tech production does not (necessarily) suggest deception or a desire to mislead the audience, but rather an understanding of the power of technology to produce fantasy, pastiche, and spectacle.

Wang Ning, the deputy director, underlined the critically important role of advanced technology for the ceremony in an interview on Chinese Radio International:

> The technology and equipment used in this Opening Ceremony is very complicated. More than 2,000 tons of equipment was used in the Opening Ceremony including an LED screen 147 metres long and 22 metres wide at the centre of the stadium. Beijing used a smokeless powder to reduce pollution from the 40,000 explosions (quoted in Tu, 2008, p. 1).

The smokeless powder not only falls generally under attempts to attend to the Green Olympics theme, but also represents technological innovation. The ceremony highlighted advanced technology in the performance of the brightly lit *fou* drum, the huge movable scroll, the athletic footsteps painting, the movable printing, and the Silk Road map. It also showcased historical Chinese culture as an integral part of modern life, as expressed in the "Glorious Time" section of the Opening Ceremony.

Connections between culture and technology were further inflected with connections demonstrated between culture and nature, represented by a famous Tai Chi artist's performance. In two acts, the artist performed *he* (harmony) to express the harmony between nature and humans and *feng seng shui qi* (the sound of wind and water rising in tandem). Immediately following this, 2008 Chinese actors collectively performed a number of Tai Chi movements.

The principles of Tai Chi derive from Taoism, which asserts that all things, animate and inanimate, have vitality. This vitality is called *qi*, or breath of life. In the main, Tai Chi is a practice of breath and movement. Every morning and evening millions of Chinese perform this activity to build up the body. The collective performance of 2008 people practicing Tai Chi displayed this ancient art writ large on modern life, a practice in which nature is as embedded in culture as culture is in modern technology.

The use of modern technology was central to the success of the Opening Ceremony. Various performances attest to this. In the "Magnificent Civilization" section, intense drumming gave way to whimsy as dozens of actors dressed as "Flying Apsaras" (mythical Buddhist goddesses, commonly translated as *celestial maidens*) soared across the stadium and created an illuminated replica of the Olympic rings raised above the arena. In "Glorious Times," space-age Flying Apsaras decked out in spacesuits soared through the air. Flying Apsaras often appear in Chinese murals inside Chinese temples and grottos, specifically at Yuangang, Longmen, and Dunhung Grottos. Buddhist scripture describes "Flying Apsaras" as gods of heaven, and as deities associated with song, music, and fragrance. They are typically depicted as young slim women with plump faces, elegant manners, and gentle moods. The Opening Ceremony performances recreate these scenes in three dimensions, in keeping with the traditional version of suitably attired actors and others in space-age suits. The point is both simple and effective, that the mythical Apsaras of the past have transmuted into space-age creatures, the new Apsaras of modern China, particularly relevant as China's reach into space heats up.

Legendary Chinese gymnast Li Ning's lighting of the cauldron was a powerful symbolic touch in these performances. Li Ning enjoyed a spectacularly successful Olympic career in the 1980s, and he made a dramatic appearance in the ceremony, suspended by cables, airborne and soaring, in a manner similar to that of the Apsaras. Li Ning's participation in the Opening Ceremony was as strategic as the inclusion of various other celebrities, including director Zhang Yimou, and Chinese basketball hero Yao Ming, who carried the Chinese flag and led the Chinese delegation into the Bird's Nest stadium for the Opening Ceremony.

Zhang Yimou: Extending the global Chinese myth market

Every myth needs a hero, whether it is a person, a force, or a place. Scholars are clear about the necessary relationship between myth and hero, and some even argue equivalence: "archetypal heroes that control powerful forces" function as myth (Cayla and Arnould, 2008, p. 100). In other words, heroes embody myth itself. The 2008 Beijing Olympics had such a hero: Zhang Yimou, a film director with a mythical status and global reputation.

A veteran Chinese director, producer, writer, and sometimes actor, Zhang Yimou has directed dozens of films. A 2008 runner-up in *Time* magazine's "Person of the Year", Zhang ranks among the most well-known film directors to emerge from China. As film luminary Steven Spielberg's (2008) glowing portrait of Zhang for *Time* reveals, Zhang's Opening Ceremony garnered widespread admiration and praise:

> Drawing from the depths of the cultural heritage and ingenuity of the Chinese people, showcasing ancient Chinese inventions – paper, printing, gunpowder, ceramics and the compass – that have shaped civilization and channelling the sensibility and spirit that unite his fellow 1.3 billion citizens, Zhang told China's story to a

watching world. He created arguably the grandest spectacle of the new millennium, and it was viewed by nearly one-third of the world's population. With this work, Zhang obtained a stature shared by very few peers.

Zhang's history of film making secured his hire as creative and art director of the Olympics Opening Ceremony. Zhang satisfied two criteria: his involvement in the Games aroused nationalistic

Figure 3.3   **Zhang Yimou, director of the 2008 Beijing Olympics Opening Ceremony**

© Ng Han Guan/AP/Corbis

pride and formally endorsed a particular brand of Chineseness already familiar amongst global audiences of Chinese films, and his visual styling and tactical recreation of a glorious and resplendent China replete with determined human spirit and ancient culture won kudos from various quarters (Xu, 2007).

Zhang is well known for several classic films. *Yellow Earth* (*Huang Tudi* in Chinese), made in 1984, for which he was cinematographer, represented the conflict between human revolution and the earth's unassuming antiquity. *Ju Dou*, from 1990, tackled the patricidal urge and sexual transgressions, and was the first Chinese film nominated for an Academy Award. His next film, 1991's *Raise the Red Lantern*, criticized patriarchal repression during the early Republican period, introduced Western audiences to both Zhang and his leading actress, Gong Li, and was also nominated for the Best Foreign Language Film at the Academy Awards. *Not One Less* (1999) dealt with modernization and rural education during the reform era. *Hero* (2002) was explicitly about heroism and the first emperor of a unified China.

China scholar Gary Xu described Zhang's 2004 film, *House of Flying Daggers*, at great length in ways that challenge the notion of China's backwardness. Xu draws parallels between the "romantic, passionate and dream-like" visual spectacles of the Beijing Opening Ceremony and movies such as *Hero* and *House of Flying Daggers* (2007). In addition to similarities between the musical and dance numbers of the Opening Ceremony and those in *Hero* and *House of Flying Daggers*, respectively, Zhang also managed to create a thematic continuity between cinematic imagination and contemporary reality, between fictional representation and a concrete sporting event. He thus effectively relocated the historical retrospection and dream imagery of *Hero* and *House of Flying Daggers* that audiences identified with Chineseness onto a veritable world stage, that of the Olympics Opening Ceremony. This masterly citation of a somewhat fictionalized account of a non-fictional nation not only constitutes, in itself, the concretization of the myth, that of China and Chinese creativity, but also represents the confidence of a cultural aesthetic at the top of its game.

In an interview Zhang gave in *Movie View* (*Kan Dianying*), a popular Chinese movie magazine, he clearly articulates the twofold goal of his recent film making: selling a particular brand of

Chinese culture and teaching the world that China has finally arrived. Zhang states:

> I was clearly aware that I made *Hero* for foreign viewers. As soon as Americans heard that Jet Li, Tony Leung, Maggie Cheung, Ziyi Zhang, and Donnie Yen were to appear together in a martial arts film, they'd want to see the film. We would easily open on 2,000 screens, but I decided not to cater exclusively to their tastes. If I were to satisfy their tastes, I would have focused more on direct physical contact in the fight scenes. Instead, I decided to focus more on spiritual communication and less on physical contact. In fact, I wanted to lure those foreigners into the theatre before exposing them to ideas of genuine Chinese arts. Impress them a little. Give them some information. This is only the first step. There are things in Chinese culture that cannot be easily understood. It would be a great achievement if a foreigner can figure out the meaning of *yijing* [ideascape] after living in China for ten years. I don't expect them to understand. All I want is gradual influence, bit by bit. What I have to sell is Chinese culture through a martial arts genre (quoted in Xu, 2007, p. 36).

Zhang's notion of Chinese culture is summed up by the phrase *yijing* (ideascape), which resonates suggestively with branding concept "ideoscape" (Askegaard, 2006).

Yijing is an abstract notion implying "a poetic sense of harmony between the human mind and surrounding nature" that is "already tinged with human emotions and is thus not subject to codes of verisimilitude" (Xu, 2007, p. 40). In one of Zhang's first interviews after the Opening Ceremony, he asserted that "passionate, romantic and dream-like" specifically described the ceremony, expressing *yijing* and opening China's story and Chinese history and culture to foreign audiences (www.Beijing 2008.cn, 2008b).

Romance is a central theme in Zhang's recent work, which also favors directness, constructed authenticity, and an aesthetic defined by beauty and grace. People, places, and things – everyone and everything, whether they are heroes and heroines, or historical figures such as Confucius and emperors – are uniformly treated by emphasizing physical beauty. This applies in Zhang's film work and in the Opening Ceremony. Even the action-packed and spiritually bound characteristics of martial arts and Tai Chi in *Hero* are filtered through romance and romanticized beauty.

Hero showcases *yijing* through the master and pioneer of modern Chinese aesthetics, Zong Baidhua, represented by means of analogy by an empty pavilion in the middle of mountains and lakes (Xu, 2007). The pavilion's emptiness, which implies human practice in nature, becomes "the converging point for the breathing and spiritual movement of the mountains and lakes" (Xu, 2007, p. 40). This, in essence, beautifully represents Zhang's notion of Chinese culture.

The central protagonists in *Hero*, such as the historical character Qin Shihuang, and associated concepts, such as *tian xia* (political sovereignty), are used as a kind of shorthand for abstract notions of civilization and the end of the barbaric fringe. Qin Shihuang was the first emperor of unified China. It was under his rule that the notion of *tian xia*, which literally means "under heaven," initially understood as the entire geographical and metaphysical realm of mortals, subsequently came to be equated with political sovereignty. In China, Qin Shihuang, therefore, constitutes a model, an archetype even, of unity and harmony, concepts that Zhang translated to the Opening Ceremony.

The Olympics are absorbed into this great Chinese story, which began in ancient times and continues through the present, and Zhang's rather abstract equivalence between Chinese unity and world harmony is difficult to miss or contest. In one performance, Chinese schoolchildren paint a simple picture with mountains, a river, and a smiling sun. The vignette of children drawing a picture frames the Opening Ceremony's first and last parts, and defines its basic storytelling structure, by which Zhang means to achieve yet another act of substitution. Not only is painting an old art form but it is also *the* art form of one of the oldest and longest civilizations in history. Consequently, all that follows this initial vignette, including the rest of the Opening Ceremony and the weeks of Games thereafter, constitute different chapters of the story.

The theatrical features of Zhang Yimou's visual style were in demand well before the Beijing Olympics. Since the 1990s Zhang has been seen as China's cultural ambassador and the new world power's artistic voice (Xu, 2007). A work outside film remains one his most well-known and successful.

In 1997, Zhang was invited to stage Puccini's *Turandot* conducted by Zubin Mehta in Florence. Italy. A year later, he staged the same opera in the Forbidden City, where the original story is set. A newly inflected Chinese focus via "authentic," quasi historically accurate costumes and tableaux aimed at fully exploring the opera's Orientalist content. Although Zhang, at the time, lacked experience in theatrical production, some observers resorted to what may be called a "primitivist" innovation argument to suggest he deftly turned the handicap to his advantage. It was precisely because he was untrained in the basics of operatic theatre that he was able to lend the story and the staging authenticity. Nobody else, Xu implies, had the wherewithal, or imaginative potential, to get to the heart of this opera, in which Western fascinations with the Orient are woven "into a colorful tapestry of exotic material culture and unfamiliar emotive expressions" (Xu, 2007, p. 43). Zhang's operatic innocence, as it were, his insistence on cultural authenticity, and "his uncanny ability to arrange crowds in a spacious setting" are precisely "what makes Zhang's amateurish opera career unique," attracting global attention (Xu, 2007, p. 39). Zhang's huge *Turandot* production has toured widely, including stops in Beijing, London, Seoul, and Taiwan, and at Olympic stadiums in Paris, Berlin, and Barcelona (Tuan, 2011).

Zhang's operatic ventures seem to have paid off for China, in that they provided grist for the Opening Ceremony. Specifically, various musical devices in the Opening Ceremony established a highly operatic ambience of melodramatic opulence of feeling. The sonorous sounds of the gong and the drum played by the Peking Opera Orchestra and the melodious sounds of the *huqin* fiddle kick off a performance of Chinese traditional opera, followed by a concert of traditional percussion instruments interpolated by sounds of drum beating in conjunction with a dance accompaniment by actors dressed as Xian terracotta warriors – attributed to Qin Shinhuang and excavated from the environs of his tomb – dancing with red flags in their hands. These performances successively represent Chinese history across space and time, and are filled with diverse folk traditions, dialects, and art forms, all of which consummately immerse the viewer in the historical complexities of Chinese culture.

Zhang's Opening Ceremony demonstrated his acute grasp of the importance of location, a faculty that is everywhere in evidence in *Hero*, which perhaps provided Zhang with a model for thinking about how to frame, introduce, and stage historical settings and places in the Opening Ceremony. *Hero* was shot in tourist destinations popular for their historical riches. The spectacular scenes of the formidable Qin army's attack on the Zhao capital, for instance, were shot in the sandstorms of Dunhuang city in Gansu province. Dunhuang, which is located in the Gobi Desert and is known as a jewel on the Silk Road, is famous for its numerous caves, once home to thousands of ancient Buddhist manuscripts, sculptures, and murals. Depictions of the Silk Road and the Flying Apsaras in the Opening Ceremony are modeled on images and artefacts found in these caves. Zhang's previous creation of a historic and mythic China in his films, his considerable success in the opera world, and his repute cumulatively made him the best candidate for creating a new global image for China. His image was a hybrid of Chinese historical culture, represented by *yijing*, and modern technological spectacle that had the immediacy required by a huge event such as the Olympic Games Opening Ceremony.

The presentation of "harmony" via the movable print performance, the gigantic rising globe called "Dream," the scroll with the footprints of all the participants, and the theme song *You and Me* represented a vision of peaceful, friendly people living in harmony. This theme is an aspiration among many people across the world. By representing this theme through a Chinese focus, the Opening Ceremony enabled China, namely its government and its creative personnel, to target a global myth.

In contrast to the frequent criticism of Chinese state control over artistic freedom, Zhang's comments to the *Financial Times* after the Games provide a different picture: "I am still an independent artist. I am not a member of the Chinese Communist Party or the Communist Youth League," says Zhang. "I am still working hard to make one new film after another. My life has not changed at all" (in Xie, 2009, p. 1). Zhang emphasizes his independent status despite working for China to direct the Opening and Closing Ceremonies. His comments seem to emphasize the importance of autonomy in artistic creativity and uniqueness. In one sense Zhang's comments cannot be picked apart for contradiction, as his work in the Opening Ceremony generally shunned obvious references to contemporary political issues.

Of course, one could offer criticism that in setting much of the Ceremony in the mythical past, Zhang shrewdly avoided stepping on governmental toes. The image of the new China was resplendent, modern, and positive, and it is hardly surprising that references to political issues, such as the Taiwan Strait, Tibet, human rights, and the Xizang and Xinjiang issues that give China a bad name, were markedly absent. If anything, the Opening Ceremony was a site of celebration, commemoration, and fantasy and although it might have provided a skewed representation of the real China, was perhaps no different from what is commonly expected at such events. The Opening Ceremony was an opportunity to unveil a brand, the new China, that had long been in the making, and that is precisely what it did.

Public discourses of the Opening Ceremony

After the Games, various debates emerged around the issue of whether the Beijing Olympics Opening Ceremony represented the "real" China. As mentioned above, Steven Spielberg, who had withdrawn from his position as adviser for the Opening Ceremony, called it "the grandest spectacle of the new millennium" (quoted in Dyer, 2009). Other audiences and media commentators continued to see China as an isolated and less developed nation in both the past and the present, partly because of the later Qing Dynasty's closed door policy between 1724, marked by the ban on Christianity, and 1842, and the first Opium War, as well as Mao's policy of economic self-sufficiency from 1949 to 1976 (Grasso, Corrin, and Kort, 2004; Xing and Xin, 1998).

Informing these discourses were the divergent histories of Europe and China. During the 18th century and the early 19th century, Europe was changing under the impact of rationalism, nationalism, colonialism, and the industrial revolution. Meanwhile, the Qing court had adopted a position of isolation toward the Western world (Xing and Xin, 1998). Later, Mao stressed the need for ideological remodeling. He espoused class struggle and advocated economic self-sufficiency, hoping that progress could be achieved through ideological motivation (Grasso, Corrin, and Kort, 2004). Since the 1989 anti-bourgeois

liberalism and pro-democracy movement, the Chinese government has promoted a four-fold strategy of modernization and
democratization directed toward four quarters: agriculture,
industry, national defense, and science and technology (Grasso,
Corrin, and Kort, 2004).

The Opening Ceremony opened the floodgates to questions about political and social freedoms. Some pointed to the
revelation that the nine-year-old who appeared to be singing
the Chinese national anthem was lip-synching, the actual singing voice belonging to a seven-year-old deemed not telegenic
enough to appear on stage. They saw the fakery as a metaphor for the various restrictions imposed on the media before,
during, and after the Games. Many in the foreign media wanted
to reveal the unseen and unreported sides of China, with accusations of air pollution, forced evictions, human rights violations,
suppression of dissidents, corruption, heavy-handed security,
political crackdowns in Beijing, Xinjiang, and Tibet, and the
forced disappearance of beggars and migrant workers.

Initial reception to the Opening Ceremony was mostly positive. Zhang Yimou's lavish display of cultural history impressed
viewers across the globe and generally silenced naysayers (e.g.,
Coles, Knowles, and Newbury, 2012; Latham, 2009; Qing et
al. 2010). But within days of the Ceremony, the shine began to
wear off. Several concerns emerged, mainly whether the Opening
Ceremony was a representation of the real China or a mostly fictional creation by a hugely talented film director. One of the first
blows arrived on August 9 2008 when the *Beijing Times* (*Jing hua
shi bao*) revealed that the giant fireworks showing footprints were,
in fact, digital images. News of the little girl's lip-synched singing
added to the controversy. These scandals fuelled fierce debates
about Olympic fakery, reasons why the Opening Ceremony could
not reveal the "real" China, and reasons why Chinese authorities were concerned about face value, and about the lengths to
which they were willing to go to ensure the portrayal of a perfect
China (Latham, 2009). Many concluded that the "real China"
was too unpleasant to be revealed, and perhaps Imagined China
was an unreal China. Others argued that reporting on the fakery
did not constitute ground-breaking news, but rather only negated
an image that was already widely contested.

Before MSNBC News Division president Steve Capus set out
to cover the Games, he said, "if there was news, in whatever form,

they would be covering it" (in Stelter, 2008, p. 1). Later, Capus revised his earlier statement, admitting that the desire to cover the Olympics might conflict with the desire to cover news, leading media critics to ask "what is sports and what is news?" (Stelter, 2008, p. 1). The US television network MSNBC reported that "a meeting had taken place between the major right-holders to broadcast the games internationally and Olympic officials requesting that the restrictions imposed upon them be lessened in order to provide 'decent coverage'" (Stelter, 2008, p. 1). Restrictions on reports of pro-Tibet protest activity and internet censorship is also mentioned here. All reports were expected to take the official line and stay away from the reality of China, though Steve Capus insisted that all manner of news deserved to be covered.

Some observers chose to remain positive and view the problems of the Opening Ceremony as an opportunity for cultural interpretation. For example, anthropologist Kevin Latham suggests that the "fake" giant firework footprints actually reveal a great deal about the pursuit of authenticity both in the Games and within cultural practice at large (2009). According to information shared with a Beijing newspaper by an Olympic official, the firework footprints were filmed a year prior to the Games and subsequently manipulated to produce digital images for use in the event of bad weather. This information suggests that while the means were deceptive, the intent was pragmatic. The Chinese officials had planned for all eventualities, and used the solutions they had had the foresight to arrange. From here, one could argue that the desire to create and sustain an authentic vision of reality was a profound concern. It applied not only to the representation of history: rather, it was comprehensive in conception, and therefore fuelled various aspects of the Opening Ceremony, including ensuring that the fireworks display was not impeded by uncooperative weather conditions. In any case, at times, these concerns seem to forget that the Opening Ceremony dwells in the realm of fabrication, fantasy, and fashion.

Fashion and the global myth

Fashion works as a system that reflects the spirit of the times and creatively reveals social concerns and scientific, and aesthetic progress (Wilson, 2005). Fashion, fuelled by urbanization, organizes modern life through the intervention of stylized, everyday products (Evans and Breward, 2005). The fashion industry does not merely produce pleasant clothing, music, sport, and other cultural forms. It also produces stylistic innovations and creative visions (Kawamura, 2005).

This is true as well in sporting event fashion, such as the Olympics. As the artist Cai Guoqiang – the visual creative director of the Opening & Closing Ceremonies Department – suggests, the Opening Ceremony used global fashion systems to represent the concern for environmental pollution through the concept of a Green Olympics, the pursuit of romantic ideals through storytelling, and the expression of peace and equality across 2008 smiling faces emerging in the fireworks (Beijing 2008.cn, 2008a, p. 1). No less noteworthy, however, is that a sporting event, in its capacity as spectacle, can reconstruct people into icons who consequently generate new styles of playing, dressing, behaving, and appearance. It is their game and personality, on and off the sports fields, that brings sports as fashion to retail counters and online boutiques. If athletes are driven by the game, audiences are driven by what athletes wear in attitude and clothing.

Themed clothing often becomes fashionable before, during, and after any big sporting event. An event as big and widely publicized as the Olympics, which forms its own cultural institution, produces its own corps of fashion images. People wearing themed clothing generate their own subculture. These include sponsors, officials, workers, athletes, attendees, and viewers across the world.

The Olympics provides a "fantastic opportunity for viewing international fashion" (Wilson, 2008). The teams' Opening Ceremony uniforms play increasingly important roles in the Olympic spectacle. Many are designed by well-known brands, and most seem to project a conservative, well-tailored identity. As one pop culture blog commented, "many countries sent out sailors and private school students with crests and heraldry adorning the breast of their sports jackets" (Tumasoff, 2008, p. 1). The Japanese team, for example, was dressed in white pants and navy vests printed with brass admiral buttons that derived from a country club sporting lifestyle. The Polish team wore dark navy vests with contrasting cream buttons. The US team's black suits with tied cravats, ascots, and contrasting white caps were designed by Ralph Lauren, inspired by the film *Chariots of Fire*; its members sported an array of sweater vests and clean-cut polo shirts with flag patches or Chinese characters reading "Beijing" (Frankel, 2008; Wilson, 2008).

Outside the stadium, the fashion industry around the Olympics boomed. The Chinese-American actress Lucy Liu, for example, in more than ten photos for *Harper's Bazaar*, showcased clothing by Chanel, Alexander McQueen, Christian Lacroix, Giorgio Armani, Versace, Givenchy, Dior, Dolce & Gabbana, and Carolina Herrera that referenced all things sporty (Harper's Bazaar Staff, 2008). Other events attempted to establish a more meaningful connection with the Games. Luxury brand Shanghai Tang used the number eight in its giveaway scheduled for 8:08 PM on August 8 2008. Eight women dressed in Shanghai Tang's signature red silk *qipao* outfits, standing at the corner of 57th Street and Madison Avenue in Manhattan, gave away 888 red envelopes containing a lucky Chinese dollar. Participants had the option to either retain the lucky dollar or chance winning an $888 shopping spree at Shanghai Tang's Midtown Manhattan boutique (Hruska, 2008).

All these events and activities represent the creation of an institutionalized fashion system, which seems to express a unified concern for the Games, and consequently for ideals associated with it. Styles of clothing, fashion shoots, advertising, and even the verbal discourse of the fashion world in the media, all constitute a consummate fashion brand that propagates its own myth and that of the Games. If the Opening Ceremony reimagined China, the fashion system constructed around the Games also generated its own vision of the already reimagined China, and thereby contributed to the global myth of Imagined China.

The global myth of the 2008 Olympic Games as represented in the Opening Ceremony derived from a number of features, such as Chinese culture and history, contemporary Chinese film, Chinese art and philosophy, and the economic wherewithal of the Chinese government's resources. Worldwide fashion systems also constituted a significant partner in this collective enterprise directed by Zhang under the aegis of the Chinese government. Not least was the role of the media, which focused on China's economic strength, its historical culture, and the reality behind the mask of progress. In short, Imagined China was constructed out of both positive and negative factors, all of which collectively helped produce a complex and comprehensive global myth market.

Global myths and Chinese culture

This case study used the Imagined China myth of the 2008 Beijing Olympics Opening Ceremony to examine the development of a global myth through the discourses of managerial workers, viewers, and the media. In this case, the myth market developed from historical Chinese culture and global fashion systems, evoking nostalgia and authentic feeling, as well as reflecting social contradictions. Myth markets typically involve an identity myth, which in this case is defined by anxiety. Specifically, China's identity anxiety derives from narratives of economic and technological backwardness, scant democracy, the taint of cheap and inferior mass production, widely publicized media restrictions during the Games, and the various "lies" of the Opening Ceremony performances. Still, many would argue that all these anxieties amounted to little in the face of the Opening Ceremony's cumulative achievement in creating a vision of a modern, beautiful, and less politically stunted society, with an incredibly rich historical culture.

Extending the global myth market represents the last and most important way to make a local brand global (Cayla and Arnould, 2008; Holt and Cameron, 2010). In the Beijing Olympics Opening Ceremony, the global myth market developed from the blurring of boundaries between Zhang's globally familiar filmic repertoire and his selective rejuvenations of Chinese history and culture, which generated a Chinese-inflected view of global concerns regarding harmony, unity, peace, and war. The global market for this myth expanded and extended through the mediation of media – which form a central feature of the myth market – and the wide range of media discourse lent an external authenticity to the mythical drama. The represented myth appears so real that it can withstand negative discourses, revealing ways in which negative discourse can solidify brand authenticity (Giesler, 2012). All these mechanisms collectively extend and expand the myth market.

We have shown how the 2008 Beijing Olympics Opening Ceremony adopted a historical and mythical approach toward

Chinese culture using global fashion resources to establish the myth of Imagined China. Zhang's direction enhanced the perception and consumption of a new Chinese way of life, and new Chineseness, through which new cultural forms became possible. In the context of the 2008 Beijing Olympics, Chinese brand culture clearly emerges – targeting markets through historical and mythical Chinese culture paired with modern technology, composing identity myths and extending them globally, and engaging with historical and cultural codes of branding.

4   Shanghai Tang: A Chinese Luxury Brand with Global Ambitions

I like Shanghai Tang. I am fascinated by its citation of Chinese traditions. For example, Chinese gold and silver ingots (yuanbao) were an important medium to exchange expensive goods in ancient China. They were typically owned by high-ranking officials, emperors, and tycoons, and used as money. Shanghai Tang has cleverly introduced gold and silver ingots in its patterns. They look very stylish, up-to-date, attractive, distinctive, and meaningful. I love Shanghai Tang's unique style!
Mrs. W, Beijing

Shanghai Tang promotes itself as the first and only luxury brand to have emerged from China. It fuses iconic elements of Chinese culture with stylish fashion for the current globetrotting shopper (Chua and Eccles, 2009). The brand includes a range of goods, from wearable and affordable luxury to bespoke tailoring for suits and dresses, all of which convey the image of a modern Chinese lifestyle. David Tang, a wealthy Hong Kong tycoon, started Shanghai Tang in 1994, offering a line of high-quality, often eccentric products made in Mainland China. Initially, the product line included Chairman Mao wristwatches, *qipao*, silver chopsticks, Chinese-designed silk panamas, leather items, and bespoke tailoring. Tang expanded Shanghai Tang's presence by taking it abroad to New York, London, and Paris, aiming to become China's first global luxury brand.

Tang's entrepreneurial acumen ensured profits within one year of expansion. However, the 1997 Asian financial crisis hit the company hard, and Shanghai Tang's fortunes turned. In 2001,

Tang sold the majority of his stake to the Richemont group, a Switzerland-based luxury retailer that counts prominent luxury brands such as Cartier, Alfred Dunhill, Piaget, and Montblanc in its portfolio. By the end of 2011, Shanghai Tang had over 40 stores in 11 countries, including 17 in China, with plans to increase that number to 30 by 2012 (Khan and Balfour, 2011).

Today, prices for Shanghai Tang's bestselling dresses hover around $700 and men's mandarin collar shirts are about $275. As Raphael Le Masne de Chermont, Shanghai Tang's French executive chairman and CEO, said in 2011, "Sir David Tang was the first person to say we could proudly brand China and the products that were made in China. He was a visionary" (Luxuryinsider.com, 2011). The company has focused recent expansion plans on China. Matt Marsden, research director at Daiwa Capital Markets, explains: "Shanghai Tang has done a fantastic job of building brand equity and has become a genuine luxury brand in Hong Kong and the West. This will help give it credibility and increase the chances of success as the company expands in China" (quoted in Khan and Balfour, 2011, p. 1).

The selective definition of historical and traditional Chinese cultural resources in conjunction with global fashion systems had the potential to transform a local and regional brand into a global presence. Drawing upon the insight that brands co-create contexts in which cultural creation can occur – which echoes the workings of fashion systems – this chapter examines the voices of consumers, managers, and the media, all of whom interpret Shanghai Tang as a vivid symbol of a culturally and historically specific China, which nevertheless represents a culture beyond national boundaries reimagined through fashion resources. The discourses of Shanghai Tang elaborate this particular vision and incarnation of China: they also elaborate ways in which the Richemont group, a Western luxury firm, reinvigorated Shanghai Tang's branding through a contemporary aesthetic imbued with Chinese dimensions. The narrative treats common storylines and overarching themes that arise through various interpretations of Shanghai Tang.

Fashion discourses involve interpretations of historical themes and current social concerns. Furthermore, many global fashion images embrace metaphorical references, which are effectively condensed and constructed from these themes and

Figure 4.1   **David Tang, founder of Shanghai Tang, in Hong Kong**
© Uden Graham/Redlink/Corbis

concerns (e.g., Cholachatpinyo *et al.*, 2002). Fashion products may reference various historical cultures; for example, modern fashion has drawn upon stylistic aspects of the Renaissance and Baroque periods (Evans, 2000). As noted earlier, these historical periods become abbreviated images that relocate and dislocate iconic characteristics of these eras (Evans, 2000). Indeed, historical references in modern fashion are subject to contemporary visions and ideas, as their designers and users invent them anew, selectively retracing, rethinking, and reinterpreting historical perspectives and events. Fashion images with historical references create layered, often contradictory meanings, and shed new light on the present (Evans, 2000). Such dialectical images in global branding refer to brand images with a historical reference that is retooled with new meanings, which might contradict the original historical source.

A sense of Chineseness is integral to Shanghai Tang. The traditional calligraphy and color palette of Shanghai Tang's logo help embody the brand's identity. Indeed, the brand exploits both common and unusual visual and verbal conventions to imply an essential equivalence between Chinese historical conventions and contemporary fashion. This flattening of difference between old and new suggests that mutually exclusive elements are potentially inclusive of one another, and give rise to metaphoric codes which potential consumers of Shanghai Tang recognize and relate to.

In the following, we examine the processes and possibilities of the co-creation of brands and brand culture by managers, consumers, and the media through the lens of global fashion systems and cultural resources from Chinese history and traditions. The study of Shanghai Tang facilitates an examination of the flow of cultural meanings.

The significance of design

Shanghai Tang's success depends upon design. Details such as store layout, colors, and clothing fasteners all play a part in the overall brand DNA (see Henderson et al., 2003). We can start at the beginning, with the company name. Many of our interview participants seemed to appreciate the innovative rendition of the brand. The Chinese name, Shanghai Tang (上海滩), reminds some of the well-known Chinese television series of the same name (上海滩), as well as Shanghai's leading attractions, such as Shanghai Bund, which represent for the average consumer a vision of what Shanghai was in its pre-Second World War heyday. The formal qualities of the brand's visual aspects are equally evocative. Shanghai Tang's logo reads right to left, following the traditional Chinese direction – a small detail, but one that enhances the brand's authenticity. The logo's gold color expresses the brand's retro glamor, which, according to consumer accounts, plays a significant part in the brand's identity. The store décor enhances the brand's image, as retail themes of light pink and green lend playfulness to the traditional gold logo.

CEO Raphael Le Masne de Chermont previously headed the Richemont group's other luxury brands serving key markets in Europe and Asia. Le Masne de Chermont brought extensive experience with luxury brands to Shanghai Tang – while working for Richemont, he gained on-the-job brand development training at Piaget. On taking over the helm at Shanghai Tang, Le Masne de Chermont hired top-class creative employees, with wide ranging international experience, such as Joanne Ooi. Ooi was born in Singapore and raised in the US, and held the position of creative director for seven years. Although Ooi had only two years of experience in the fashion arena, having worked with French shoe designer Stephane Kélian in Asia, she quickly grasped the problems holding back Shanghai Tang.

At the time of Ooi's hire, Shanghai Tang mainly offered expensive and fashion-insensitive Chinese emporium goods to local Chinese consumers. Its high-end market was naturally very narrow, and most tourists were likely to patronize it only as a once-in-a-lifetime shopping opportunity. Le Masne de Chermont and Ooi redeveloped Shanghai Tang into a more fashion-conscious, Chinese-styled establishment offering highly wearable clothes with some eccentric features. Further, the management team jointly aimed to recast Shanghai Tang as a lifestyle brand encompassing not only clothing, but also home accessories and curiosities. Opening the Shanghai Tang café further expanded the lifestyle motif.

Ooi connected the brand with its culture: "For each collection, Ooi chooses and researches a China-related theme. 'I decided it was really imperative to create cultural roots for every single product'" (Tischler, 2006). These measures paid off, and the brand's sales increased rapidly. In 2005, its New York store's sales revenue jumped 50 percent.

In an article in *Fast Company*, le Masne de Chermont proposed that Shanghai Tang could be a peer of Gucci, the high-end global luxury brand: "It's no surprise that the company's principals have been recruited from the carpet-bagging global creative class. We're a melting pot of multicultural people who work on the same vision: a Chinese lifestyle brand that has relevant ambivalence" (Tischler, 2006, p. 3). These global, cosmopolitan managers/employees – members of various diasporas – reflect Shanghai Tang's version of Chineseness. In an interview from MediaTV's series on luxury brands' marketing strategies, Le Masne de Chermont, who has lived in Hong Kong since 1999, stated:

> The rise of China as a luxury powerhouse, not only as a market of consumers, but also as a breeding ground, will produce high-end brands of its own. Rising costs of production in China mean it is losing its competitive edge to other Asian markets, so it will begin to develop its own luxury labels to fill the needs of this new upmarket culture [...] You see, China is doing it with telephones and computers, like Lenovo and Haier, but you haven't seen China yet doing it with fashion and lifestyle [...] there will be some emerging, and it is good news (in Davis, 2009, p. 1).

As part of its resolution to create a fashion-based brand culture of Chineseness across the globe, Shanghai Tang also launched the Mandarin Collar Society in 2009, "a club with the goal to promote an elegant Chinese-inspired style for men. It's an alternative that allows you to reorient yourself, to be stylish while being yourself" (from shanghaitang.com).

Shanghai Tang employs seven in-house designers who renew, renovate, and upgrade their growing product line (Chua and Eccles, 2009). Within this group, five are of Chinese extraction, a number that indicates Shanghai Tang's commitment to Chineseness. Designers are expected to factor in sales and costs when creating new designs or introducing changes. The most challenging aspect of the designer's work might reside in the "open to buy" principle, wherein Shanghai Tang retailers and franchisers have the freedom to create their own sales inventory each time a final collection is made available in a viewing (Chua and Eccles, 2009). The aims of this strategy are simple – optimize sales by enabling retailers and franchisers to select the best mix of products suitable for their respective stores and clienteles. Naturally, there are implicit downsides to this principle. Despite their creative features, some designs might not sell well. Orders will be canceled. In short, Shanghai Tang's design strategy suggests a strong market orientation in brand philosophy, which undoubtedly helps Shanghai Tang stay on top of market changes, consumer inclinations, and international fashion demands.

Shanghai Tang's business focuses on its core collection, several seasonal collections, and holiday promotions. The core collection remains fundamental, as it comprises a stable selection of bestsellers, including cashmere and silk sweaters, home furnishings, and other gift goods, all of which amount to 50 percent of total revenue (Chua and Eccles, 2009). Seasonal collections, however, keep Shanghai Tang fresh, up-to-date, and abreast of global fashion trends – critically important for maintaining status in the global fashion industry.

Shanghai Tang chooses its retail locations carefully, with an eye toward symbolic luxury (ShanghaiTang.com, 2010a). For example, the Xin Tian Di outlet evokes old Shanghai's storied heritage, the JinJiang Hotel store appeals to official Chinese governors and other consumers interested in the age of Mao Zedong, and the Beijing Ritz Carlton Hotel store exudes luxury and pleasure. As for product designs, Shanghai Tang draws on a number of significant icons and symbols from the vast lexicon of Chinese cultural and historical meanings, which evoke a variety of associations, from nostalgia and historical pride to cultural curiosity and sensual confidence.

As attitudes to luxury brand image and conspicuous consumption change, so does the notion of "Chineseness." Consumers, of course, interpret and define Shanghai Tang's brand meanings largely through the filter of their own cultural backgrounds, tastes, and experience. Shanghai Tang's role within the fashion system is shaped through both active and passive consumption, which, while functioning at the behest of fashion, also help to shape fashion, and thereby reform its principles. Consumption, interpretation, and identity projection are, it would seem, equal parts flattery and correction, and constitute central factors in the development of brand meanings, for example, pertaining to apparel, logo design, and lifestyles spaces, such as the Shanghai Tang café.

The myth of the modern Chinese lifestyle

Shanghai Tang targets cosmopolitan consumers. Political theorist Pippa Norris contends that in contrast to consumers who identify primarily with national symbols, "cosmopolitans can be understood as those who identify more broadly with their continent or with the world as a whole, and who have a greater faith in the institutions of global governance" (2000, p. 159). The process by which individuals construct cosmopolitan identity is constituted by *codes*, signs, and symbols that both communicate and ask to be interpreted. We argue that Shanghai Tang provides a set of codes that consumers might embrace or reject in identity construction and maintenance.

Specifically, non-Chinese consumers of Shanghai Tang can attempt to establish cosmopolitan identity by consuming Chinese culture, or Chineseness, through the Shanghai Tang brand attributes. Consuming Chineseness also may sustain a cosmopolitan identity, inflected with distinctive Chinese features, which provide a touch of the exotic to their style. On the managerial side, designers, store managers, and sales associates are collectively responsible for generating cosmopolitan identity through their designs, strategies, and marketing tactics. They occupy a key position in brand meaning because they produce the products, spaces, and commercial habitat that meet consumer demands for brand cosmopolitanism.

Asia can be understood as a transnational brand that has reanimated and repackaged historical culture to reveal a new Asian image of modern, multi-cultured lifestyles (Cayla and Eckhardt, 2008). Fashion is a powerful mechanism for expressing the subjectivity of modern life, interrogating consumer lifestyles, and integrating social desires (Evans and Breward, 2005). Swiss-owned Shanghai Tang deploys global fashion to repackage historical Chinese cultures and showcase a modern Chinese lifestyle, nonetheless enriched by multiple traditional cultural codes. Many codes are dialectically redefined and reconfigured in Shanghai Tang through new images of modernity. Our interviews revealed that Shanghai Tang's cultural meanings often encompass anti-trendiness and anti-brand worship. What this suggests is that Shanghai Tang has already entered the realm of modern style and fashion, which allows for the kind of self-scrutiny and self-reflexivity that scholars believe characterizes modern life (Giddens, 1991). If Shanghai Tang is a modern take on Chinese cultural codes, it is also an assessment of culture itself, repackaged as a multi-dimensional lifestyle.

Various interviewees in our study of Shanghai Tang illustrated this point. Some stated that fashion – and Shanghai Tang in particular – was a ladder for professional and personal success. Some admitted to enjoying the pseudo-authenticity and playfulness of Shanghai Tang's use of cultural symbols. Others perceived the brand as a way to reflect education and good background. Fashion, one participant said, was a means to flaunt wealth, as in the case of the Shanxi coal mine bosses – who run mines that are among the most dangerous working places in the world. This participant's censure of the coal mine bosses reinforces the notion that fashion, along with beauty, grace, and glamor, can also provide a space for interrogation and scrutiny.

One might further consider how fashion interrogates myth by reconsidering Shanghai Tang's quotation of old Shanghai, when the city was brimming with growth, speculation, glamor, adventurer seekers, and poverty. The Shanghai Bund, an urban icon, and one of the city's most famous attractions, represents two worlds – modern skyscrapers and colonial heritage. In the late 19th century and the early 20th century, the Bund served as the financial centre of East Asia and was a political hub of the international community in China. The Bund was witness to chaotic politics, a vigorous economy, a society fragmented by vicious class divides, crime, extravagance, and urban waste.

For this reason, the Bund represents everything that was mysterious, seductive, and exciting about old Shanghai, and has been widely featured in various Chinese movies and dramas, such as *Shanghai Bund, Shanghai Triad, Jasmine Women*, and *In the Mood for Love*, and novels such as *Fate of Half a Life* and *Love in a Fallen City*. Shanghai Tang's product references mine these associations, thereby throwing up a whole panorama of cultural possibilities and meanings with which consumers can align, depending on their cultural and political predilections.

The use of the red star in Shanghai Tang's portfolio marks another invocation of myth and history. Both the red star and Mao Zedong's portrait appear on Shanghai Tang products. In China, Mao remains a controversial figure. Supporters believe Mao helped China transform from an agrarian society into a major world power. Others think of him as a villain who damaged China through the famine and targeted violence of the Great Leap Forward and the Cultural Revolution. Despite related contradictions, Mao's portrait hangs in Tiananmen Square and he appears on all Renminbi currency. Shanghai Tang's use of Mao's portrait forms a provocative dialectical gesture in the light of their concurrent references to Puyi, the last Chinese emperor who reigned right up to the period before the rise of old Shanghai. Puyi remains a tragic figure in Chinese history. He ended the monarchy, brought China to ruin with poor governance, became a puppet of imperial Japan, and eventually, during Mao's time, emerged a "model citizen" who was successfully "reformed."

Shanghai Tang's employment of three key moments – Puyi's image, references to old Shanghai, and Mao's portrait – suggests a multi-layered and polyvalent panoply of modern Chinese history. The case of Shanghai Tang demonstrates the ways in which brands link cultural history, and its associated symbols and controversies, to brand meaning and value. Specifically with respect to quotation of Chinese sources, Shanghai Tang's fashion provides an array of conflicts and resolutions, all or some of which can be potential myth markets for brand positioning. Combining sign-experimentation and sign-dominant approaches, the following sections explore how consumers using notions of fashion and design interpret Shanghai Tang, Chinese cultural codes, and brand meaning.

Distinctive cosmopolitan identity projection through Chinese cultural codes and global fashion resources

Wearing Shanghai Tang might smarten someone's look and improve their job prospects, provide someone else with a sartorial impression of cultural immersion, and help others enhance their sex appeal. Conversely, Shanghai Tang aesthetics might repel others and motivate them to assume an anti-fashion stance, itself an alternative variety of fashion trendiness. In short, fashion stimulates a variety of effects and responses. Following the lead of cultural theorist Ray Williams, who emphasizes "the historical legacy of an ongoing social dialogue over the societal

consequences of fashion phenomena" (1994, p. 15), our interpretation of historical culture in fashion focuses on consumer
experience as on-going social dialogue. Social dialogues express,
or negotiate, individual identity, often mediated by brands, and
constituted by personal and social identity. Consumption of
Shanghai Tang reveals ways in which some consumers construct
a distinctive cosmopolitan identity.

For some global citizens, cosmopolitan identity manifests
itself through the use of products that construct the notion of
"who I am" in conjunction with others' perceptions of "who
you are." Along these lines, we present the stories of Mr. L, who
is Chinese, and Miss J, Singaporean-Chinese, who use Shanghai
Tang to co-create cosmopolitan identities.

Mr. L from Beijing, a 40-year-old entertainment industry
CEO, is a "red consumer." The term red consumer refers to
people whose parents or relatives either worked for the Mao
administration or were highly influenced by Mao-age culture.
Mr. L was interviewed in a tea bar near the Shanghai Tang store
in the Grand Hyatt Hotel, Beijing. He was dressed in a black
Shanghai Tang vest.

Mr. L's comments express his convictions about the construction of personal identities and social roles as highly tran-
sitory in nature. His narrative reveals that being perceived as
a cosmopolitan citizen is extremely important to him from a
professional standpoint. Shanghai Tang's high-level functionality facilitates this desired look in international and Chinese
social contexts. He said:

> My years as marketing director gave me the opportunity to meet
> lots of foreign clients. The first impression is very important when
> meeting people. To make a good first impression, I often wear
> Shanghai Tang's Tang suit or jacket. It makes me feel good in
> social and professional conversation. But I do not mean that I fol-
> low fashion. The word fashion sounds very *shi shi de* [pretending
> to do something, pseudo]. The thing about my view of fashion is
> that we were never meant to look like someone else or be someone
> else. I think I feel confident, when I wear [Shanghai Tang's] Tang
> suit or jacket. For instance, if someone looks elegant and has good
> taste, I think I would like to talk more with them. [He laughs.] I
> think they are healthy, well-educated and disciplined. They make
> new friends easily.

Mr. L believes that fashion enables him to attract people and thereby meet more people potentially useful for his business. His use of the *shi shi de* expression suggests that although he does not think of himself as focused on fashion, he believes that good fashion can only do him good. Mr. L's comments about fashion are also an example of sign-experimentation, by which we mean Mr. L interprets his relationship to fashion through a set of psychological codes (Murray, 2002). Fashion makes him feel good: it expresses good taste, education, and polite manners. Shanghai Tang specifically helps him achieve these social goals. He continued:

> I wear it [the Tang suit] to Chinese weddings and to other Chinese formal occasions. On formal occasions, people often wear Western suits [*xi zhuang*]. I wear a Tang suit or shirt. Its style looks Western, but it doesn't require a tie. So you can imagine, everyone is in a suit and tie, and I am not. Also, its quality is very good. It has a neatly pressed design and the material has enough give. It takes to my body. And its colors and design are very smart and stylish. Shanghai Tang often uses bright green or bright pink in the collar or wristband or lining. This sets Shanghai Tang clothes apart from competitors. I think that the traditional Chinese collar, buttons, and cufflinks give the clothes a unique, meaningful touch. When my foreign friends see me in this kind of suit or shirt, they often say: "Oh! Nice suit! I love this color! Or collar!" and then they often ask me about the meaning of the traditional Chinese collar, or of the Chinese character *shòu* on the cufflinks. I am happy to explain the meanings to them. The clothes are a great conversation starter. Moving into business is very easy after that.

Mr. L's detailed description explains the appeal of Shanghai Tang to him. The Western orientation with Chinese detailing, high-quality material, flattering cuts, and vibrant and distinctive coloration collectively suit his tastes and satisfy his needs. China gave the world innovative fashion details such as mandarin collars, frog closures, and butterfly buttons. Mr. L claims that Shanghai Tang's strategic citation of these Chinese features is among the most appreciated features by people who compliment him. If, on the one hand, flattering cuts and quality materials add to up to cosmopolitan style, the color detailing, collars, buttons, and cufflinks seal the deal with a Chinese kiss. This is to say, Shanghai Tang has clearly figured out the right combination that offers enough of both worlds to customers like Mr. L who seek to enhance their image toward professional ends.

Shanghai Tang gives Mr. L confidence and facilitates the construction of a cosmopolitan identity that straddles international and Chinese realms. In Chinese contexts, Mr. L's cosmopolitan identity looks international. He has a talent for looking good, and his friends often seek his advice on fashion and dressing. Mr. L defines his cosmopolitan identity not through money but through taste, refinement, and quiet fashion. He explains this point by reference to an example that patently does not apply to him:

> I do not want to be labeled "a Shanxi mine boss." [He explains this term.] Last year, in a much-publicized event, a group of mine owners in Beijing from northern Shanxi paid cash for 10 Hummers at 1.3 million yuan each, or one hundred and seventy thousand US dollars, and flamboyantly drove them back to Shanxi in a convoy! Then about six months ago, a coal mine boss from the Shanxi province brought 20 Hummer jeeps in one deal for cash!

When we replied, "Wow! Why do they like Hummers and paying in cash?," Mr. L explained, "They really like to burn money and show off. The Hummer jeep is powerful and safe. Maybe it protects their nerves, which must be weak from having made so much blood money so quickly!"

These social contrasts differentiate Mr. L from those groups that blindly follow fashion, or seek Westernized fashion trends that some consumers equate with liberty (Dong and Tian, 2009). Mr. L's refusal to consume well-recognized international fashion brands implies his disapproval of fashion conformity and shameless spending. It also implies his resistance to embracing a vulgar lifestyle. Mr. L's comments about fashion, Shanghai Tang, and personal identity as it relates to dress express the attitude of a Confucian businessman, *ru shang*, which refers to rich and knowledgeable businessmen who maintain a strong sense of social responsibility.

One could say that Mr. L's resemblance to the modern, international Confucian businessman partially derives from reflective taste, good education, professional savvy, positive attitude, and international travel. His preference for the traditional Chinese collar (mandarin collar) is consistent with the Confucian busi-nessman identity, in that Chinese intellectuals and nobility typi-cally favored the mandarin collar. Achieving this status was a common ambition among people from all walks of life. The notion of the Confucian businessman has parallels with the notion of the Western gentleman, and stands in sharp contrast to ostentatious parvenus, *bao fa hu*, such as nouveau riche mine bosses from northern Shanxi province, *Shanxi mei laoban*.

Beyond his own market segment, Mr. L's comments explicitly point to this group of conspicuous consumers of luxury goods in China. Their extravagant displays of money are so notoriously frequent and visible that common practice now deems anyone displaying ostentatious spending worthy of the Shanxi coal mine boss epithet. Despite the humorous undertone, this is no ordi-nary expression, for it programmatically accuses: Shanxi coal mine bosses have flourished from running some of the most dangerous working spaces in China. Mr. L's slightly facetious comments seem to reveal the ugly side of consumption rampant in modern Chinese society.

We would argue that Mr. L's cosmopolitan identity, deriving in part from his choice of Shanghai Tang clothing, which com-bines functionality with modern and traditional codes, does not express an anti-conformist position, yet nonetheless is more than aware of fashion's downsides. To him, fashion is a number of appreciable things, from appearance and positive psychological feeling to good business sense and social conversation. Fashion is also, when expressive of venal acquisition and arrogant dis-play, an ugly phenomenon that does little credit to the positive aspects of modern Chinese society, and therefore merits censure.

Miss J, another Shanghai Tang customer, puts a fine point on cosmopolitan identity in her views of fashion, brand mean-ing, and brand consumption. Miss J is Malaysian-Chinese. She is a well-educated young lawyer in the intellectual property rights industry in Shanghai. She explains her cosmopolitan identity and interest in Shanghai Tang by reference to old Shanghai, around the 1920s and 1930s:

Shanghai Tang captures the essence of old Shanghai – freedom, fashion, multi-cultures – mmm [...] metropolis, and civilization. Lots of movies, dramas, and novels are set in Shanghai of that time.

They showcase dazzling neon lights, sexy and elegant female curves
sheathed in exquisite *cheongsam* [or *qipao*], and seductive melodies!

Like Mr. L, Miss J suggests that Shanghai Tang provides a
picture of the modern, though this is a nostalgic notion of
modern. It is glamorous, sensual, and reminiscent of movie stars:

> I don't want to attract too much attention by dressing oddly, like a
> gallery line-up at the zoo! I only like to be noticed by people I like.
> [She laughs slightly.] I think Shanghai Tang not only attracts the
> right people's attention; it also makes me feel good about myself.
> For example, this black jacket, it never goes out of style, even with
> its bright pink lining and traditional Chinese patterns. It looks
> good even at parties. You know, the most noticeable person should
> not be the guest, but the host of the party, though it would be
> fine if some people said "I like the bright pink lining" or the meta-
> phorical Chinese pattern on my jacket! I love this kind of feeling! I
> only need some people to understand me, not everyone!

Miss J's insistence that fashion should not make her a curiosity
suggests that she wants to stand out without standing out, that
there exists a fine line between attractive distinction and unap-
pealing oddness. Her inclination, it seems, is for small details
picked out by color and design that are still generalized enough
to be in sync with the crowd. Her aesthetic might be called subtle distinction, which is a kind of reserved and defined taste.

In other words, fashion consumption helps navigate the
tension between being distinctive and conforming. This is
also Miss J's fashion preference, which specifically comprises
wearability, part-fantasy and part-identity projection, and
selective distinctiveness. This combined appeal, in which the
fantasy ingredient of identity construction plays a central part,
has been a long-standing strategy in the promotion of mass-
standardized fashion products (Alhoff et al., 2011). Superficially
anti-conformist signifiers in such products make it possible for
consumers to satisfy the desire to fit in and stand out, maintain
acceptability, and flirt with incomparability. Miss L's comments
about wearing Shanghai Tang clothing imply that the brand
facilitates such identity maneuvers within social contexts.

In this sense, Shanghai Tang represents the happy marriage
of two differing aspects of consumption, whereby the weft of

identity aspirations smoothly interweaves the warp of fixed brand meanings. The result is an identity fabric with distinctive features that speak in the common language of social acceptability, an end that both Miss J and Mr. L seem to seek in buying and wearing Shanghai Tang. In other words, Shanghai Tang's Chinese detailing crossed with a modern aesthetic remains flexible. Whereas Miss J perceives retro glamor in Shanghai Tang's design, Mr. L seeks a Confucian businessman sensibility – differences of meaning that eloquently express the notion that "brands are more like discussions than they are like monologues" (Kay, 2006, p. 747).

A ladder for success

Miss L is a slim, 27-year-old Chinese model. Prior to her interview, she had just finished shopping at Shanghai Tang – she was happy to be interviewed but said it would have to wait a day. As scheduled, we met at her office in a top-end Beijing shopping mall the next day. Unlike Mr. L and Miss J, Miss L's fashion tastes are aligned with her professional choices. In a sense, she likes fashion because she has to. She expressed a desire to purchase more fashion items, but her budget prevented her from doing so: "There are a lot of beautiful, up-to-date clothes and designs, and they will help me shine in a crowd, but I cannot afford them." She expressed pride in being a devoted follower of trends and in her preference for Western brands:

> This spring season, 3D and masculinity are a big deal. Like this. [She points to a color picture.] 3D camellia in D&G's skirts, 3D peach blossom in Alexander McQueen's clothing, 3D rose in Fendi's dresses, and bold geometric prints with leather and canvas to make women look tougher, more masculine even.

Miss L affirmed that she consumed fashion to stand out. Adopting the *qipao*, or *cheongsam*, is, from her perspective, a means to achieving that goal, and climb the social ladder. In seeking social mobility she found most Chinese apparel and fashion products too "local" (*tu*) or out-of-date in comparison with Western fashion. She used the phrase "country bumpkin," implying her dislike of the "raw" look of Chinese products, and said that they seemed to lack a contemporary feel. However, her selective preference for the Shanghai Tang *qipao* helps her to stand out at a Western party. Wearing Shanghai Tang, which blends Western and Chinese themes, and appearing fashionable at parties seemed for her to constitute climbing the ladder of success:

> The only thing I bought was a traditional *qipao* [from Shanghai Tang's store]. One of my friends, who's a foreigner, is having a big party tomorrow night and I'm going to be there. I had nothing to wear but now I have the *qipao* I bought yesterday. Maybe wearing it will make me stand out. This dress's style is so different from Western clothing, don't you think? [...] I don't like the traditional *qipao* because it's too Chinese! I don't want to look like a country bumpkin at tomorrow's party. I don't want to be excluded because I'm not fashionable. I buy Shanghai Tang because it's a global brand. Its designers are Western. I think this dress appeals to Westerners, and its distinctive Chinese features will make me stand out!

Miss L deploys fashion to the strategic end of competing successfully in social life. "Standing out" seems to enable Miss L to harvest appreciation among her social peers, snag career opportunities, and enhance her personal life. Her comments offer a cogent example of the extent to which dress can denote a consumer's self-worth, which, on gaining the benefits of symbolic capital, can bring economic and social rewards. Miss L prefers Shanghai Tang's *qipao* in Western contexts because it kills two birds: it functions as a symbol of individuality and it suggests cosmopolitanism because of its international feel. However, beyond such contexts Miss L prefers to patronize Western brands, which, to her, signify difference in Chinese social contexts.

A plump woman of 35 from Yiwu city, Zhejiang province, Mrs. L is a stationery manufacturer. We met her at the Shanghai Tang store in Hangzhou. She had accompanied a friend on a shopping trip to Shanghai Tang, where she bought two black Tang jackets, one short with light green cuffs and the other long with light pink cuffs. Mrs. L was open and talkative.

Once inside the store, we told the sales associate we wanted to buy gifts for foreign female friends. The sales associate indicated the gifts section and said, "A lot of people overseas like these products, such as the dumpling bags." She pointed to a red leather bag. Mrs. L smiled and said: "Looks good, very good! This kind of item will express your taste. It is a big international brand, isn't it?" She turned to the sales associate, waiting for her answer, and the sales associate agreed. Asked what she had bought previously, Mrs. L answered, "I only bought two jackets to have a try. Looks very modern! My friend loves Shanghai Tang. She finds their products very cultured. So I look like a well-educated person." She laughs in front of the mirror in the Tang jacket. "This kind of product is a big international brand, high-class [*shang dang ci*], and is presentable and valuable enough [*na de chu shou*] for gifting to a boss or friends." Her comments that Shanghai Tang could serve as a shortcut for success had a touch of snobbery, seeming to suggest her avid consumption of branded products was determined by fashion trends and notions of social status; and that Shanghai Tang was an easy means to provide the impression of being a well-educated person.

Both Miss L and Mrs. L represent a type of consumer who conforms to fashion trends in order to sustain an impression of personal distinctiveness, a practice that is common enough in the current climate of relatively de-personalized social life (Evans and Breward, 2005). In these patterns of consumption, fashion functions in part as symbolic capital or social capital, which consumers deploy in keeping with the prevalent ideology that fashion sets one apart, and sets things in motion. Fashionable clothes thus resemble money in the pocket that enables one to buy a variety of things – attention, pleasure, conversation, and professional networks – as one migrates across social and cultural contexts. Its power is enormous because its signifying potential is highly flexible, not only because perceptions of fashion differ, but also because individual expectations of fashion are in constant flux.

Follow the monkey: Anti-fashion and anti-brand attitudes

A number of anti-conformist participant narratives in the study suggest consumer autonomy with regard to fashion and brand discourses. Mr. W, vice general manager in a Chinese consulting firm, is a good example of this kind of consumer. He studied art history in college, and can be considered a red consumer. He was interviewed in his office in Shanghai. During the interview, he was wearing a dark blue mandarin collar shirt.

Mr. W: I buy Shanghai Tang products, but that does not mean that I like following so-called fashion and marketing. In my opinion, fashion and brand is just some bamboo pole someone set up in an open and vacant ground that has many monkeys around it. With the sound of the gong beating, the monkeys begin scrambling up the pole. I am not this kind of monkey that follows fashion trends and brand meanings. I just like beautiful things!
Interviewer: What do you think of Shanghai Tang?
Mr. W: There are too many details! Too many! They look flimsy. Honestly, I do not like some of Shanghai Tang's color combinations, especially on the jackets. They show a much too strong color contrast, between the bright pink and black or the bright green and black, which hurts my eyes. In the Chinese mind, we generally tend to harmonious color combinations.
Interviewer: So, what do you like about Shanghai Tang?
Mr. W: I like some unique designs, such as the mandarin collar, and harmonious color combinations. The pattern of this collar is similar to the traditional mandarin collar, but the height is lower than the traditional one, which runs up nearly half the neck and feels clumsy and stiff. But this is more comfortable and looks more beautiful. The slits in the two sides make this shirt more strikingly vivid and more crease-proof than the general shirt without slits.
Interviewer: What do you think of the mandarin collar?
Mr. W: I am used to it, so I like it!

Mr. W's narrative expresses an anti-fashion and anti-brand position. His metaphor, of fashion being a bamboo pole for monkeys to scale at the sound of a gong, indicates that he views fashion and brands as encouraging blind imitation and mass instinct. The description plays with a common Chinese proverb about "monkey tricks," which refers to someone playing tricks or making a fool of someone. This suggests that Mr. W thinks of fashion and brands as tricks that marketers use to make fools of consumers.

Mr. W's impressions of Shanghai Tang describe his disapproval of pseudo-aesthetics and superficial authenticity. He claims to love Shanghai Tang for its design and functional features. He reveals his preference for Chinese styles when he criticizes Shanghai Tang for having what he thinks are too many details. Although he does not go so far as to correlate fashion and identity, what he does say expresses self-confidence. That he wears mandarin collars because he likes them suggests that he does not shy away from Chinese styles because they are Chinese. In fact, he likes how the collar, which was popular during the Mao era, makes reference to his "red" background, perhaps subtly embodying his status.

A reflective, authentic reservoir of historical Chinese references

Shanghai Tang products often express subtle meanings, their dialectical images, or the collusion of conflicting meanings or associations, offering complexity. Almost all the Shanghai Tang consumer participants in the study appreciated the brand's introduction of isolated Chinese style elements into more normative styles to make them fashionable, for example, iconic patterns and the strategically located signature colors on cuffs and collars.

Fashion has the ability to turn yesterday's emblems into tomorrow's commodities (Evans, 2000). Shanghai Tang does precisely that. Even a quick perusal of the products, whether in stores or online, shows that the brand depends on yesterday's emblems for its fashion statements. Chinese styling is the key to its success. This is particularly evident in the brand's seasonal collections, in which designers focus on small, distinctive details that provide immediacy to cultural citations. It is almost as if Shanghai Tang has taken recommendations from fashion theorist Evans, who argues that re-actualizing the past is a way to refine the overwhelming ideology of myth, though expressing it suitably is equally important for the myth to exert the desired impact. Mrs. W from Beijing illustrates this:

> I like Shanghai Tang. I am fascinated by its citation of Chinese traditions. For example, Chinese gold and silver ingots [*yuanbao*] were an important medium to exchange expensive goods in ancient China. They sometimes took the form of a smiling face to represent

happiness and wealth. They were typically owned by high-ranking officials, emperors, and tycoons, and used as money. Today, we see them at Chinese New Year parties. Shanghai Tang has cleverly introduced gold and silver ingots in its patterns. They look very stylish, up-to-date, attractive, distinctive, and meaningful. Images of the ingots are light brown and white or silver and golden, and there are many of them together on shining silk. I love Shanghai Tang's unique style!

Mrs. W embodies Shanghai Tang's sophisticated target consumer, readily recognizing and appreciating the brand's cultural references.

Shanghai Tang's citations of Chinese cultural symbols are typically positive, though slightly anarchic images sometimes appear in certain products, as pointed out by Miss K, who is originally from Shanghai but now lives in Europe:

> I was really attracted by this bag. [She points to the "old Shanghai" message bag she has purchased with old Shanghai images of social upheaval.] I like the gray and white color combination, which makes me think of old Shanghai life – lots of opportunity and danger, rogues and heroes, luxury and poverty. This bag's design is fashionable, don't you think?

Regardless of whether it deploys ingots or images of social upheaval in old Shanghai, Shanghai Tang's design strategy consists in first isolating, then re-introducing familiar features into novel arrangements that defamiliarize the old and the new. Once-precious ingots become more commonly available and wearable if you buy a Shanghai Tang dress, as does a blast into a socially complicated past if you buy a Shanghai Tang bag. This fashion strategy, which engages the cultural interest of consumers by re-engaging the old within the new, does not elaborate citations but rather represents them figuratively across designs. Clearly, the tactic of developing a "dialectical theatre of fashion" has been successful for Shanghai Tang. Backed by strong marketing, striking fashion shows, savvy retail strategy, and catchy advertising, Shanghai Tang has created a brand identity that is equal parts glamorous and sexy *and* aloof and interesting.

The dialectical ambivalence of the erotic and the chaste

Intense desire becomes all the more intense when unrequited. This is sometimes true of desire between people, and almost always true in the case of fashion. Piecemeal quotation of the past serves to maintain a necessary distance from the past, which defines the success of the dialectical image, one that is both erotic and chaste, or desirable because it cannot be fully had. This psychological conundrum resonates nicely with the formal aesthetics of Chinese dress, in which ambiguity of meaning is a central aim, in that it is both sensual and unsullied. The latter aspect, of purity in Chinese dress, was influenced by communist party politics during Mao's reign, and by an earlier era of Chinese feudalism. Concealment, denial, and calculated ambivalence of intention thus became the central poles of Chinese sartorial aesthetics.

That said, Chinese fashion has been courting the enemy for some time. The formal penetration of Western fashion into China began around 1981, when French designer Pierre Cardin mounted shows of his work in Beijing and Shanghai. Further influenced by Western thoughts of individualism, identity expression – particularly via brand adoption – has become increasingly popular in China. Shanghai Tang, in particular, has been able to successfully marry Chinese ambivalence with the emphasis on direct allure, which is a defining feature of Western dress (Davis, 1992). The collective semiosis, or means by which designs, images, logos, and texts interact with consumers to create meaning and value, derives from the dialectical ambivalence of the erotic and the chaste that manage one another. Fashion theorist Davis has argued that "allusiveness and ambiguity are endemic in clothing" and that fashion communicates "because of its semantic incapacities to encourage creativity in the delineation and expression of ambivalence" (1992, p. 22). However, identity development and projection are founded on tensions and ambiguities within Western clothing discourse, and Shanghai Tang's resolution of the contrast between traditional Chinese and modern Western is only in keeping with related identity paradigms.

Fashion advocates have found various ways to incorporate the erotic in fashion. But, according to some, theories only deflect from the obvious love affair with lust that lies at the heart of the erotic in women's fashion (Davis, 1992). Shanghai Tang's retro references to old Shanghai can be better appreciated by first acknowledging what they are – juxtapositions of very selective quotations that eschew discomfiting aspects of the past. In stores stocked with sexy *qipao* and shiny, silky dresses with images of gold and silver ingots, the bag with the image of old, struggling Shanghai is more likely to evoke nostalgia than it is a sense of activism or social concern.

As a *New York Times* travel writer describes it, "At the end of the 19th century, Shanghai, a port city near the mouth of the Yangtze River, was a flourishing international trading and financial center that was known for its decadence – an intoxicating mix of brothels, cabarets, opium dens, and privileged foreign settlements" (Barboza, 2012, p. 7). The insistent appeal of retro glamor marks a quality Shanghai Tang designers have firmly grasped. The most obvious result of their understanding is Shanghai Tang's women's *qipao*, which is both chaste-looking and sexy, its shiny fabrics and side slits evoking the retro glamor of erstwhile nightclubs and cabarets, and the attendant attractions of rubbing elbows with the likes of respectable elite, wealthy rogues, and well-heeled prostitutes. This piece of clothing embodies a melting pot of associations that more or less fit the notion Davis advances – that, at heart, fashion is going for a good time, and what's the harm in that?

Sexiness can be a lonely quality. It needs the company of the chaste to become erotically charged. The chaste is an apparel-receptive value, which develops through a set of linked aesthetic features. In fashion, this could be the slightly misaligned blouse button, which fetchingly reveals the bosom, or the facility of translucent fabric to both veil and expose (Davis, 1992). In a classic formulation from fashion journalist Bernadine Morris, "clothing is sexy when it is not too revealing" when "it is body-conscious dressing – showing some skin and shape but not too much!" (1989, p. 87). Broadly speaking, chasteness and sexiness are highly subjective impressions, though Shanghai Tang designs, according to some customers, address this point with appealing results. Mrs. G is a Singaporean-Chinese Shanghai Tang enthusiast based in the UK:

> I love Shanghai Tang's jackets and scarves. The colors are simple and common. They will not draw too much attention in public. But

they create designs that make people look sexy and shapely. I also like the embroidered flowers on this jacket. They stand for chastity and purity in China. I absolutely love it, and as if the sexy design and chaste flowers weren't enough, there is also a cerise pink lining, which stole my heart. The loose black jacket slightly reveals the cerise pink lining. It makes me look very sexy and attractive. We call this quality of the Chinese woman's personality "manshow," which refers to simmering sex appeal never breaking the surface. The jacket is slightly split on the side. I love this split, too! Shanghai Tang products look very, very erotic and exotic!

Mrs. G's account, which implies that Chinese women can be both chaste and erotic, parallels Miss J's statement of selective reserve in Shanghai Tang clothing. Both women are referring to the brand's varied features, connoting diverse associations and impressions. Many Chinese love dark colors with bright detailing that draws attention, the combined effect of which is encapsulated by the Chinese buzzword *menshao*, or "manshow." It is used to describe people who are ostensibly reserved but actually volatile, like a dormant volcano. The term can also be used to describe duplicity, though without malice. So, *menshao* describes a kind of hide and seek, which Shanghai Tang represents through bright linings, collars, and cuffs, and skirt slits at strategic locations, lending a sensual edge to the latent bubble under the surface of restraint.

A lexicon of Chinese symbols

Shanghai Tang showcases various aspects of Chinese historical and traditional symbols pertaining to values and beliefs that relate to social relations, social groups, and social orders, which collectively constitute culture. In this way, Shanghai Tang's symbols take on aspects of Chinese ideology. For its part, Shanghai Tang employs diverse Chinese symbols to interpret the lexicon of luck through its store design, clothing, and accessories. Shanghai Tang's retail environments are designed to influence consumer shopping experiences and decisions. Store "atmosphere" refers to the creation of those purchasing environments that could generate particular emotional effects that enhance purchase possibility (Spies, Hesse, and Loesch,

1997). They elaborate that the store's environmental stimuli can affect the consumer's emotional states relating to pleasure, and these can impact on purchasing behavior. Here, pleasure refers to the extent to which the store environment impacts on consumer happiness and satisfaction, encouraging arousal to the extent that the store environment facilitates the impression of the consumers being in control of themselves, and free to act according to their will.

Researchers have proposed that the interplay of ambient cues and social cues, which affect arousal in the store environment, impact on consumer pleasure levels (e.g., Baker, Grewal, and Levy, 1992). In other words, the more social cues are manifest in the store environment, the more the subject is aroused, within limits. In Shanghai Tang's case, the ubiquitous Chinese symbols in its stores evoke emotional effects and hence enhance purchase possibility, as attested by Miss U, a dancer from Shanghai:

> I like its [Shanghai Tang's] Xin Tiandi store. The store's exterior details, such as the antique walls and tiles, resemble traditional Shikumen buildings of old Shanghai, while the interior combines 1930s Shanghai with 21st-century urban spaces. I love it. I was impressed by a lot of things. I like the vibrant pink and green color, the sexy mannequins in the shop windows, the bright pink and green old Shanghai logo, the grey patina of the store address plaque, the Chinese *lu* handles, and so on. Oh! I also like the China-inspired designs, such as the pink and light green wall décor, the high, light green ceiling decorated with square patterns, traditional Chinese double happiness paper cut-out patterns. I think it is wonderful! What's more, there are many Chinese symbols in the apparel, such as the endless knots, gold fish cups, and the spider-jade bag.

Miss U clearly enjoys the many citations of historical symbols in the store and in the products. Her comments about Shikumen buildings refer to the "stone gate" or "strong gateway" that is a unique architectural feature of Shanghai residences, a style that developed during the Taiping (Heavenly peace) Rebellion, or China's civil war (1850–64). At that time, many rich businessmen in Shanghai and the surrounding areas took refuge in the city's foreign compounds, known as concessions. These buildings are essentially two- or three-story townhouses enclosed within high, heavy brick peripheries. The residences are linked on

straight alleys – called *long dang* in Shanghai-nese – marked by
stylish stone arches commonly seen in Anglo-American nations.
The residences contain interior courtyards that are common in
traditional Chinese domestic architecture. Shikumen residences
thus combined Western and Chinese architectural features,
a hybrid style on which the Xin Tiandi Shanghai Tang store,
positively referred to by Miss U, is modeled.

Mrs. W admits to a fondness for Shanghai Tang's Chinese
symbolism, while her husband favors the red star symbols, which
correspond to his "red" family background – his parents worked
for the Mao regime. Mrs. W says:

> I like the Shanghai Tang store at the Beijing Grand Hyatt Hotel.
> The shiny gold of Shanghai Tang embedded in the white gate, the
> traditional Chinese red, sky blue, and light green on the walls, all
> make it look very luxurious and glamorous. I love the "double fish"
> cap sleeve *qipao*; "dumpling," or *jiao zi*, bags; the "firecracker"
> silver resin earrings; and the coin cufflinks. They appear very mean-
> ingful to me, though my husband doesn't like them. He only likes
> the simple red "star" symbols in the leather collection and in the
> hats. At first I couldn't understand why he liked the red stars, but
> now I think it has to do with the background of his military family.
> His parents were members of the Red Army, and he was very
> present in the Cultural Revolution.

The Chinese symbols of Shanghai Tang describe a particular
way of life from the past and the present, and represent ideas,
values, and beliefs. In this way, Shanghai Tang expresses Chinese
ideology and other regional ideologies that reflect Chinese identity. For example, Shanghai Tang's quotation of luck symbols
from the Chinese cultural lexicon not only provides denotation,
or the literal meanings of distinctive Chinese symbols, such as
longevity, symbolized by the Chinese character *shòu*, or love,
harmony, and abundance associated with the Chinese double
fish symbol; it also provides the second order of signification,
or connotation, by which a word or a symbol elicits memories,
such as the red star symbol that Mrs. W's husband seems to like,
possibly because it reminds him of a bygone era and his own
childhood.

Fashion can stimulate people's memory of history. It can
reconstruct for them the remembered and the forgotten: "in

fashion, quotation is sartorial remembrance; fashion activates the past in the present by rewriting its own themes and motifs through historical quotation" (Leslie, 1999, p. 308). Mrs. W's account of Shanghai Tang's use of ingots, for example, confirms that cultural codes expressed through fashion products carry subtle connotations, which conjure memories, remembered in whole or in part. On the other hand, Miss K's account related to images on a Shanghai Tang bag reveals historical quotation in fashion producing dialectical images. The images cited the 1920s and 1930s, when Shanghai was brimming with economic speculation, crime, poverty, and disease. In harnessing these images, the bag's design aims for the effect of cinematic montage, in which juxtaposed images enable a chain of associations that may not occur in an ordinary plot-driven narrative. Accordingly, various images of old Shanghai appearing side by side on a new substrate, or bag, redefine the old, though precisely how is up to the consumer.

Miss K's comments about the bag expressed nostalgia for a bygone era, the glamor of which lies in its being firmly in an inaccessible past, and precisely for that reason all the more attractive: utopia looks good partly because it is not within reach. This is the point fashion observers advance to demonstrate fashion's facility in grappling with contemporary social contradictions through retrospection. Fashion responds to fantasist desires for escape from the present by relocating the past into new surroundings (Evans, 2007). Dialectical branding, which is founded on montage and quotation, and on hypothesis, contradiction, and some variety of resolution, creates an aura of authenticity, or "the quality of being perceived as genuine and natural," which, in turn, can become a central strategy for brand development (O'Guinn, Allen, and Semenik, 2008, p. 610).

The consumer interviews and our subsequent reflections dealt with how global luxury brand identity and market-oriented creativity strategically satisfy global consumers. Shanghai Tang managers offer further insight into the brand. In the following, we examine their interpretations of historical Chinese culture as it appears in Shanghai Tang products and their brand meanings.

Strategically satisfying global consumers: Identity and social dependency

Interviews with store managers, store supervisors, and sales associates suggest that Shanghai Tang helps its consumers address contradictions between self-identity and social dependencies. In this sense, Shanghai Tang's particular styles satisfy its consumers' diverse identity expression needs for various social occasions. Mrs. A, about 30 years old, is a manager at the Shanghai Tang store in the Shangri-la Hotel. She explained the reasons behind Shanghai Tang's popularity among customers. Her account revealed the success of Shanghai Tang's strategic marketing practices, which help consumers construct distinctive cosmopolitan identities:

> We have a range of products with fashionable styles, designs, and colors that fit all occasions. For example, last week one of my [Chinese] friends wore this black cashmere turtleneck sweater [she points to the item] for her Spanish conference. She was very happy with that. I think the clothes she picked up here were suitable for that occasion. The cashmere turtleneck sweater is one of our top-ten items for its fashionable and best sale features. The turtleneck suggests Chinese tradition while the whole design is fashionable. This product is also popular with foreign customers, though they prefer the red version. It's pretty common for Western customers to go for the bright colors.

Mrs. A implies that Shanghai Tang enables its Chinese and foreign customers to meet their social appearance needs. Shanghai Tang's Chinese details seem to be appreciated in international contexts by both Chinese and foreign customers. She emphasizes that the Chinese like dark colors while Western customers prefer bright colors. Her insights suggest that Chinese tastes are generally more conservative than Western ones, in her experience.

Another informant, Mrs. Z, a manager of the Shanghai Tang store in Xin Tian Di, Shanghai, points to Shanghai Tang's international fashion status using examples of the brand's fashion shows. She states that well-defined Chinese elements in Shanghai Tang goods enable consumers to express their Chinese individuality and adapt to Chinese contexts:

Our customers love our products. I think our products are fashionable in style and color, use high-quality materials, and well-defined Chinese symbols. Every season, Shanghai Tang has a fashion show. It introduces new fashion trends to its customers. For example, the shiny colors are central elements in the current fashion season [winter 2008]. You'll find that many of our products have bright, shiny colors, like this [ingot] dress. You know, we always use exquisite designs and materials to showcase Chinese details in our products, such as the images of ingots, traditional Chinese buttons and collars, golden fish, and so on. It's for this reason that Chinese and foreign customers like buying our products to show their international or fashionable taste with Chineseness.

Miss T, a 27-year-old sales associate at Beijing's Yintai store, describes an exceptional aspect of Shanghai Tang. At the time of the interview Miss T, an open and talkative woman, had been working at Shanghai Tang for six months. She enthused:

I think our products satisfy the needs of both foreign and Chinese consumers. For example, when foreigners visit China, they prefer to buy Chinese-styled goods, but they are often disappointed by the low quality and functionality of Chinese goods. That's why these consumers prefer the Tang suit to the traditional Chinese suit, which is high, and the tight mandarin collar makes breathing difficult. What's more, the traditional Chinese red maybe makes people feel a little bit stiff, don't you think? [Interviewer: Yes!] Even though our products only have one or two Chinese details, they look very fashionable and modern in design, color, and material. You feel comfortable in them. For instance, this black jacket has a fashionable design. Without this Chinese embroidery, it looks like a Western brand jacket. But with the Chinese embroidery, the whole jacket looks very vivid and attractive, don't you think? [Interviewer: Mmm!] The Chinese, especially successful and well-educated Chinese elites who work in an international environment, want to express their Chinese identity. A lot of Chinese goods are not fashionable and suitable for international occasions. The one or two Chinese details in our products satisfy their Chinese needs.

Miss T's quote suggests how Shanghai Tang helps foreigners in China to resolve the tension between social dependency and personal autonomy.

In the past, foreigners who wanted to purchase Chinese-styled products to express their social roles in China were disappointed by the quality and styling of local products. Shanghai Tang succeeded where others failed. Moreover, Shanghai Tang also helps the Chinese to address tensions between personal identity, aspiration, and suitable social roles in the international arena.

Employees as consumers

Nearly all of Shanghai Tang's employees are either long-standing consumers or potential consumers. When asked whether they buy Shanghai Tang clothes, most responded in the positive. Miss E, a Shanghai store employee, explained:

> I can afford to buy them when they are on sale. That's when it's really worthwhile to have them. Now, I have the brown double-fish scarf that I bought last year. I also bought one men's scarf to give to a friend. It has yellow tiles on silk stain. This year I am going to buy that kind of polo shirt. [She points to the polo shirt section.] But right now the classic ones are not on sale. So I'm saving up.

Although Shanghai Tang store employees intend to please customers and promote their products, their explanations are no less reasonable and persuasive for that reason. Their answers suggest that they, too, think like customers, and buy Shanghai Tang products when they are on sale. This suggests that even employees really do appreciate Shanghai Tang products. They might be loyal to the brand but they are not foolish in their purchases, a natural extension of the fact that employee consumption behavior will differ from that of the brand's regular consumer with the means to shop often and widely.

Shanghai Tang's executives are known for wearing Shanghai Tang clothes in public, an obvious branding strategy, as they would hardly embody their brand if they did not wear it. Thus, in their capacity as temporary consumers, managers can become better acquainted with consumer perspectives, which ultimately affect brand consumption. One is able to take managers' eulogistic accounts of Shanghai Tang seriously precisely because their testimonies are based on actual consumption, and not just marketing speak.

In its capacity as an aspiring world-class luxury brand, Shanghai Tang attracts well-qualified, international employees, many with Chinese backgrounds, including creative designers. Creativity and innovation are central in any brand's development, but Shanghai Tang's success depends on the exceptional negotiation of Chineseness across its global product portfolio, retail design, and marketing communication. As Chinese branding consultant Mary Bergstrom notes in her book *All Eyes East: Lessons from the Front Lines of Marketing to China's Youth*, notions of Chineseness have been around for some time. Interesting for today's changing China, she suggests, is "the idea of recent Chinese history fitting into a modern luxury framework" (2012, p. 177).

Shanghai Tang is not alone in pursuing this branding strategy. Shang Xia, "a brand for the art of living," was founded in 2008 by Chinese designer Jian Qiong Er and the French luxury brand Hermès (www.shang-xia.com). Bergstrom argues that Shang Xia has invested in creating a common recent history, not embedded in a luxury lifestyle lineage; but one that resonates with a broader range of contemporary Chinese consumers' personal memories. At its core, Shang Xia offers low-key luxury products that relate to a shared cultural activity, the tea ceremony. In this case, Chineseness maintains a connection to cultural practices, but with a historical fluidity. That Shanghai Tang has achieved the right balance is evident in its international presence and growing base of consumers, who find the brand styling suitable for all occasions.

In interpreting Shanghai Tang, we can trace the broad contours of the Imagined China myth, in which modern life is a heady mix of history, style, and culture as well as a myth defined not by falsity but by an authentic pursuit of style. Still, regardless of how authentic an imagined myth might be, it remains necessarily incomplete and fragmented, because no myth can adequately represent all the voices it contains. This incompleteness constitutes part of what makes a myth seem authentic.

Global store locations and environments

Shanghai Tang has over 40 stores worldwide (ShanghaiTang.com, 2013). All of the stores are located on top-end fashion streets, such as Shanghai Xin Tian Di plaza in Shanghai and Sloane Street in London; in first-class shopping malls, such as the BurJuman Shopping Centre, Dubai; in top-end luxury hotels, including the Beijing Ritz-Carlton Hotel, the Beijing and Hangzhou Grand Hyatt Hotels, and the Shanghai Shangri-La Hotel; and airport shopping centers. Its store interiors and facades are also modeled on the brand principle of crossing Chinese and Western styles. Mrs. G's detailed account illustrates the significance of location and Shanghai Tang store design:

> I like the locations of Shanghai Tang stores. I have visited a lot of them and they are often located on important business streets with distinctive characteristics. For example, Shanghai Tang's Xin Tian Di store is located in Shanghai Xin Tian Di plaza. The plaza is a major tourist attraction in Shanghai and a fashionable pedestrian street due to the historical and cultural legacies of the city. There you can enjoy the antique grounds, walls, tiles, windows, and architecture of old Shanghai's Shikumen culture. The Shanghai Tang name plaque is bronze. The English lettering – SHANGHAI TANG – is in capital letters. The Chinese lettering has been rendered from right to left in traditional, Kai-style calligraphy. Below the signage is an image of a fashionable model wearing Shanghai Tang. The brand logo appears in pink and green on the shop window. When you walk into Shanghai Tang's corridors with traditional black brick flooring, you'll find the rusty address mark and the Shanghai Tang logo, followed by stylish mannequins against the bright green background. You will be surprised by the modern decoration and fashionable products with distinctive Chinese details. For example, the ceiling is decorated in bright green, but with the traditional Chinese paper cut-out pattern. The shelves are black outside, but bright green, pink, and blue on the inside. When you move around the shelves, the sales associates in purplish red clothes and black trousers slowly follow you and then smilingly explain the products in your hands, even if you're just looking at them. When you find a dress you like, they will suggest that you try it on. They are nice and polite even if you decide not to buy anything. You know they will not push you to buy something. I like this kind of environment: no pushing!

Mrs. G's comments about the store's location, design, and service underscore Shanghai Tang's positioning as a top-tier retail establishment.

Figure 4.2 **Shanghai Tang storefront**
© James Leynse/Corbis

The enduring axiom "location, location, location" has taken on new meaning in the retail race. The Shanghai Tang store in Shanghai Xin Tian Di plaza sits amidst a busy shopping and tourist area that also has historical interest. Securing a prime location through a large, semi-permanent commitment of resources remains one way to begin to ensure the store's growth and profitability. Moreover, location sometimes cancels out losses that would be sustained during an economic slump, and trumps competition when the economy is good and growth potential is high (e.g., Lamb, Hair, and McDaniel, 2008).

Other Shanghai Tang stores in luxury shopping malls and hotels partake of the unique glamor of their locations. One of its stores is located in the Ritz-Carlton Hotel at 83A Jian Guo Road, close to Hua Mao Shopping Mall, one of Beijing's most exclusive shopping malls. The Ritz-Carlton Hotel itself is a top luxury hotel, which itself is enough to entice consumers to visit. The Shanghai Tang experience is exciting – the store is located in a sumptuous hotel replete with lights, color, and lots of action. This store also enjoys spur-of-the-moment visits by customers wandering over from the nearby Hua Mao Shopping Mall, which attracts thousands of customers to its many top-end stores.

Grand Hyatt Beijing's Shanghai Tang store provides another example of how location works to the brand's advantage. Shoppers from nearby Dongfang Xintiandi shopping mall can conveniently pop over – as they are walking through the main Wang fu jing thoroughfare, consumers are unlikely to miss the Grand Hyatt Beijing. Inside the hotel, the ambience exudes grandeur, luxury, and glamor – and the first sight in the lobby is the striking signage of the Shanghai Tang store, its lettering embedded in a white gate against a ground of light yellow marble illuminated by soft yellow light. The second sight is the gold Shanghai Tang name set in the black gate opposite the white marble stairs with golden handrails. The wall décor's color combination is traditional Chinese red, sky blue, and light green.

In our interview, Mrs. G indicated that the ambience at Shanghai Tang exudes harmony. The friendly, non-pushy service culture helps make customers feel relaxed. Shanghai Tang aims at a wealthy market segment that demands excellent service, pleasant ambience, and glamorous locations. Additionally, Shanghai Tang employees are well trained and encouraged to control their eagerness, reduce customer stress, be helpful – but not insistent – and charitably assist customers in the shopping process, which involves looking for products in different colors, locating the right size, and evaluating fit and feel. At Shanghai Tang, customer service also involves micro-interactions, such as offering advice and suggestions, contacting other stores, and providing tailoring assistance.

Expressing dynamic and stylish Chinese lifestyles

Brands, fashion products, and advertisements constitute central elements in the scenery of modern life. Shanghai Tang, as part of this scenery, expresses the dynamics, stylistics, and aesthetics of modern life through fashion, inflecting everyday objects with design, style, and iconic color. Shanghai Tang's designers and marketers pursue up-to-date international fashion. For example, like many global designers during the year 2008, they favored silk designs with a lot of shine, interpreted in classic Shanghai Tang style. They used traditional motifs, such as ingots on *qipao*, but translated into international fashion, as pointed out by Mrs. Z, the manager at the Xin Tian Di store, and Miss N, the sales associate at the London store. But Shanghai Tang consumers are not always likely to follow the latest fashion trends. Many Chinese consumers claim that they do not care whether Shanghai Tang products are fashionable or seasonally appropriate. They insist they do not follow fashion trends.

This stance especially applies to Mr. L (Mrs. W's husband) and Mr. W, so-called red consumers. Mr. L grew up in the People's Liberation Army Navy (PLA) while Mr. W's parents worked in the Ministry of Ordnance Industry. Their childhood and teenage years were spent listening to Chinese revolutionary songs – so-called red songs. They experienced remarkable freedom growing up, as their parents were often away tending to the heavy work load during the Cultural Revolution. Mr. W's father went away for long periods during his childhood. (Once, on his father's return home, Mr. W was unable to recognize his father immediately, and mistakenly called him "uncle.") According to Mr. L, a childhood spent entertaining himself resulted in a high regard for independent thinking and secured his personal wherewithal, and he felt that he was personally unlikely to become a blind follower of fashion trends.

Hong Huang, CEO of China Interactive Media Group, is another red consumer with strong views on Chinese fashion. Her grandfather on her mother's side was a pioneer of the Chinese Communist Party, her mother was an outstanding diplomat, and her stepfather was a minister of PRC Foreign Affairs during Mao's era. Via her publishing outlets, she has offered strong criticism of Chinese brands. For example, in her fashion magazine *i-Look*, Hong Huang criticized global luxury brand managers in China for acting like *Hong Wei Bing* – the group that safeguards Chairman Mao's reputation – in protecting their brand identities. She strongly disapproved of their practice of using only celebrities to endorse their brands. She maintained that such brands paid little attention to separating brand image from celebrity image, and expected the media to slavishly cover all their activities. She also revealed that such brands refused to advertise with media that did not support their branding efforts.

At the time, Chinese fashion media were in their infancy, and might have become a puppet of global brands. However, Hong Huang was reluctant to have such brands dictating to her and Chinese consumers. She responded by encouraging Chinese brands that focused on Chineseness. She introduced new Chinese designers, brands, and brand cultures in *i-Look* magazine, and became one of the most influential channels through which Chinese consumers learned about Chinese brands, including Shanghai Tang.

Consumers typically have one of two responses to the Chinese themes employed by Shanghai Tang. One kind of consumer appreciates and understands the cultural quotations – even finds them fashionable. They believe that Shanghai Tang defines these codes well and deploys them in practical ways. Mr. L, Mr. W, and Miss J were of this view. The second kind of consumer finds Shanghai Tang's cultural quotations out-of-date or much too "folksy" to be truly appealing. Our interviews demonstrate the complexity of interpretations invoked by Shanghai Tang's liberal use of Chinese cultural quotations.

With regard to Chinese aesthetics, it has been suggested that the Chinese favor perceptual thinking based on ethics over logical thought based on science, which is preferred in Western society; and that the Chinese are more concerned with the whole structure and the total expression of harmony than with details expressing individual identity or personality, commonly favored by Western thinking. Even in matters of human beauty, the Chinese favor harmony. They appreciate faces with porcelain smoothness and eyes that are in keeping with the subtlety of the whole. In contrast, Westerners like strong faces with well-defined contours, large eyes, and sensuous lips. As regards the body, Westerners express sensuality and beauty by exposing the body rather than covering it up. These cultural differences in notions of bodily beauty appear in Shanghai Tang designs, which use subtle details, such as translucent fabric or slightly misaligned buttons, to expose body parts.

Mr. W's comments about Shanghai Tang products underscores this emphasis on subtlety in Chinese aesthetics. Grandness, when it is expressed in Chinese aesthetics, appears in representations of landscape, which exemplify the harmonious convergence of diverse formal patterns and designs. Grandness, to all intents and purposes, resides in nature, and not in individual things. This contrasts with the broad strokes of Western aesthetics that focus on details, which might explain the emphasis on close looking in Western art criticism (Wang, 2001). In particular, grandness in Chinese aesthetics develops from abstract symbols and icons that merely point to the essence of truth and beauty, rather than representing it directly. These aesthetic preferences have a long-standing history in China as testified by one of the founders of Taoism, Lao-tzu. He wrote: "Tao bears one, one bears two, two bears three and three bears all in the universe" (1891, p. 42).

For the most part, Shanghai Tang products are aligned with notions of harmony. The designs, colors, fabric quality, and cuts are uniformly subtle and pleasing in aspect: When details do stand out they do so without disturbing the peace of the whole. They are meant to capture the eye but ultimately enhance the effect of the harmonious whole. This aesthetic contributes to the meaning of the brand, and frequent consumers, active and passive, would be able to read the various aesthetic codes that make up the lexicon of Shanghai Tang designs.

Reading codes in a branding lexicon constitutes brand literacy. Specifically, brand literacy means "the ability of the consumer to make sense of and compose the signs of a brand culture and to understand the meaning systems that are at play" (Bengtsson and Firat, 2006, p. 377). As brand consultant Anders Bengtsson and consumer researcher Fuat Firat argue, brand lit-

eracy typically divides consumers into three groups. In the first
case, the consumer's understanding of the brand barely extends
the immediate surface meanings of words and symbols associated with the brand. In some cases, having little or no knowledge of symbolic brand meanings, these consumers might be
considered brand illiterate. The second case includes consumers
who know the brand name. They also know that symbols associated with it do not merely function to distinguish one manufacturer from another, but bear additional cultural meanings. This
group of consumers has the ability to read and understand the
cultural meanings and strategies underlying brands. They are
termed brand knowers. The third group includes consumers and
cultural intermediaries who contribute to the life and meaning
of the brand. Their role is reformative and transformative. These
consumers fully participate in the culture of brands, in that they
do not merely follow the brand's cultural meanings, but are able
to play with and redefine brands through their co-creative activities. This kind of consumer is known as a brand professional
(Bengtsson and Firat, 2006).

Going by these definitions, it might be argued that the coal
mine owners of Shanxi province may be brand knowers while red
consumers, such as Mr. L and Mr. W, might be brand professionals. It may also be that participants who have grown up and worked
in Beijing for a long time are more brand literate than those from
Shanghai, as red consumers are typically based in Beijing.

As this basic analysis of brand literacy reveals, a brand culture perspective on brands such as Shanghai Tang can shed
light on how brands interact with cultural history, dialectical
images, and the formation of identity. In its cumulative capacity
as such a brand culture, carved from diverse groups – variously
self-reflexive, innovative, and dynamic – Shanghai Tang represents the perceptions and interpretations of an emergent hybrid,
multi-cultured Chinese lifestyle.

The co-creation and circulation of brands and cultures

Fashion systems can co-create, convey, and circulate brand
meanings among various brand actors, who, in turn, co-develop
the imagined myth. In Shanghai Tang's case, fashion co-creates

and circulates cultural meanings pertaining to Chinese culture and history through brand products via the activities and
narratives of brand actors. Shanghai Tang brand actors project
individual identities through brand consumption in social situations and professional contexts, and within personal relationships. Through their experiences of meaning appropriation,
brand actors interact with various folk and regional theories in
an attempt to interpret the brand's version of Imagined China.

For its part, in its capacity as the self-proclaimed "pioneering
China luxury lifestyle brand" with global presence, Shanghai Tang
has the onerous task of acting as "the global ambassador of contemporary Chinese Chic" (ShanghaiTang.com, 2010d). Shanghai
Tang has become responsible for developing the Chinese blue-
print of "contemporary luxury lifestyle products," ranging from
clothing and accessories to homeware and lifestyle items, such as
lounge music collections (ShanghaiTang.com, 2010d).

One insight into the task at hand – for Shanghai Tang to continue as a leader in the world of Chinese global fashion – was
provided by Miss S, the sales associate supervisor at the Shanghai
Tang store in the Beijing Ritz-Carlton Hotel, and by Mrs. W, a
consumer in Beijing. Both respondents enthused that Shanghai
Tang had started a Chinese cultural revolution worldwide. They
used the inauguration of the Mandarin Collar Society in 2007
that "banned" the necktie to illustrate this point. What this suggests is that in order to stay on top of the market, Shanghai Tang
needs to continue to develop and redefine its brand ideology – to
promote Chinese cultural symbols through distinctive styles.

The Mandarin Collar Society was the brainchild of top brand
managers at Shanghai Tang, including Le Masne de Chermont.
The Mandarin Collar Society eschews Western neckties, and
instead champions the mandarin collar – portrayed as a chic,
modern alternative and a means to explore modern Chinese
lifestyle. Here's how Shanghai Tang describes the venture:

> The timely, compelling and slightly cheeky initiative unites men
> who are shaping the world in diverse fields, such as sports, busi-
> ness, politics and the arts. To spearhead the effort, Shanghai Tang
> has appointed MCS Ambassadors, including British sprint cham-
> pion Linford Christie, Michelin star chef Pierre Gagnaire, world-
> renowned pianist Lang Lang, and Gavin Newsom, Lieutenant
> Governor of California (ShanghaiTang.com, 2010b, p. 1).

Beyond the formation of the club, Shanghai Tang has further cultivated its brand identity through the lifestyle product of the Shanghai Tang Café, following in the footsteps of leading fashion names such as Giorgio Armani.

The Shanghai Tang Café is an extension of the brand's mission to convey a lifestyle vision of modern Chinese chic. The café

> [...] extends the distinctive Shanghai Tang vibrant, witty, multi-sensory retail experience with an oriental sense of service into a full-service café restaurant and bar that will please the most discerning taste palates. It is a sophisticated offering of modern Chinese cuisine and innovative cocktails that reflects Shanghai Tang's unique, vibrant energy, bold colors, witty humor and cultural richness" (ShanghaiTang.com, 2010c).

This venture is essentially one more way to underscore that modern Chinese lifestyle is culture reinvented. The Shanghai Tang Café is headed by Jereme Leung, an award-winning chef famous for his creative and innovative "New Chinese Cuisine" style of cooking, which stretches the envelope in the styling and presentation of traditions of regional Chinese cuisine. Beyond its culinary achievements, the café also offers the brand's "signature colors in vivid accents, Chinese cultural motifs, rich textures & Chinese craftsmanship such as silk, embroidery, lacquer, as well as other Shanghai Tang home products, enveloping the guests in a multi-sensory world of Shanghai Tang" (ShanghaiTang.com, 2010c, p. 1).

That fashion represents creativity and innovation reveals itself through Shanghai Tang's logo, store décor and location, and range of products and their designs. It exemplifies a successful meaning transfer model, by which brands redefine, reinvent, and co-create meanings from a culturally constituted world for consumer consumption. In Shanghai Tang's case, numerous testimonials and the brand's history demonstrate that Shanghai Tang has found various ways to re-substantiate meanings drawn from the world in highly contrived contexts.

Brand culture at Shanghai Tang

Fashion as a system represents modernity and the reflexivity of modern life. Shanghai Tang, in its role within the fashion system, not only helps people develop a metropolitan or cosmopolitan identity, but also reflects the growth of consumer culture and the progress of democracy, a system that facilitates and encourages contemplation and criticism (Evans and Breward, 2005; Lipovetsky and Sennett, 2002). The discourses of Shanghai Tang, constituted by consumers, managers, and producers, and the consumption of Shanghai Tang can be seen as an example of Imagined China at work. This Imagined China develops from traditional and mythic elements interweaving a modern framework of production, commerce, and consumption. Shanghai Tang thus represents how historical Chinese cultural codes with the support of global fashion resources can develop cosmopolitan consumer identity. For some, Shanghai Tang represents a ladder to success. For others, it embodies authentic and nostalgic emotion. For most, it expresses a hybrid aesthetic of international style and know-how. All these differences emerge across various interpretations of sex appeal, hide-and-seek, sophistication, and social responsibility. Shanghai Tang managers reveal how the brand's use of global personnel, market-oriented creative designs, diverse product ranges for various occasions, top-end store locations, and service cultures can affect consumer interpretations. Collectively, these processes convey how the novel meaning transfer model works, and demonstrates the co-creation and circulation of brand meanings and culture among various brand actors.

Brand culture constitutes the very foundation on which global brands depend for support and growth. Elements of Shanghai Tang's brand culture – consumers, managers, retail stores, and of course, design – have demonstrated here that diverse contributions are essential for the co-creation and development of brand meanings and brand growth, as well as a rationale for potential myth markets, represented in Shanghai Tang design, marketing, and consumption patterns. Shanghai Tang provides a model of conceptualizing a culturally conceived branding system – based on principles of global branding – by marrying global fashion systems with a Chinese imaginary.

5 From Chinese Brand Culture to Global Brands

Chinese-styled branding, conceived as a process that generates cultural meaning and value, can be productively considered in a conceptual space located between managerial strategy and consumer interpretation, with implications for brand management and research. Creating a frame for this space directs attention to a perceived gap between managerial intention and market response. We suggest that the potential of Chinese branding can be elaborated through the notions of co-creation and circulation between brands and cultures.

We conclude this book by introducing the concept of global ethnic diaspora reach as a strategic global branding approach that contributes to current managerial perspectives in research pertaining to brand development. Thereafter, we revisit the construct of Imagined China, and its reconstructions of the identity of modern Chinese lifestyle and Chinese brand culture. In concluding, this chapter makes an attempt to demonstrate how Chinese brands contribute to, and draw from, Chinese culture, and thereby to show that an understanding of Chinese brand culture can reduce the limitations of the managerial approach to brand development, including global brands, and enhance the existing meanings of consumer culture in China.

Global ethnic diaspora market reach as a global branding approach

As a recent feature in *The Economist* reported, diaspora networks continue to prove a strong economic force. Diaspora networks "speed the flow of information;" help spread ideas and money; and further "by linking the West with emerging markets, diasporas help rich countries to plug into fast-growing economies" (2011, p. 13). Our three case studies offer possible visions for global brands – brands marketed not just to a Western audience, or a local Chinese market, but also to a worldwide ethnic diaspora. Global ethnic diaspora refers to the movement of people, forced or voluntary, from one or more nation-states to others. Accordingly, "diaspora results from movements of people in space and refers to their relationship to two or more locations, a place of origin and a place of living. Diaspora refers to a situation in which a religious or ethnic group lives outside of original places" (Jacobsen, 2004, p. 140). A diaspora includes people who reside outside their origin country and away from its citizens.

In international marketing and consumer culture research, scholars have been increasingly focused on global branding, namely on examining global brand meanings, analyzing the advantages and pitfalls, and exploring conditions that ensure success in global brand development. We have defined "global brand" as one that reaches multiple markets around the world, even if those markets are primarily diasporic, that is, serving mainly the home market living in other countries. Our research has suggested how Chinese global brand contexts can draw upon the reach and extent of diaspora to develop brand meaning and image.

Brands can gain a strong foothold in global markets by targeting diaspora markets worldwide because diasporic consumers typically eliminate the need to translate a foreign brand (Anholt, 2005). For example, Jollibee, a Philippine fast-food brand, markets successfully in Hong Kong, the Middle East, and the US because there is a vast Philippine diaspora in those regions. These types of brands have been called pedigree brands, those that are "strongly influenced by the brand's internal legacy and internal conventions" (Gelder, 2005, p. 111). The strength of a pedigree brand often derives from outstanding people, such as a legendary founder, or a place rooted in myth, and from being able to meet social needs pertaining to belonging among diaspora (Gelder, 2005). Another example comes by way of Welsh whisky brand Penderyn, which is the first genuine Welsh whisky to have emerged in the past century and has done well among expatriate Welsh around the globe (Gelder, 2005).

Of course, not all brands enjoy the advantage of a diasporic, expatriate consumer base. Our three case studies suggest that images of modern Chinese life animated by global fashion resources can be used as leverage in appealing to Chinese expatriate populations. In other words, cultural similarities, such as abstract Confucian values, and common cultural symbols that exist among ethnic Chinese, who constitute a vast untapped market across the globe, can become the basis for developing Chinese brands globally. The three cases reveal that the symbolic value of global brands functions as a substantial resource to satisfy cultural needs that exist among ethnic diaspora (Gelder, 2005).

For instance, his highly successful global tours demonstrate the immense appeal of Jay Chou, his brand of music, and his cultural affiliations among young expatriate Chinese in the US, Canada, and European countries. In his capacity as a Chinese music artist, Chou expands the symbolic value of his origins through his quotation of Chinese poetry, martial arts, and myths, and through his hybridization of traditional Chinese music and various Western pop genres (Brown, Hirschman, and Maclaran, 2000). These strategies of multi-dimensional cultural mining not only establish Chou's authentic credentials for a Chinese fan base in China, but also augment perceptions of him as a highly desirable icon of modern China amongst fans across the Pacific Rim and further overseas, as hundreds of Chou fan sites attest.

Our second example, the Beijing Olympics Opening Ceremony, reveals how addressing a national identity anxiety can bring forth new identities. The narratives of two sources illustrate the specifics of China's identity anxiety. Mr. F, who now lives in Shenzhen, China, lived in England for more than six years. Mrs. L is the director of a Washington, DC-based research foundation. Both stated that China's identity anxiety has to do with its economic and technological backwardness prior to 1949, the absence of political democracy, a reputation for manufacturing cheap and inferior quality export items, media restrictions during the Olympics, and fakery during the Opening Ceremony performances.

Nevertheless, the 2008 Beijing Olympics Opening Ceremony can be said to have successfully grappled with the issue of China's identity anxiety. Specifically, it helped present a new China – strengthened by economic success, technological growth, and modernization, but nonetheless grounded in the values of its rich and proud cultural past. The Opening Ceremony tapped into the emotions of domestic Chinese and the Chinese diaspora worldwide through performances that evoked nostalgia and authenticity, and generally elicited pride in national and cultural identity. In particular, elements such as the old Silk Road tableau, the Beijing opera vignette, and the expansive gesture of thousands of performers playing the *fou*, grounded the Opening Ceremony in historical Chinese culture, and provided a common cultural experience for many Chinese observers. These emotive effects of the Opening Ceremony were essential to revitalize the notion of China's image through the imaginary of a new China. Our various informants, as well as the media and other commentators, confirmed the positive impact of the Opening Ceremony on the image of China.

Shanghai Tang's brand success shows that using Chinese cultural symbols – old and new, positive and controversial – can successfully launch a brand onto a global stage. Some scholars have stated that a cosmopolitan image remains important in catering to the expatriate Chinese population (e.g., Roll, 2006). We propose that Shanghai Tang proves much more. It shows that cosmopolitanism is simply not enough, and that it is more the use of traditional Chinese images filtered through contemporary design and fashion systems that really speaks to Chinese communities worldwide.

Global brand success also depends on the cultural wherewithal of the brains behind the brand. There are various examples of diasporic talents that succeeded in overseas markets. For example, the Indian companies Infosys and Wipro have successfully developed Indian software brands worldwide (e.g., Pandit, 2005). Turning back to Shanghai Tang, its cosmopolitan image is Chinese-styled and themed, a hybrid effect that enjoys high appeal among consumers. One of our informants from Shanghai, now living in Europe, liked the old Shanghai references in the brand products. Another, who grew up in China and pursued advanced schooling in England, liked the Chinese-styled sexiness and well-designed clothing that connotes a world-class fashion sense. The sales associate at Shanghai Tang's London store, who is an ethnic Chinese born in Malaysia, stated that Shanghai Tang's cosmopolitan image is nicely forged by crossing Chinese symbols such as ingots with clothing conventions such as the *qipao*, but made with modern design quality fabrics. Finally, a Malaysian-Chinese informant suggested that Shanghai Tang was able to create a cosmopolitan image in its products through references to old Shanghai, which in the pre-Second World War period was one of the biggest financial hubs in East Asia.

The Chinese diaspora

Furthermore, there is the economic and technological strength of Chinese diaspora in Southeast Asia and other regions. For example, the Chinese diaspora in Singapore generates 81 percent of Singapore's GNP (Roll, 2006). Jay Chou World Tour Live in Singapore 2010 was presented by Mobile One and its key partners were the Overseas Chinese Banking Corporation (OCBC) and Pure-Flo. The chairman and CEO of Mobile One, Teo Soon Hoe and Karen Kooi Lee Wah, are both Chinese-Singaporeans. The founder of OCBC is from Fujian province, China, and the CEO of Hyflux responsible for developing Pure-Flo is Olivia Lum, also Chinese-Singaporean. In other words, these Chinese diaspora-run companies help promote Chinese brands in Singapore, and some important Chinese brands worldwide.

Similarly, the case of the Beijing Olympics Opening Ceremony revealed contributions of the Chinese diaspora in Hong Kong. Hong Kong is a special administrative region of China and is home to substantial numbers of the Chinese diaspora. For example, Li Ning, the six-time Olympic medallist who ignited the cauldron at the Beijing Olympics Opening Ceremony, was born in China but has lived in Hong Kong for many years. He founded the Li Ning brand, which offers footwear and sporting apparel in China and abroad, and serves as the chair of the Li-Ning Company Limited's board of directors. Another example is the current chief executive of Hong Kong Special Administrative Region (HKSAR), Sir Donald Tsang Yam-Kuen, whose father is from Foshan City, Guang Dong province, Mainland China.

Among the Hong Kong organizers, Donald Tsang provides an exceptional case of expatriate initiative. Tsang strove hard to ensure that Hong Kong was the site of the relay route opening ceremony held at the Hong Kong Cultural Centre, the torch relay, and the equestrian events. The torch relay of the 2008

Olympic Games traveled across four regions worldwide, namely through Greece, Hong Kong, Macau, and Mainland China. The equestrian events were held in two locations. The Jumping and Dressage events took place at the Hong Kong Olympic Equestrian Venue (Shatin) and the Cross-Country section of the eventing competition took place at the Hong Kong Olympic Equestrian Venue (Beas River). Hong Kong also organized 13 training arenas for jumping and dressage at the Hong Kong Sports Arena and Penfold Park (Beijing2008.cn, 2008b). Prior to these events, Tsang was responsible for inspecting the preparation work for the Olympic Equestrian competition, especially for the security check procedure at the Hong Kong Olympic Equestrian Venue (Beijing2008.cn, 2008b). His example and others demonstrate the economic weight of Chinese diaspora in Hong Kong, and the impact of their outstanding entrepreneurial, leadership, and marketing acumen on the success of the 2008 Beijing Olympics.

Shanghai Tang's case illustrates the impact of Chinese diaspora in Malaysia. The Chinese diaspora in Malaysia produces some $40 billion, which amounts to more than 40 percent of Malaysia's gross national product (Roll, 2006). To harness the potential of this diaspora, Shanghai Tang employed a marketing campaign immersed in Asian cultural traditions to promote its 2009–10 Autumn–Winter season. This campaign was showcased at the historical Cheong Fatt Tze Mansion in Penang, Malaysia, considered to be the epitome of the Chinese country home (ShanghaiTang.com, 2009). Such a strategic location naturally attracted scores from the Chinese diaspora. Furthermore, almost all Shanghai Tang's in-house designers are ethnic Chinese, and those who are not have either lived or worked in Chinese contexts for long periods before starting at Shanghai Tang. The Chinese diaspora provides a key ingredient in the global success of the brand.

Imagined China: Reconstructing the identity of modern Chinese lifestyle

Although Anderson has explored the concept of imagined community in terms of nation building, nation is only one instance of imagined community: "Communities are to be distinguished, not by their falsity/genuineness, but by the style in which they are imagined" (Anderson, 2006, p. 6). Recall that imagined community has been defined further in terms of collective identity, in that "just as national identity takes the form of identification with representations of the nation, so can ethnic groups, feminists, classes, new social movements and other communities of action and identity be understood as imagined" (Barker, 2004, p. 99). The three cases under scrutiny here draw upon these definitions of imagined community and collective identity to suggest that China, as a brand, represents both the nation and a pan-national Chinese identity that crosses domestic borders and encompasses much of the world.

Jay Chou's case tackles the issue of cultural hybridity. The 2008 Beijing Olympics Opening Ceremony posits a China that is old, new, and forward-looking. Shanghai Tang presents a world of cultural anachronisms and historical simultaneity. In all these cases, China becomes a complex, polyvalent imaginary that necessarily demands complex and polyvalent mechanisms of expression. With Jay Chou, we see musical mixing, verbal citation, and metaphoric imagining. In the Opening Ceremony, we see China re-imagined through the classic trope of storytelling, by which China is recreated as a picture with ancient roots and a brilliant, almost infinite future. Shanghai Tang triangulates popular memories and counter memories, contemporary fashion, and identity aspirations by means of icons, palette, and design that collectively evoke but do not pinpoint cultural memories, enabling its products to reside in a fascinating realm of ambiguity and suggestiveness. Despite the differing strategies, all three cases occupy common ground. They all are implicitly dependent on a concrete and historical China, which they imaginatively, innovatively, and always selectively mine for their respective aims.

The representation of historical Chinese culture refers to the representation of Chinese religion, history, tradition, and cultural myths. As we have detailed, culture and history can offer important contextualized contrasts to managerial and information processing interpretations of global branding's interaction with consumer society (Schroeder, 2009). Intricate and diversified ways of involving social, cultural, and historical resources, whether local or distant, provide an opportunity for the productive grounding of brand development. Historical

Chinese culture animates myth through the ideological shaping of popular memories and counter-memories, in conjunction with the competition for identity value, and thus reconfigures the Imagined China and modern Chineseness as a global brand.

Fashion and irrelevance

Fashion does not operate separately from historical culture; rather, fashion systems engage cultural aspects to build a vision of the present, past, or future. Fashion systems and historical culture co-create circulations of past and present, or irrelevant and fashionable, often under the misleading veil of cause and effect. Indeed, it may seem that because something new has emerged, something else has become obsolete. Nevertheless, one might wonder how a new season of womenswear eclipses the qualities and denigrates the colors of last year's offerings to make them appear so "last year." Furthermore, when a particular technology replaces another, one may ask whether this marks the emergence of a truly superior technology, or whether it is a question of fashion. Old-fashioned technologies, as well as multiple seasons of vintage clothing and over a century of recordings, exist side-by-side with contemporary versions. Thus doubts, comparisons, and questions can be raised about the superiority of contemporary aesthetic products. After all, retro-revivals and resurrections continue to occur. Sites such as YouTube allow simultaneous access to music and images from many eras, exposing viewers to supposedly surpassed, not merely out-moded, genres and styles. There can be a surprised sense upon listening: "This sounds as good as music being made and recorded today." In fact, debate continues over qualities of music technologies, with many new listeners confused when a vinyl lp does not produce a scratchy surface noise or a tinny sound, but rather a reproduction of a musical performance as alive, compelling, and warm as any they have heard.

Thus, some questions must be raised regarding the interactions of historical culture and fashion systems whose purposes may have included the latest production's washing-away of anything of yesterday into defunct oblivion. With multiple eras and genres and styles available from various outlets in the current present, consumers may find themselves doubting the judgment of fashion systems regarding what is superior and essential,

wondering whether fashion should not be more appropri-
ately limited to presenting what is the "latest." Consumers
who make these connections and experience this simultaneity
of eras, styles, design, and quality may find themselves more
amenable to engaging with the past as though it were the
present, and also finding the superiorities that extend throughout historical pasts and possibilities.

To play out the example, some recorded music fans have
grown accustomed to believing that all aspects of sound quality,
mixing, reproduction, and delivery, and even creative ideas,
have improved over the years. Listen to the sounds of ten years
ago? Well, maybe the nostalgic favorites, but do not expect to
find anything else of value there. However, in many cases a
vinyl record from the 1950s, if played on a high-quality sound
system – including audiophile amplifier, turntable, cables, and
so forth – carries a quality of sound and recording that is a revelation (e.g., Felton, 2012). If one has only heard such music on
a mediocre radio, a mid-level stereo, or a cheap record player,
one might reckon that older recording and sound technology
was inferior, not one's own equipment.

These considerations are not esoteric, and they throw into
question the notion of progress and evolution and the emergence
in all cases of the "better" over time and in the future, thus
casting a different light upon the directional force of fashion
systems, if not levels of innovation. Indeed, this suggests that
fashion would be misunderstood as pressing only forward to
leave the current behind, rather than working to create a sense
of the contemporary and relevant, and the defunct to which
markets and consumers are expected to respond.

What Chinese brand culture reveals in these cases is that
fashion systems circulate, pulling forward, washing back, and
drawing in new and unknown, as well as already familiar,
notions and entities – such as brands. In this way Chinese
historical culture need not be understood as qualities
and characteristics and narratives dredged up out of some
nearly unreachable, hazy past, but rather always a reinvention
and presentation co-creating itself by the mechanisms of the
fashion system. Thus, we are duped if we come to believe
that the past has been surpassed, innovatively outdone,
by the new and fashionable; yet the circulation of brands
and cultures, especially when stripped of distortions

about the inferiority of the past, offers current, contemporary, and relevant, if hybrid, opportunities in the co-creations of global brands. In this way, we argue for comprehending the circulation of brands and cultures, including historical culture, and see here compelling paths of transformation from Chinese brand culture to global brands.

Cultural myths lack a definitive point of historical origin, a fact that the three case studies deploy in positive ways to re-imagine China for branding purposes. Nevertheless, re-tracing genealogical threads can evoke the origins of pivotal historical moments until they coalesce into a form that is consistent with the popular memory of that myth. The three cases studies suggest that these are critical and controversial times for the re-germination of the myth of Imagined China, which is still variously rooted in images of imperial glory, colonial-era political humiliations, and the age of Mao despite more than 30 years of a market-oriented economy. This might be precisely because the modern commercial entity of China is deeply indebted to narratives about the magnificent imperial China prior to the 19th century, the controversial period between the end of the monarchy and the age of Mao, and to subsequent politics and policies implemented by Mao until his death in 1976. By drawing on such a heterogeneous mythology of old and recent, brand builders set themselves up to compete, through ideological framing, for the identity value of popular memories.

Until very recently, the mass media in China circulated a variety of products, such as music, art, movies, television series, and consumer goods, from Japan, South Korea, and Western countries. Jay Chou went against the grain and reinvigorated national cultural production. He was responsible for popularizing Chinese music, ancient poetry, martial arts myths and icons, and war myths. Zhang Yimou did for Chinese culture and history what Jay Chou did for its musical landscape. He unfolded the vast cultural riches of a historical China for the world to see as one long, unbroken cultural story, still moving, now into the future. Shanghai Tang also performed what is no less than a sleight of hand in renewing interest in modern China by focusing on an old Shanghai aesthetic. Its products project a flattering picture of a period during which Shanghai was a veritable sin city, thriving at a time when the Western world was suffering in the throes of the Great Depression. The strategy here could be counter-memory awareness, which develops from challenging popular notions of an old myth. In this way, Shanghai Tang's products re-configured old Shanghai, and the beginnings of modern China in the pre-Second World War period into an object of cultural desire.

The circulation and co-creation of brands and cultures revisited

We have drawn upon the notion that culture refers to the products and representations of a group, expressed not merely by cultural forms and relationships, but also by artefacts in their capacity as texts with symbolic content and agency. Brands can be thought of as such texts, which express both symbolic content and the everyday meanings of different brand actors. Culture can be used to develop brands, and brands can develop new brands or new cultures, and the new cultures can be re-integrated into developing other new brands.

This book aimed to reveal these integrated tissues of production and consumption through the example of the circulation and co-creation of Chinese brands and cultures. Chinese-styled branding should not be under-valued as merely a mode of communication, but newly considered as both a process of cultural production and a creation of cultural meaning. New Chinese culture can circulate globally and construct new global meanings worldwide.

Aesthetics in Chinese-styled global brand culture

The term aesthetics applies not merely to general art theory and art history. Properly speaking, aesthetics is "a specific regime for identifying and thinking about the arts or the aesthetic regime of art" (Ranciere and Rockhill, 2006, p. 82). We have argued that Chinese-styled global branding can be treated as a specific aesthetic regime of cultural forms or arts in order to examine the creative aspects of authenticity, retrospection, and re-invention deployed in brand building. Chinese-styled global branding aesthetics are expressed in habits of Chinese life practices, such as conventions of salutation and social interactions, food preparation, and principles of organizing space and religious rituals (Leuthold, 1998).

A Chinese-styled global brand culture approach can reveal the cultural perspectives of various brand actors toward brand development. Iconic brands generate cultural conversations in relevant ways and, in the process, brands take on new meanings (Holt, 2004). This book has presented three brands – Jay Chou, Imagined China in the 2008 Beijing Olympics Opening Ceremony, and Shanghai Tang – each highly valued by customers, managerial workers, and the media for their symbolic content. Such brands are more than just brands – they are also cultural icons and aesthetic objects.

The aesthetics of a Chinese-styled branding approach can be examined by looking at how brands address social concerns, such as identity myths and anxieties. Identity myths are subjective, but sometimes brands succeed because they are able to prise out and grapple with the objective qualities of identity myths (Mandoki, 2007). One solution to tackling identity myths is to create a myth, which can be grafted onto the objective aspects of an existing identity myth. Using powerful symbolism, such created myths can appease collective anxieties resulting from acute social and economic changes. The current era in China is such that masses of urban and rural Chinese want to escape from the negative images of China that derive from its political history and manufacturing reality. Brands such as Jay Chou, the Opening Ceremony performances, and Shanghai Tang have created their own identity myths that reveal a heightened awareness of what people need from brands. Their myths have crafted new identities that share common ground in history and locally perceived available culture that are clearly visible within their branding practices. They have used what some scholars have termed reputational capital resources that are locally available to unveil the meanings of historical Chinese culture through the use of modern fashion resources (Askegaard and Kjeldgaard, 2007).

Identity myths and their aesthetics are not value free. They have their ups and downs, their truths and their lies. Brand aesthetics can solve targeted problems by affiliating with appropriate moral codes. In other words, the morality of aesthetics plays a key role in brand development. The three brand cases presented here represent a common morality, which primarily derives its strength and convictions from historical myths, historical narrative, and cultural exemplars. The morality of brand aesthetics in this case is intertwined in the references it selects and the contexts within which they are re-engaged. The stories of managerial workers in these case studies provide ample evidence of this choice in brand aesthetics. In all three cases, we have testimonies that suggest a profound conviction in the authenticity of the imaginary, that the nostalgia is not gratuitous, but rather genuinely involved in creating a new image of and for China, and rejuvenating the best of the China of old. The morality of aesthetics in this case can be understood as the morality that history makes possible.

According to sociologist Peter Berger, "authenticity" refers to identifying what is real in our lives (1973). Accordingly, one could argue that brand authenticity refers to the search for the real behind brand development. In other words, in Chinese-styled brand development, the democratic and free discourses around brand meanings of brand actors manifest real desires. The employment of historical Chinese culture suggests the desire for authentic Chinese culture. Authentic in the present must reflect modern realities, such as the desire for cosmopolitanism, social mobility, and professional success that Shanghai Tang mobilizes through its product line, club ventures, and lifestyle enterprise. At the same time, the use of global fashion mechanisms suggests that consumers and managers are not just searching for the authentic but also for the authentic as it is possible today. However, it may be that desire is fueled by the impossibility of achieving true authenticity (Griffiths, 2013).

Global fashion systems represent a market-fueled circulation of consumer desire and demand, and examining these systems facilitates the interrogation of modern life. Brand fashioning in the three case studies shows how consumers create new brand mythologies, interrogate history, engage with authentically re-imagining the past, and deal with social concerns about status, appearance, education, and national pride. The various conquests of fashion have compelled scholars to take it seriously, from social scientists and economists to marketing experts and consumer researchers.

Implications of the brand culture approach to Chinese-styled global branding

Although marketing and consumer research has generated vast amounts of literature, it has yet to produce adequate theoretical frameworks based on a cultural perspective for the study of branding in the global marketplace and in emerging markets, such as Chinese markets. This research represents an effort to fill the gap between brand development studies focusing expressly on Western brands and their markets and culture-specific global brand development in emerging markets, such as India and China.

Our approach to global brand development in China has integrated a number of research techniques and concepts, such as the multi-sited ethnographic study, brand actor perspectives, and interpretation. Our interest lies in studying how brand actors co-create, circulate, and re-configure existing meanings of brands and their cultures. The research has been peripatetic and culturally diverse, exposing a variety of voices and cultural vantage points such as anti-fashion, anti-conformism, brand devotees, and brand illiterates, revealing that brand culture is a complex field of meanings, people, and modes of being that both influence the market and are influenced by it. In other words, brand culture encompasses diverse scenarios of emerging and established cultural forms, including new, co-created cultural forms.

A brand culture approach to Chinese branding in global markets also addresses the problem of the low repute of Chinese export brands as compared with prominent global brands, as well as demonstrating that a global ethnic diaspora reach strategy can develop global brands. Beyond China, a global ethnic diaspora reach strategy is particularly valuable to brand builders and marketers in other developing countries, which, like China, have large expatriate populations. These considerations emphasize the weaknesses of branding approaches that focus too narrowly on locally appreciated and available resources.

A global brand culture approach to Imagined China takes the concept of the imagined community out of the political realm into a global cultural field. Branding beyond nation building addresses a variety of concerns stemming from questions of identity, belonging, and social status. Identity myths arise from various sources, which share common ground across the world, especially among diasporic communities. Brands become vehicles for meaning co-creation and re-configuration across national boundaries through the discourses of production and consumption. Brands emerge in the social and cultural arena. This would suggest that the Imagined China myth extends cultural myth creation to non-Western contexts with social implications, recognizing commercial culture in identity politics in part via conflicts between the public and private arenas.

The Imagined China myth negotiates the ideological parameters of popular memory and the socio-political significance of counter-memories, helps address the shortages of brand development in non-Western countries, and adds to the growing evidence of evolution in global brand culture. Imagined China provides a wake-up call to Chinese brand builders, producers, managers, and marketers, recommending that they pay attention to the complexities and potential of Chinese brand culture. Global branding implies that brand builders are not merely promoting individual brands, but also certain cultures or lifestyles. As has been noted, Starbucks offers an American lifestyle of coffee drinking, while McDonald's sells visions of convenience as a deserved reward for a busy day's hard work.

Historical Chinese culture and modern Chineseness have become global brands. These are no ordinary brands, but rather ones that attract millions of consumers worldwide and thousands of managerial workers both within and outside China. The enormous market success of Jay Chou, the 2008 Beijing Olympics Opening Ceremony, and Shanghai Tang proves that the landscapes of Chinese brand development are vast and growing, with huge untapped potential. These explorations and reflections should provide impetus both to other Chinese brand builders and to brand builders overseas to rethink their brand development strategies in terms of culturally aware brand strategies, that include the role of local cultures in the development of recognizable global brands. However, brand builders must also factor in the potential negative impact of such brand building, for example repercussions for local cultures. Excessive cultural reproductions and representations can lead to a vogue for inauthentic and meaningless versions of local cultures, and the related denigration of these.

Despite having suggested some implications for brand managers and brand builders, this book is not content to offer only managerial advice. Rather, it examines the open discourses of brands by managerial workers, consumers, and the media in an effort to analyze the negative and positive co-created meanings and circulations of brands and cultures. It blends theory-building research from the social sciences with cultural analysis tools common in the humanities, and thereby draws the study of brand culture and branding into the social sciences and cultural studies. Global brand literacy is expanding rapidly, as is the appeal of brand culture, for a growing band of brand-conscious Chinese consumers. The Chinese brand panorama is expanding.

Shifting Chinese brands away from a focus on cheap commodities, toward global brand development, allows clues to emerge from brand culture. Aesthetic values and historical culture offer possibilities and inform a global reception of branded products, services, and experiences. These opportunities are informed by ever-evolving brand culture, and more specifically, by the co-creation and circulation of brands and cultures.

Appendix

Notes on method

Throughout the book, information from multiple case studies gathered from multi-sited interviews and observation data from managers, consumers, and other related resources combine methodological individualism with interpretive logic to offer access to intersections of consumer meaning making and brand development. We attempt to combine consumer-based approaches with managerial concerns within an overarching framework of brand culture to highlight how brands interact with multiple actors, and how they interact with culture to produce meaning and value.

The case study method is a common approach to the examination of brand management (Carson et al., 2001). Case studies are based on the value of empirical examination; however, there are some limitations to its application, mainly that a few cases become the basis for making general statements about the issues under examination (Bengtsson and Östberg, 2006). The multi-case study serves as a means to mine multiple sources and voices and develop a holistic examination of empirical data. It is a complex method that is capable of dealing with the complex intricacies and broad strokes of cultural and social phenomena (Miles and Huberman, 1994; Yin, 1994). A multi-case method reflects a process of exploration providing insights and asking questions that lead to a better understanding of brand development in the chosen context. As one recent observer pointed out, multi-case studies can offer a holistic understanding of cultural formulation processes through interactions between cultural forms and varied contexts (Mills, Eurepos, and Wiebe, 2010).

Methodological concerns: An ethnographic approach

We allowed multiple relevant cases to present themselves as the research questions developed. Multi-case studies are particularly useful for investigating interplays between a specific mechanism and diverse aspects of varied contexts, and gaining solid configurations and clear temporal sequences that avoid quasi findings (Mills, Eurepos, and Wiebe, 2010). In other words, the multi-case study can address precisely how uniqueness intersects with generalities. A multi-sited ethnographic approach combined with a multi-case study approach is particularly valuable in that it provides the opportunity to discover paradigmatic parallels and thereby integrate varied viewpoints under a common umbrella of conceptual hypothesis and theoretical proposition. It is, in effect, a way to acknowledge the limitations of case studies and expand their applications as much as possible (Eisenhardt, 1989).

This book investigates the global possibilities and play of Chinese brands; we have necessarily adopted a multi-sited ethnographic method. Despite the upsides, cross-cultural methods, which are widely used in cultural marketing and consumer research, are often self-contradictory. Adapting research instruments to individual domestic cultures is necessary to ensure cross-cultural comparability and external validity. But, keeping tests applicable to several nations can also imperil reliability and internal validity (Douglas and Craig, 1997; Usunier, 2000). Specifically, a confined set of so-called universal traits may be used to measure and compare cultures and arrive at conclusions (Kjeldgaard, Csaba, and Ger, 2006), the application of which can sometimes cause the loss of crucial cultural meanings, of cultural difference, and consequently of new meanings. In a nutshell, the cross-cultural method is torn between acknowledging local specifics and abiding by non-specific, international values applicable to more than one country.

Fortunately, culturally contextualized consumer research is a wide field and provides ample checks and balances. One of them is the ethnographic method, which can equalize the effects of cross-cultural analysis. The ethnographic method enables the study of the circulation of meanings and the emergence of cultural forms. The one-sited ethnographic method is typically used to examine the impact of global culture on local cultures, and is particularly valuable in assessing the erosion of local cultures as well as their resistance to aspects of neo-colonialism and global capitalism (Gupta and Ferguson, 1997). Arguably, the ethnographer need only stay in one place in order to study these cultural forms.

Multi-sited ethnographic studies are among the most widely used methods to study global and local contexts (Kjeldgaard, Csaba, and Ger, 2006), with some scholars maintaining the centrality of interview and observation in the arena of data collection (Moisander and Valtonen, 2006). At the same time, Bengtsson and Östberg (2006) have suggested that the managerial approach to studying brand development suffers from certain limitations, such as the use of unique situations rather than general ones, and a supposition of intentionality, personal and professional, behind informant narratives. Our choice of a multi-sited ethnographic method combined interview and observation in an effort to examine the problems surrounding Chinese brand globalization and investigate the impact of Chinese brand cultures on global markets.

Marcus (1998) has emphasized that multi-sited ethnography provides a useful way to acknowledge micro–macro relationships. A multi-sited ethnography reconciles the implied antagonism between consumers and marketers and reconceives them as limited actors in global markets. This study understands consumers and marketers as linked and interdependent entities, with extended links with producers, consumer advocates, and various authorities.

The concept of multi-sited ethnography was concretely conceptualized in anthropology as "multi-locale" by Marcus (1986, 1989) in the late 1980s. Later, in the 1990s, the term underwent conversion to "multi-sited" (Marcus, 1995, 1999), and it was subsequently embraced by others around the world. Marcus advocates multi-sited ethnography in interdisciplinary work, or cultural studies, where analyses are not limited to "a clearly bounded object of study," but where "distinct disciplinary perspectives that participate in them tend to be challenged" (Marcus, 1995, p. 97). According to him, multi-sited ethnography is particularly useful in examining the circulation of cultural meanings, objects, and identities across time and space (Marcus, 1995). Beginning in the 1990s, the multi-sited ethnographic method increasingly drove media studies and social and cultural studies of science and technology, though it was more recently introduced into marketing research.

Ekström (2006) describes the multi-sited ethnographic method as a way to study global and local contexts. The multi-sited ethnographic study approach compels researchers to acknowledge the existence of differing experiences and varying relationships between different brand actors and to use micro perspectives to throw light on the macro context. Researchers thereby gain a better understanding of the wider principles of cultural formation by learning precisely how meanings, objects, and identities circulate in contemporary society, as well as learning how different groups of brand actors are able to contribute to brand formation and brand development. Multi-sited ethnography thus shows how brand meanings and brands are co-creatively developed and come to include positive and negative meanings.

That brand meaning is a product of co-creation is not a new concept. Many observers have addressed this phenomenon (e.g., Holt, 2002, 2004; Pongsakornrungsilp and Schroeder, 2011). Co-creation, in turn, has been addressed via issues of materiality – the basic process of identity formation (Borgerson, 2005). The cultural meaning of a brand is often developed by "various authors," such as the brand owner and consumers, as these intersect with popular culture and other important stakeholders (Bengtsson and Östberg, 2006). The consumers of brands (including employees, managers, and executives) also contribute to these cultural meanings through social and ethical negotiation (Borgerson, 2011; Borgerson et al., 2009; Cova and Dalli, 2009; Zwick, Bonsu, and Darmody, 2008).

Consumer researcher Karin Ekström has provided a detailed summary of cultural research applying Marcus's method of multi-sited ethnographic study (2006). It includes migration studies (Czarniawska, 1998); generational migration of things (Curasi, Price, and Arnould, 2004); the body's immune system (Martin, 1994); plot and story (Czarniawska, 2004); and anti-caste activists in India and England (Hardtmann, 2001), to name a few exemplars. A similar summary pertaining to the impact of Marcus's method in marketing and consumer research has been provided by Kjeldgaard and colleagues (2006). The studies thereof include marketers' structuring of global markets through transnational activities (Applbaum, 2000); unknown brand meanings in the commodification of Nike shoes (Klein, 1999); the construction and production of transnational brand identities (Cayla and Eckhardt, 2008); the history of iconic brands and their impact on popular culture (Holt, 2004); and "doppelgänger" brand images – negative cultural references to popular brands (Giesler, 2012; Thompson, Rindfleisch and Arsel, 2006). The cultural and marketing research examples follow the rise of globalization from local vantage points, or the structuring of the global "from within" (Kjeldgaard, Csaba, and Ger, 2006).

Numerous researchers have applied the multi-sited ethnographic method to study brand development. Klein (1999), for example, used this method to examine the links in Nike's chain of commodification. Her method took her to "sweatshop" factories in China, Indonesia, and other Asian countries. In another example, work on global cultural experiences plays out in surfing scenes in Indonesia (Canniford, 2005). Canniford interviewed surfers in a number of Indonesian surfing locations, reviewed surfing films and media, and historical archives, in an effort to examine how local sovereignty manifests itself on a global stage. Earlier, Belk and colleagues' study on desire (2003) in the US, Turkey, and Denmark, and Belk and Costa's case studies (1998) on the mountain man myth in various locations lasting several years also employed the multi-sited ethnographic approach.

Consumer culture theory (CCT) calls for the development of alternative concepts of culture that explore "the heterogeneous distribution of meanings and the multiplicity of overlapping cultural groupings that exist within the broader socio-historic frame of globalisation and market capitalism" (Arnould and Thompson, 2005, p. 869). This approach enables analysis of diverse experiences that influence different groups, and investigation of relevant networks, their mobility, and their reach within the economic infrastructure of globalization (Kjeldgaard et al., 2006). In this book, managerial perspectives, consumer vantage points, their networks, and the interactions between these participants are examined across locations to come to an understanding of how Chinese brand development crosses national boundaries and intersects with a global context. As a result of pursuing multi-sited ethnographies, our case studies gave us a rich understanding of the cultural formation of each of the selected brands, including how brand meanings circulate.

Acknowledging the interplay of individual and society

In this book, we understand consumer society to be structured, in part, by the actions of individuals, brand builders, the media, and consumers. We interviewed participants who, in addition to being brand builders, are also consumers. They function as individuals even though they represent larger, sometimes corporate, entities. Methodological individualism constitutes an apposite method to investigate a society because it begins by examining individual behavior rather than collective behaviour, enabling consumers, producers, marketers, consumer advocates, and various authorities to come to terms with the varied nature of their experiences (Hodgson, 2007). This is to suggest that the study of individual participants does in fact provide a dependable picture of the larger, macro, context of Chinese brand globalization.

A market system approach (e.g., Giesler, 2008), which studies individuals rather than society as a whole, certainly has its detractors. Heath's call for "holism" in methodological individualism (2005) implies that society is greater than the sum of individuals and their actions. In contrast, Udehn (2001) views society as established by the sum total actions of individuals in it. Methodological individualism, or methodological reductionism, refers to a reduction of the description of all larger entities by reference to smaller ones (Udehn, 2001) and explains and comprehends "broad society-wide developments as the aggregation of decisions by individuals" (Cooper and Finklestein, 2008, p. 55). Methodological individualism grasps a society-wide situation where the individual constructs society and the aggregation of individual behaviors constitutes society. The logic here is that since it is individuals, prior to their membership in groups, who constitute society, the examination of contexts must begin with them in their capacity as basic units. Hodgson (2007) states that methodological individualism can offer a better understanding of the relations between individuals, who, because they are the stuff of society and social structure, are also the builders of society. That said, it is evident that individual behavior and intentions are varied. They cannot represent the whole phenomenon that is society. Some concerns regarding these negotiated understandings have been addressed through a focus on materiality.

Cultural anthropologist Daniel Miller has argued that a theory of consumption needs a theory of *materiality*, or a way of understanding relationships between subjects, objects, and environment (Miller, 1987). Consumer research has tended to confuse materiality with *materialism*, or "the role of material objects in affecting terminal goals such as life satisfaction, happiness, and social progress" (Claxton and Murray, 1994, p. 422). With respect to consumers, a theory of materiality "helps map agency and effects in relations between consumers, objects/relations of consumption, and identity construction" (Borgerson, 2005, p. 440). Discussions of materiality explicitly raise questions around the use of objects, images, and symbolic resources by consumers in their identity work, and the ways in which consumers are altered by consumption objects, practices, and meanings. It has been suggested that individuals construct identities as much through engagement with material objects and practices as they do through human relationships (Borgerson, 2009).

Different models of materiality – including theories of co-creation and actor network theory – offer different approaches, distinct research questions, and diverse outcomes. Examining the ways in which consumers, managerial workers, and the media co-create brand meanings – including perceptions of brand identity and image – in conjunction with objects, experiences, and other symbolic resources in the world calls for a materiality-aware approach.

Attending to methodological individualism in cultural and marketing research involved face-to-face interviews with each participant, note taking, data collection, analysis, observing individual websites, attending concerts and events, and visiting stores related to each case. Individual interviews and observations made thereof reflect individuals influenced by brands, brand culture, and culture more generally, as well as individuals constructing society through discursive, cultural, and material practices.

Interpretation and interviews

Interpretive logic helps facilitate the emergence of new meanings and new understanding (Moisander and Valtonen, 2006). Moreover, interpretive methods push researchers to fruitfully second-guess themselves and begin to reread cultural practices that were previously taken for granted. In order to comprehend the data, we employed an interpretive case study method because it provides tools to generate macro implications from interpretations of participant experiences. Specifically with respect to cultural and marketing research, Thompson and Haytko (1997) argue that interpretive logic provides an in-depth explanation of individual consumer culture as opposed to mass consumer culture. An interpretive method in cultural marketing and consumer culture research allows us to examine brand development, namely the circulation and accumulation of brand meanings, as demonstrated by studies of Harley-Davidson through activities related to its products (Schouten and McAlexander, 1995), of *Star Trek* through its enthusiasts (Kozinets, 2001), and of Apple and its fanatical brand fans (Muñiz and O'Guinn, 2001).

Brand meanings are not fixed. Aspects of intended meanings – brand identity – might be expressed by text and images in marketing communications and other brand stimuli, but consumer perception, experience, and aspiration may intervene with unintended meanings – brand image. The cultural knowledge of consumers filters brand communications, as consumers comprehend and sometimes reconstitute meaning into forms that are not fully consistent with brand builders' intentions (Puntoni, Schroeder, and Ritson, 2010; Scott, 1994). It has been suggested, however, that brand authors can understand and reconstitute what would function as relevant brand meanings only if they possess a minimal level of competency or brand literacy, which facilitates the reading and digesting of brand messages. Competency is desirable as it helps determine how authors will conduct themselves *vis-à-vis* brands in commercial and social situations (Peñaloza and Gilly, 1999). Meaning construction in relation to brands and brand messages operates through flexible socio-cultural codes written by and decoded between varied authors whose interpretation of brand messages exerts a powerful effect on brand development and brand success. Market interpreters focus on reading and decoding consumer codes, partially accessed through consumer activities and choices, and partially through messages relayed by mass media and shareholders (Kates, 2006). This suggests that brand meaning and brand culture are a complex bundle of personal and socio-cultural meanings (e.g., Allen, Fournier, and Miller, 2008; Schroeder, 2009).

Interview techniques

As suggested by McCracken (1988b) and Thompson and his colleagues (1989), we aimed to create a relaxed interview environment in which the participants experienced ease and comfort, which included allowing participants to suggest a context and location. To maintain privacy, no one apart from the interviewer and the interviewee was present during these meetings. Interviews typically began with a grand tour question, as McCracken calls it (1988b). This involved inquiries regarding background, such as age, gender, occupation, citizenship, and personal interests. The general flow of the ensuing questions was in keeping with interpretive consumer research conventions regarding the face-to-face interview (e.g., Thompson, Locander, and Pollio, 1989).

Prior to each interview, the participants were given a brief idea of the process to follow, and the objective of the study was explained – that it was intended to acquire an understanding of their experiences and perceptions pertaining to the relevant case study subjects and, through these examples, to gain a better understanding of Chinese brand globalization. The interviews lasted anywhere between 26 minutes and 2 hours. The tone of the interviews was largely casual, with questions sometimes improvised on the basis of answers provided by participants. Sometimes, participants were asked to elaborate on points included in their responses to acquire detailed reflections. Questions were designed to glean as complete a description of specific experiences as possible, with breathing room for participants to introduce unsolicited stories and narratives, which ultimately proved enriching. Therefore, although the design of the interviews was fixed by the desire to gain a full understanding of brand author perspectives, the questions themselves did not follow a preordained format.

Participants were encouraged to provide details about specific experiences relating to their general perceptions. This measure minimized digressions and maintained a dialogue that was relatively free of abstractions. The subsequent portions of the conversations spanned various topics, including perceptions of their experiences related to relevant social groups, for example managerial circles. The concluding questions factored in their opinions, suggestions, and recommendations for Chinese brand builders desiring brand globalization. In reproducing interview quotes and insights, in many cases the names of the informants have been changed.

Researcher participation related to the case studies included attending concerts, visiting stores, and taking pictures; and in each instance taking notes and transcribing them at the earliest opportunity. Data gathered from these contexts provided an authentic grounding in surface and ambient details. Following Thompson's and his colleagues' (1994) guidelines, we used interpretation to reflect on the cultural meanings in, and beliefs behind, participant descriptions. Situating the discovered meanings in relation to existential research theories on brand globalization helped develop an understanding of conflicts and paradoxes as perceived by the participants, and also understandings of strategies implied in their descriptions and observations of the case study subjects. To these results we added the results of visual analysis of websites, store location events, and photos, as the analysis of visual records provides pattern and meaning to the differing experiences of participants (Collier, 2001). The studies discussed here developed in phases, and the following section provides some details regarding how they were conducted.

Developing the cases

In discussing his concerns about the global visibility of his company's brands and the possibilities of an enhanced retailing strategy, one of the two participants working for a prominent Chinese apparel manufacturer invoked Asian musical superstar Jay Chou, which sparked our interest in Jay Chou as a case study subject. One of the authors visited Beijing, Shanghai, and Wenzhou to interview three consumers, including a student and a vice general manager from China and France, aged between 24

and 36 years. Two were male and one was female. The interviews were conducted in relatively private places selected by
participants, such as participants' offices and coffee shops. The
interviews typically began with general background questions.
Subsequent questions were relaxed, such as the location of
recent concerts. Questions thereafter focused on perceptions of
Jay Chou and understandings of his popularity. Two interviews
were conducted in Chinese and one was conducted in English.
Fifteen months later, in March 2010, two of these Jay Chou fans
were interviewed again to capture shifts in perceptions. These
were conducted in Chinese, then transcripts were translated into
English.

To gather background information for the Jay Chou case,
one of the authors attended four Jay Chou concerts between
2005 and 2008, one each in Beijing, Shanghai, Hangzhou, and
Wenzhou. These concerts lasted two to four hours, and audience
numbers ranged between 10,000 and 80,000. In addition, five
Jay Chou-related websites were observed for a period of more
than three years. Three of the five websites were fan-related,
and two were official. (Three of the five were in English.)
Other online data, television shows, and printed materials on
Jay Chou were observed for a longer period. Further investigation included listening to eight of his albums and analyzing lyrics, song names, and musical instruments. We also used
secondary data from Asian music researcher Anthony Fung, who
has studied Jay Chou's fan bases and related information for
several years (2008).

All these sources of data provided varied interpretations of
Jay Chou, namely how Jay Chou's cultural meanings circulate,
and how he, in his capacity as a cultural form, has developed as
a brand. Jointly, the interview and observation data, in conjunction with the secondary data from Fung, made possible a theoretical framework that cuts across geopolitical spaces and crosses
cultural barriers. Such a framework also provides insights into
existing marketing strategies in the global marketplace, and into
ideologies of evolving Chinese culture.

To investigate how the Beijing Olympics Opening Ceremony
has enabled China to grow as a global brand, we interviewed
international consumers, CEOs, and brand managers from
universities, corporations, and market research firms located in
the UK and China. We conducted interviews online, via tele-

phone, and in person, corresponded by email, and visually analyzed recordings of the Opening Ceremony. All these steps and
measures followed an interpretive approach, and focused on
the activities of consumers and other brand authors in order to
understand how authors construct brand meanings.

Some stages of the Beijing Olympics Opening Ceremony
study began prior to the ceremony. For example, the first
author trained and then served as a volunteer for the Opening
Ceremony. In August 2008, two days after the ceremony, we
posted a bilingual English and Chinese notice on a pre-existing, individual MSN account (which included 82 Chinese and
foreign friends) asking "Did you watch the Beijing Olympics
Opening Ceremony?" and "What do you think of it?" MSN
friends were asked to write back with comments and examples. We also sent 112 emails, with these enquiries attached,
to marketing executives, managers, and CEOs of prominent Chinese brand firms, including Lenovo, Lining, Haier,
Geely, Quanjude, Maotai, and Tsingtao beer. The list of
email recipients produced three interviewees for the Jay
Chou case and six interviewees for the Chinese brand globalization focus. We acquired 52 respondents, 37 of whom
answered the questions with detailed replies, though most
provided rather brief answers. We sent follow-up emails to the
52 respondents requesting them to agree to in-depth interviews,
and 13 agreed to participate. In August, one of the authors
interviewed six participants in Beijing, Jinan, Shenzhen, and
Shanghai. Later, in December 2008, we interviewed two participants in Hangzhou. Both worked for a top Chinese automobile
corporation. Further, during the Shanghai Tang study, two
participants employed with the company offered their opinions
on the Beijing Olympics Opening Ceremony. More recently,
in 2010, four participants, previously interviewed in December
2007 for their views on Chinese brand globalization, were invited
to discuss the 2008 Beijing Olympics Opening Ceremony.

We also gathered a convenience sample of people who had
seen the Opening Ceremony and were willing to be interviewed.
A total of 16 informants, including CEOs, brand managers, and
consumers, were involved in semi-structured interviews over a
period of eight months. The interviews lasted between 60 and
75 minutes and were conducted in English and Chinese, the
latter translated into English. After the more general questions,

we asked for participants' observations of the Beijing Olympics Opening Ceremony, and specifically asked the CEOs and brand managers about their current business situations. This was followed by detailed questions about the use of advanced technology to stage Chinese historical culture in the Opening Ceremony, and its implications for using Chinese historical culture to build and develop Chinese brands.

Information was also collected from Chinese print media, online and televized advertisements, and from newscasts on the Beijing Olympics Opening Ceremony. *The Financial Times*, *The New York Times*, beijing2008.cn (the official website of the Beijing Olympics), *Movie View* (Kan Dianying), China's most popular film magazine, and five useful interviews conducted by CRI (China Radio International) were also selected. By examining these different sources, we constructed a varied description of informant responses to China's staging of the Beijing Olympics Opening Ceremony, and their perceptions of Chinese international branding. We place the Opening Ceremony within a larger context of the 2008 Beijing Olympic Games, Chinese branding, and global cultural branding, in an effort to conceptualize an alternative framework that sheds light on Chinese branding contexts relevant to cultural theories around consumption practices and processes.

The Shanghai Tang case study served to address an important unanswered question: How to make historical Chinese culture in branding and branded products not only accessible and practical, but also fashionable? As the CEO and a brand manager from the Chinese automobile corporation offered: "We used historical Chinese elements in our brands and products to market them overseas [...] but how do we make these kinds of products and branding activities popular?"

Seeking answers to these questions, we posted an English and Chinese notice on an MSN account asking people for their thoughts on how to make products that evoked historical Chinese cultural elements fashionable in global markets. We requested that people send answers that included examples. We also sent 123 similar emails to brand managers and marketers in China and abroad. Out of 69 respondents, 12 named Shanghai Tang, which garnered the most mentions. Seven informants consumed Shanghai Tang products, and three of these agreed to in-depth interviews. Through this case study, we investigated how a sample of Shanghai Tang consumers, as well as a number of managerial workers, perceived the metaphorical and emotional meanings of historical Chinese culture, which they associated with branding activities and found fashionable.

Further, we interviewed Shanghai Tang managers, as well as international consumers at universities, corporations, and market research firms in the UK and China. This research approach included online contact, phone calls, and face-to-face interviews, followed by email correspondence, and visual analysis of the Shanghai Tang brand identity. We interviewed managerial and consumer participants, personally observed activities in retail stores in China and the UK, and consulted several relevant online interviews.

The Shanghai Tang stores we visited are located in Shanghai (three stores), Beijing (four stores), Hangzhou (one store), Guangzhou (one store), and London (one store). We interviewed 11 store managers and sales associates. All the Shanghai Tang stores were located on main thoroughfares, in luxury hotels, or in centrally located shopping malls. Shop design characteristics were similar: fashionable, luxurious, and glamorous.

In the first interview at the Shanghai Tang store in the Shangri-La Hotel, Shanghai, the store manager suggested that it would make more sense if the interviewer posed as just another consumer in future interviews with Shanghai Tang employees. We followed her advice and withheld our identity and intentions from subsequent Shanghai Tang interviewees. In this way, we interviewed Shanghai Tang store managers and sales associates. These interviews lasted 60 to 120 minutes. On leaving the stores, we documented details of the store managers' and sales associates' conversations, comments, and insights. All the participants spoke in Chinese, and the notes were translated into English by the first author. As required by their retail positions, each participant competently introduced the products and even helped us pick out certain items, which we tried on in the stores. Six of the managerial participants were current Shanghai Tang consumers and five were potential consumers. Each provided reasons for his or her keenness to patronize Shanghai Tang. In total, there were 22 consumer participants, including 11 managerial workers who were also avid Shanghai Tang consumers.

We returned to the locations to take pictures of the stores, and found suitable methods for observing the consumers and their consumption practices unnoticed. We were able to inter-view seven who had just completed their shopping at the stores. These interviews lasted 25 to 45 minutes, typically taking place at coffee shops located nearby. Later, we emailed our Shanghai Tang consumers for follow-up interviews, and three respondents accepted the requests. These interviews were conducted in their offices in China, and lasted about an hour.

Thereafter, we sent related emails to a sample of staff and students at a university in southwest England and received four responses. We selected two informants for further interviews, one from the UK and another from Singapore. We recorded both interviews, which were conducted in English, and tran-scribed verbatim.

A note about the consumers among the participants: the four males and seven females ranged between the ages of 25 and 52 years. Interviews with the Chinese participants were conducted in Chinese, subsequently translated into English. The rest of the interviews were conducted in English. The interviews began with general questions about the participants' background and working experience. Thereafter, we asked participants why they purchased Shanghai Tang products. They tended to respond with stories and narratives often expressing emotional bonds with the brand. Three of the women, who were diasporic Chinese, favored the accessories. Their Western female counter-parts also expressed this preference, and added that the Chinese cufflinks would make good gifts for male friends. Most of the male consumers expressed their interest in the Chinese Tang suit, and generally admired Shanghai Tang designs.

Our research allowed us to shed light on the macro context and appreciate and gauge the process of cultural formation via the circulation of meanings, objects, and identities in contemporary society. The micro-level data collected for Shanghai Tang from managerial workers, consumers, and the media was employed to interpret the larger landscape of circulating of meanings between brands and brand authors. As a result of interviewing global consumers and marketers of Shanghai Tang in different loca-tions and by observing its stores, related consumption behav-ior, relevant websites, and other media resources, the final case study reveals the possibilities and processes of understanding and engaging Chinese cultural resources through fashion codes in Chinese global branding strategy.

182

References

Aaker, D. A. 1996. *Building strong brands*. New York: The Free Press.

Aaker, D. A. and Joachimsthaler, E. 1999. The lure of global branding. *Harvard Business Review*, 77(6), 137–44.

Aaker, D. A. and Joachimsthaler, E. 2009. *Brand leadership: building assets in an information economy*. New York: The Free Press.

Aaker, J. and Williams, P. 1998. Empathy versus pride: the influence of emotional appeals across cultures. *Journal of Consumer Research*, 25(4), 241–61.

Alashban, A. A, Hayes, L. A., Zinkhan, G. M., and Balazs, A. L. 2002. International brand-name standardization/adaptation: antecedents and consequences. *Journal of International Marketing*, 10(3), 22–48.

Alhoff, F., Wolfendale, J., Kennett, J., and Baumgardner, J. 2011. *Fashion – philosophy for everyone: thinking with style*. New York: Wiley.

Allen, C., Fournier, S., and Miller, F. 2008. Brands and their meaning makers. In C. P. Haugtvedt, P. M. Herr, and F. R. Kardes, eds. *Handbook of consumer psychology*. Mahwah, NJ: Lawrence Erlbaum Associates, pp. 781–822.

Anderson, B. 2006. *Imagined communities: reflections on the origin and spread of nationalism*, new edition. London: Verso.

Anholt, S. 2005. *Brand new justice: how branding places and products can help the developing world*. Oxford: Butterworth-Heinemann.

Appadurai, A. 1990. Disjuncture and difference in the global economy. In M. Featherstone, ed. *Global culture: nationalism, globalization and modernity*. London: Sage, pp. 295–310.

Applbaum, K. 2000. Crossing borders: globalization as myth and charter in American transnational consumer marketing. *American Ethnologist*, 27(2), 257–82.

Arnould, E. J. and Price, L. L. 2000. Authenticating acts and authoritative performances: questing for self and community. In S. Ratneshwar, D. G. Mick, and C. Huffman, eds. *The why of consumption: contemporary perspectives on consumer motives, goals, and desires.* New York: Routledge, pp. 140–63.

Arnould, E. J. and Thompson, C. J. 2005. Consumer culture theory (CCT): twenty years of research. *Journal of Consumer Research*, 31(4), 868–82.

Arnould, E. J. and Tissiers-Desbordes, E. 2005. Hypermodernity and the new millennium: scientific language as a tool for marketing communications. In A. J. Kimmel, ed. *Marketing communication: emerging trends and developments.* Oxford: Oxford University Press, pp. 236–55.

Arsel, Z. and Thompson, C. J. 2011. Demythologizing consumption practices: how consumers protect their field-dependent identity investments from devaluing marketplace myths. *Journal of Consumer Research*, 37(5), 791–806.

Askegaard, S. 2006. Brands as a global ideoscape. In J. Schroeder and M. Salzer-Mörling, eds. *Brand culture.* London: Routledge, pp. 91–102.

Askegaard, S. and Kjeldgaard, D. 2007. Here, there, and everywhere: place branding and gastronomical globalization in a macro-marketing perspective. *Journal of Macromarketing*, 27(2), 138–47.

Azhari, N. 2008. Textiles and clothing trade post-agreement on textiles and clothing: Can trade facilitation help? In M. Mikic, ed. *Unveiling protectionism: regional responses to remaining barriers in the textiles and clothing trade.* New York: United Nations Publications, pp. 171–83.

baidu.com 2010. *Zhou, Jielun or Jay Chou* [in Chinese]. Available at: http://baike.baidu.com/view/2632.htm.

Baker, J., Grewal, D., and Levy, M. 1992. An experimental approach to making retail store environmental decisions. *Journal of Retailing*, 68(4), 445–60.

Balmer, J. M. T. 2009. Scrutinising the British monarchy: The corporate brand that was shaken, stirred and survived. *Management Decision*, 47(4), 639–75.

Banister, E. N. and Hogg, M. K. 2006. Consumers and their negative selves, and the implications for fashion marketing. In T. Hines and M. Bruce, eds. *Fashion marketing: contemporary issues*. Oxford: Butterworth-Heinemann, pp. 217–29.

Barboza, D. 2012. Easy China through three doors. *New York Times*, May 6, Travel Section, pp. 6–7, 11.

Barker, C. 2004. *The Sage dictionary of cultural studies*. Thousand Oaks, CA: Sage.

Barnard, M. 2002. *Fashion as communication*, 2nd edition. London: Routledge.

Barnhill, D. L. 2005. East Asian aesthetics and nature. In B. Taylor, ed. *The encyclopedia of religion and nature*. London: Continuum, pp. 16–19.

Barthes, R. 1990. *The fashion system*. M. Ward and R. Howard, trans. Berkeley: University of California Press.

Beijing2008.cn 2008a. *Press conference: fireworks for opening & closing ceremonies*. Available at: http://en.beijing2008.cn/live/pressconference/mpc/n214469220.shtml.

Beijing2008.cn 2008b. *Hong Kong*. Available at: http://en.beijing2008.cn/news/olympiccities/hongkong/n214486735.shtml.

Belk, R. W. and Costa, J. A. 1998. The mountain man myth: a contemporary consuming fantasy. *Journal of Consumer Research*, 25(4), 218–40.

Belk, R. W., Ger., G., and Askegaard, S. 2003. The fire of desire: a multi-sited inquiry into consumer passion. *Journal of Consumer Research*, 30(4), 326–51.

Belk, R. W., Wallendorf, M., and Sherry, J. F. Jr. 1989. The sacred and the profane in consumer behaviour: theodicy on the Odyssey. *Journal of Consumer Research*, 16(2), 1–38.

Bengtsson, A. and Firat, A. F. 2006. Brand literacy: consumers' sense-making of brand management. *Advances in Consumer Research*, 33, 375–80.

Bengtsson, A. and Östberg, J. 2006. Researching the cultures of brands. In R. W. Belk, ed. *Handbook of qualitative research methods in marketing.* Cheltenham: Edward Elgar, pp. 83–93.

Benjamin, W. 1999. *The arcades project.* H. Eiland and K. McLaughlin, trans. Cambridge, MA: Harvard University Press.

Bently, L., Davis, J., and J. Ginsburg, J., eds. 2008. *Trade marks and brands: an interdisciplinary critique.* Cambridge: Cambridge University Press.

Berger, P. L. 1973. "Sincerity" and "authenticity" in modern society. *The Public Interest,* 31, 81–8.

Berger, P. L. 1990. *The sacred canopy: elements of a sociological theory of religion.* New York: Anchor Books.

Bergstrom, M. 2012. *All eyes east: lessons from the front lines of marketing to China's youth.* New York: Palgrave.

Beverland, M. B. and Farrelly, F. J. 2010. The quest for authenticity in consumption: consumers' purposive choice of authentic cues to shape experienced outcomes. *Journal of Consumer Research,* 36(6), 838–56.

Bidgoli, H. 2010. *The handbook of technology management: supply chain management, marketing and advertising, and global management,* Volume 2. New York: Wiley.

Biel, A. 1991. The brandscape: converting image into equity. *Admap,* October, 41–6.

Blackburn, S. 2005. *Dictionary of philosophy.* 2nd edition. Oxford: Oxford University Press.

Blaszczyk, R. 2007. *Producing fashion: commerce, culture, and consumers.* Philadelphia: University of Pennsylvania Press.

Borgerson, J. L. 2005. Materiality, agency, and the constitution of consuming subjects: insights for consumer research. *Advances in Consumer Research,* 32, 439–43.

Borgerson, J. L. 2009. Materiality and the comfort of things: drinks, dining and discussion with Daniel Miller. *Consumption Markets & Culture,* 12(2), 155–70.

Borgerson, J. L. 2011. Bad faith and epistemic closure: challenges in the marketing context. In R. ten Bos and M. Painter-

Morland, eds. *Business ethics and continental philosophy.* Cambridge: Cambridge University Press, pp. 220–41.

Borgerson, J. L. and Schroeder, J. E. 2003. The lure of paradise: marketing the retro-escape of Hawaii. In S. Brown and J. F. Sherry, Jr., eds. *Time, space and the market: retroscapes rising.* Armonk, NY: M. E. Sharpe, pp. 219–37.

Borgerson, J. L., Schroeder, J. E., Escudero Magnusson, M., and Magnusson, F. 2009. Corporate communication, ethics, and operational identity: a case study of Benetton. *Business Ethics – A European Review,* 18(3), 209–23.

Bourdieu, P. 1993. *The field of cultural production.* London: Polity.

Boyer, M. 1992. Cities for sale: merchandising history at South Street Seaport. In M. Sorkin, ed. *Variations on a theme park: the new American city and the end of public space.* New York: Hill & Wang, pp. 181–204.

Bradshaw, A., McDonagh, P., and Marshall, D. 2006. No space: new blood and the production of brand culture colonies. *Journal of Marketing Management,* 22(5), 579–99.

Brady, A.-M. 2009. The Beijing Olympics as a campaign of mass distraction. *The China Quarterly,* 197, 1–14.

Broudehoux, A.-M. 2007. Spectacular Beijing: the conspicuous construction of an Olympic metropolis. *Journal of Urban Affairs,* 29(4), 383–99.

Brown, S. 1995. *Postmodern marketing.* London: Routledge.

Brown, S. 1999. Retro-marketing: yesterday's tomorrow, today. *Marketing Intelligence and Planning,* 17(7), 363–76.

Brown, S. 2001. *Marketing – The Retro-revolution.* London: Sage.

Brown, S., Hirschman, E., and Maclaran, P. 2000. Presenting the past: on marketing's re-production orientation. In S. Brown and A. Patterson, eds. *Imagining marketing: art, aesthetics, and the avant-garde.* London: Routledge, pp. 145–91.

Brown, S., Kozinets, R., and Sherry, J. 2003. Teaching old brands new tricks: retro branding and the revival of brand meaning. *Journal of Marketing,* 67(July), 9–33.

Brownell, S. 2009. The Beijing Olympics as a turning point? China's first Olympics in East Asian perspective. *The*

Asia-Pacific Journal. Available at: www.japanfocus.org/ -susan-brownell/3166 [Accessed September 29 2012].

Bruner, E. 1994. Abraham Lincoln as authentic reproduction: a critique of post-modernism. *American Anthropologist*, 96(2), 397–415.

Bruzzi, S. and Gibson, P. C., eds. 2000. *Fashion cultures: theories, explorations and analysis.* London: Routledge.

Buck-Morss, S. 1991. *The dialectics of seeing: Walter Benjamin and the arcades project.* Cambridge, MA: MIT Press.

Calarco, M. and Atterton, P., eds. 2004. *Animal philosophy: essential readings in continental thought.* New York: Continuum.

Canniford, R. 2005. Moving shadows: suggestions for ethnography in globalized cultures. *Qualitative Market Research: an International Journal*, 8(2), 204–18.

Carson, D., Gilmore, A., Perry, C., and Gronhaug, K. 2001. *Qualitative market research.* London: Sage.

Carter, B. and Sandomir, R. 2008. A surprise winner at the Olympic Games in Beijing: NBC. *New York Times*, August 18. Available at: www.nytimes.com/2008/08/18/ sports/olympics/18nbc.html.

Cayla, J. and Arnould, E. J. 2008. A cultural approach to branding in the global marketplace. *Journal of International Marketing*, 16(4), 86–112.

Cayla, J. and Eckhardt, G. M. 2008. Asian brands and the shaping of a transnational imagined community. *Journal of Consumer Research*, 35, 216–30.

Charters, S. 2006. Aesthetic products and aesthetic consumption: a review. *Consumption Markets and Culture*, 9(3), 235–55.

Chen, C. C., Colapinto, C., and Luo, Q. 2012. The 2008 Beijing Olympics Opening Ceremony: visual insights into China's soft power, *Visual Studies*, 27(2), 188–95.

Cheng, H. 1997. Toward an understanding of cultural values manifest in advertising: a content analysis of Chinese television commercials in 1990 and 1995. *Journalism and Mass Communication Quarterly*, 74(4), 773–96.

Cheng, H., and Chan, K., eds. 2009. *Advertising and Chinese society: impacts and issues.* Copenhagen: Copenhagen Business School Press.

Cheng, H. and Schweitzer, J. C. 1996. Cultural values reflected in Chinese and US television commercials. *Journal of Advertising Research*, 36(3), 8–35.

China Daily 2005. Bo: *800 million shirts for one Airbus A380.* Available at: www.chinadaily.com.cn/english/doc/2005-05/05/content_439584.htm.

Cholachatpinyo, A., Padgett, I., Crocker, M., and Fletcher, B. 2002. A conceptual model of the fashion process – part 1: the fashion transformation process model. *Journal of Fashion Marketing and Management*, 6(1), 11–23.

Chua, R. Y. and Eccles, R. J. 2009. *Managing creativity at Shanghai Tang.* October 22. Boston, MA: Harvard Business School Publishing. Available at: http://ssrn.com/abstract=1467615 [Accessed August 8 2009].

Claxton, R. P. and Murray, J. B. 1994. Object–subject interchangeability: a symbolic interactionist model of materialism. In C. T. Allen and D. Roedder John, eds. *Advances in consumer research*, Volume 21. Provo, UT: Association for Consumer Research, pp. 422–6.

Cochran, S. 2006. *Chinese medicine men: consumer culture in China and Southeast Asia.* Cambridge, MA: Harvard University Press.

Coles, P., Knowles, C., and Newbury, D. 2012. Seeing the Olympics: images, spaces, legacies, *Visual Studies*, 27(2), 117–18.

Collier, M. 2001. Approaches to analysis in visual anthropology. In T. van Leeuwen and C. Jewitt, eds. *Handbook of visual analysis.* Thousand Oaks, CA: Sage, pp. 35–60.

Cooper, C. L. and Finklestein, S. 2008. *Advances in mergers and acquisitions*, Volume 7. Bingley, UK: Emerald Group.

Corral, C. D., Pérez-Turpin, J. A., Vidal, A. M., Padorno, C. M., Patiño, J. M., and Molina, A. G. 2010. Principles of the Olympic movement. *Journal of Human Sport & Exercise*, 5(1), 3–14.

Costa, J. and Bamossy, G. 1995. Culture and marketing of culture: the museum retail context. In J. Costa and G. Bamossy, eds. *Marketing in a multicultural world: ethnicity, nationalism, and cultural identity.* Thousand Oaks, CA: Sage, pp. 299–328.

Coulter, R. A., Price, L. L., and Feick, L. 2003. Rethinking the origins of involvement and brand commitment: insights from post-socialist central Europe. *Journal of Consumer Research*, 30(3), 151–69.

Cova, B. and Dalli, D. 2009. Working consumers: the next step in marketing theory? *Marketing Theory*, 9(3), 315–39.

Craig, E., ed. 1998. *Encyclopedia of philosophy.* London: Routledge.

Craig, S. C. and Douglas, S. P. 2000. Configural advantage in global markets. *Journal of International Marketing*, 8(1), 6–21.

Crane, D. 2000. *Fashion and its social agendas: class, gender, and identity in clothing.* Chicago: University of Chicago Press.

Crang, M. 1996. Magic kingdom or a quixotic quest for authenticity? *Annals of Tourism Research*, 23(2), 415–31.

Crewe, L. and Goodrum, A. 2000. Fashioning new forms of consumption: the case of Paul Smith. In S. Bruzzi, and P. Church-Gibson, eds. *Fashion cultures.* London: Routledge, pp. 25–48.

Csaba, F. and Bengtsson, A. 2006. Rethinking identity in brand management. In J. Schroeder and M. Salzer-Mörling, eds. *Brand culture.* London: Routledge, pp. 15–45.

Cui, G. 1997. The name game: foreign and PRC brands race to build their reputation and market shares in China. *China Business Review*, 24(6), 40–3.

Cui, J. and Zhou, G. 2001. *Freestyle* [in Chinese]. Guangxi: Guangxi Normal University Press.

Curasi, C. F., Price, L. L., and Arnould, E. J. 2004. How individuals' cherished possessions become families' inalienable wealth. *Journal of Consumer Research*, 31(4), 609–22.

Czarniawska, B. 1998. *A narrative approach to organization studies, qualitative research methods.* London: Sage.

Czarniawska, B. 2004. The uses of narrative in social science research. In M. Hardy and A. Bryman, eds. *Handbook of data analysis.* London: Sage, pp. 649–66.

Dale, C. H., ed. 2004. *Chinese aesthetics and literature: a reader.* Albany: State University of New York Press.

Davis, A. 2009. *MediaTV: Shanghai Tang's luxury strategy.* Available at: http://www.cei.asia/searcharticle/2009_09/ MediaTV-Shanghai-Tangs-luxury-strategy/37282.

Davis, D. S. 2000. Introduction: a revolution in consumption. In D. S. Davis, ed. *The consumer revolution in China.* Berkeley: University of California Press, pp. 1–22.

Davis, E. L., ed. 2004. *Encyclopedia of contemporary Chinese culture.* London: Routledge.

Davis, F. 1992. *Fashion, culture and identity.* Chicago: Chicago University Press.

Dawson, M. M., ed. 2003. *Ethics of Confucius,* Montana, MT: Kessinger.

de Chernatony, L. 2001. *From brand vision to brand evaluation: strategically building and sustaining brand.* Oxford: Butterworth-Heinemann.

de Chernatony, L. and Dall'Olmo Riley, F. 1998. Defining a 'brand': beyond the literature with experts' interpretations. *Journal of Marketing Management,* 14, 417–43.

de Chernatony, L., Halliburton, C., and Bernath, R. 1995. International branding: demand- or supply-driven opportunity? *International Marketing Review,* 12(2), 9–21.

de Mooij, M. 2009. *Global marketing and advertising: understanding cultural paradoxes,* 3rd edition. Thousand Oaks, CA: Sage.

Dickie, G. L. 1997. *Introduction to aesthetics: an analytic approach.* Oxford: Oxford University Press.

Dimofte, C., Johansson, J., and Ronkainen, I. 2008. Cognitive and affective reactions of U. S. consumers to global brands. *Journal of International Marketing,* 16(4), 113–35.

Dong, L. and Tian, K. 2009. The use of Western brands in asserting Chinese national identity. *Journal of Consumer Research,* 36(3), 504–23.

Douglas, M. and Isherwood, B. 1982. *The world of goods: toward an anthropology of consumption.* New York: Norton.

Douglas, S. P. and Craig, C. S. 1997. The changing dynamics of consumer behaviour: implications for cross-cultural research. *International Journal of Research in Marketing,* 14, 379–95.

Draeger, D. F. 1992. *Ninjutsu: the art of invisibility.* North Clarendon, VT: Tuttle.

Du Gay, P. 1996. *Consumption and identity at work.* London: Sage.

Dyer, G. 2009. My life has not changed at all: Zhang Yimou on his creative independence. *Financial Times,* 12–13 December, Life & Arts, 13.

Eckhardt, G. M and Bengtsson, A. 2007. *Pulling the white rabbit out of the hat: consuming brands in imperial China.* Paper presented at the Association for Consumer Research European Conference, 10–14 July, Milan, Italy.

Eckhardt, G. M and Bengtsson, A. 2010. A brief history of branding in China. *Journal of Macromarketing,* 30(3), 210–21.

Editor 2011. The magic of diasporas. *The Economist,* November 19–25, 13.

Eisenhardt, K. M. 1989. Building theories from case study research. *Academy of Management Review,* 14(4), 532–50.

Ekström, K. M. 2006. The emergence of multi-sited ethnography in anthropology and marketing. In R. W. Belk, ed. *Handbook of qualitative research methods in marketing.* Cheltenham: Edward Elgar, pp. 497–508.

Eliade, M. 1959. *The sacred and the profane.* New York: Harcourt Brace Jovanovich.

Ellingham, F. and Fisher, J. 2004. *The Rough Guide to Spain,* 11th edition. London: Rough Guides.

Elliott, R. and Davies, A. 2006. Symbolic brands and authenticity of identity performance. In J. Schroeder and M. Salzer-Mörling, eds. *Brand culture.* London: Routledge, pp. 155–71.

Elliott, R. and Wattanasuwan, K. 1998. Brands as resources for the symbolic construction of identity. *International Journal of Advertising,* 17(2), 131–44.

Erickson, M. K. 1996. Using self-congruity and ideal congruity to predict purchase intention: a European perspective. *Journal of Euromarketing,* 6(1), 41–56.

Escalas, J. E. 2004. Narrative processing: building consumer connections to brands. *Journal of Consumer Psychology*, 14(1/2), 168–79.

Evans, C. 2000. Yesterday's emblem and tomorrow's commodities: the return of the repressed in fashion imagery today. In S. Bruzzi and P. C. Gibson, eds. *Fashion cultures: theories, explorations, and analysis*. London: Routledge, pp. 93–113.

Evans, C. 2007. *Fashion at the edge: spectacle, modernity and deathliness*. New Haven, CT: Yale University Press.

Evans, C. and Breward, C. 2005. *Fashion and modernity*. Oxford: Berg.

Fairbank, J. K. and Goldman, M. 2006. *China: a new history*, 2nd edition. Cambridge, MA: Harvard University Press.

Featherstone, M. 1991. *Consumer culture and postmodernism*. London: Sage.

Felton, E. 2012. It's alive! Vinyl makes a comeback, *Wall Street Journal*. 27 January, D8.

Ferrarotti, F. 2007. *Social theory for old and new modernities: essays on society and culture, 1976–2005*. Lanham, MD: Lexington Books.

Ferroa, P. 2003. *China*, 2nd edition. Tarrytown, NY: Marshall Cavendish.

Ferry, L. 2005. Neither man nor stone. In M. Calarco and P. Atterton, eds. *Animal philosophy: essential readings in continental thought*. New York: Continuum, pp. 148–56.

Fournier, S. 1998. Consumers and their brands: developing relationship theory in consumer research. *Journal of Consumer Research*, 24(1), 343–73.

Fowler, G. A. and Meichtry, S. 2008. China counts the cost of hosting the Olympics: social programs are weighed beside image building. *Wall Street Journal*, 16 July. Available: http://online.wsj.com/article/SB121614671139755287.html [Accessed September 29 2012].

Francis, J. N. P., Lam, J. P., and Walls, J. 2002. The impact of linguistic differences on international brand name standardization: a comparison of English and Chinese brand names of Fortune 500 companies. *Journal of International Marketing* 10(1), 98–116.

Frankel, S. 2008. Who won gold in the fashion Olympics? *The Independent*, August 9. Available at: www.independent.co.uk/life-style/fashion/features/who-won-gold-in-the-fashion-olympics-889295.html.

Friedman, J. 1990. Being in the world: globalization and localization. *Theory Culture & Society*, 7(2), 311–28.

Friedman, J. 1995. Global system, globalization and the parameters of modernity. In M. Featherstone, S. Lash, and R. Robertson, eds. *Global modernities*. London: Sage, pp. 69–90.

Fung, A. Y. 2008. Western style, Chinese pop: Jay Chou's rap and hip-hop in China. *Asian Music*, 39(1), 70–80.

Gale, C. and Kaur, J. 2004. *Fashion and textiles: an overview*. Oxford: Berg.

Geertz, C. 1973. *The interpretation of cultures*. New York: Basic Books.

Gelder, S. V. 2005. *Global brand strategy: unlocking brand potential across countries, cultures and markets*. Philadelphia: Kogan Page.

Ger, G. 1999. Localizing in the global village: local firms competing in global markets. *California Management Review*, 41(4), 64–83.

Gerth, K. 2003. *China made: consumer culture and the creation of the nation*. Cambridge, MA: Harvard University Press.

Giddens, A. 1991. *Modernity and self-identity: self and society in the late modern age*. Cambridge: Polity Press.

Giesler, M. 2008. Conflict and compromise: drama in marketplace evolution. *Journal of Consumer Research*, 34(April), 739–53.

Giesler, M. 2012. How doppelgänger brand images influence the market creation process: longitudinal insights from the rise of Botox Cosmetic. *Journal of Marketing*, 76, 55–68.

Gram, M. 2007. Whiteness and Western values in global advertisements: an exploratory study, *Journal of Marketing Communications*, 13(4), 291–309.

Grasso, J. M., Corrin, J. P., and Kort, M. 2004. *Modernization and revolution in China: from the opium wars to world power*, 3rd edition. Armonk, NY: M.E. Sharpe.

Grayson, K. and Martinec, R. 2004. Consumer perceptions of iconicity and indexicality and their influence on assessments of authentic market offerings. *Journal of Consumer Research*, 31(3), 296–312.

Grayson, K. and Shulman, D. 2000. Indexicality and the verification function of irreplaceable possessions: a semiotic analysis. *Journal of Consumer Research*, 27(2), 17–30.

Greenberg, Y. K. 2007. *Encyclopaedia of love in world religions*. Santa Barbara, CA: ABC-CLIO.

Greyser, A. 2008, *The three levels of branding at Beijing*. Boston: Harvard Business School Press.

Gries, P. H. 2005. *China's new nationalism: pride, politics, and diplomacy*. Berkeley: University of California Press.

Griffiths, M. 2013. *Consumers and individuals in China: standing out, fitting in*. London: Routledge.

Grimaldi, V. 2006. Getting beyond 'made in China'. *Brand Channel*. Available at: www.brandchannel.com/features_effect.asp?pf_id=338.

Gronow, J. 1997. *The sociology of taste*. London: Routledge.

Gu, E. X. 2001. Who was Mr Democracy? The May Fourth discourse of populist democracy and the radicalization of Chinese intellectuals (1915–1922), *Modern Asian Studies*. 35(3), 589-621.

Gupta, A. and Ferguson, J. 1997. *Anthropological locations: boundaries and grounds of a field science*. Berkeley: University of California Press.

Hall, S. 1996. Introduction: who needs identity? In S. Hall and P. du Gay, eds. *Questions of cultural identity*. London: Sage, pp. 1–17.

Hamilton, G. and Lai, C. 1989. Consumerism without capitalism: consumption and brand names in late imperial China. In H. Rutz and B. Orlove, eds. *The social economy of consumption*. Lanham, MD: University Press of America, pp. 253–80.

Hardtmann, E. 2001. Motståndsrörelse mot kastväsendet: glimtar från Indien och England [Resistance movement against the caste system: glimpses from India and England]. In U. Hannerz, ed. *Flera fält i ett, socialantropologer om trans-*

lokala fältstudier [Several fields in one, social anthropologists on translocal field studies]. Stockholm: Carlssons.

Harper's Bazaar Staff. 2008. Fashion Olympics. *Harper's Bazaar*, August. Available at: www.harpersbazaar.com/fashion/ fashion-articles/lucy-liu-fashion-olympics-0808 [Accessed September 29 2012].

Harrison, J. 2001. *Synaesthesia: the strangest thing*. Oxford: Oxford University Press.

Hassan, S. S., Craft, S., and Kortam, W. 2003. Understanding the new bases for global market segmentation. *Journal of Consumer Marketing*, 20(5), 446–62.

Heath, J. 2005. Methodological individualism. In E. N. Zalta, ed. *Stanford encyclopedia of philosophy*. Available at: http://plato.stanford.edu/archives/spr2005/entries/ methodological-individualism/.

Henderson, P. W., Cote, J. A, Leong, S. W., and Schmitt, B. 2003. Building strong brands in Asia: selecting the visual components of image to maximize brand strength, *International Journal of Research in Marketing*, 20(4), 297–313.

Hines, T. and Bruce, M. 2006. *Fashion marketing: contemporary issues*, 2nd edition. Oxford: Butterworth-Heinemann.

Hirschman, E. C. 1991. Point of view: sacred, secular, and mediating consumption imagery in television commercials. *Journal of Advertising Research*, 30(6), 38–43.

Hirschman, E. C. and Holbrook, M. B. 1982. Hedonic consumption: emerging concepts, methods and propositions. *Journal of Marketing*, 46(3), 92–101.

Hodgson, G. M. 2007. Meanings of methodological individualism. *Journal of Economic Methodology*, 14(2), 211–26.

Holbrook, M. B. 1994. Nostalgia proneness and consumer tastes. In J. A. Howard, ed. *Buyer behavior in marketing strategy*, 2nd edition. Upper Saddle River, NJ: Prentice-Hall. pp. 348–64.

Holbrook, M. B. 1999. *Consumer value: a framework for analysis and research*. New York: Routledge.

Holbrook, M. B. and Schindler, R. M. 1989. Some exploratory findings on the development of musical tastes. *Journal of Consumer Research*, 16(2), 119–24.

Holbrook, M. B. and Schindler, R. M. 1996. Market segmentation based on age and attitude towards the past: concepts, methods and findings concerning nostalgic influences on consumer taste. *Journal of Business Research*, 37(1), 27–39.

Holbrook, M. B. and Zirlin, R. B, 1985. Artistic creation, artworks and aesthetic appreciation. In R. W. Belk., ed. *Advances in non-profit marketing*. London: JAI Press.

Holden, P. and Ruppel, R. J. 2003. *Imperial desire: dissident sexualities and colonial literature*. Minneapolis: University of Minnesota Press.

Holt, D. B. 2002. Why do brands cause trouble? a dialectical theory of consumer culture and branding. *Journal of Consumer Research*, 29(2), 70–90.

Holt, D. B. 2004. *How brands become icons: the principles of cultural branding*. Boston, MA: Harvard Business School Press.

Holt, D. and Cameron, D. 2010. *Cultural strategy: using innovative ideologies to build breakthrough brands*. Oxford: Oxford University Press.

Holt, D. B, Quelch, J. A., and Taylor, E. L. 2004. How global brands compete. *Harvard Business Review*, 82(9), 1–9.

Hooper, B. 2000. Globalisation and resistance in post-Mao China: the case of foreign consumer products. *Asian Studies Review*, 24(4), 439–70.

Hruska, R. J. 2008. *888 red envelopes from Shanghai Tang*. Available at: http://guestofaguest.com/from-our-inbox/888-red-envelopes-from-shanghai-tan/.

Hsieh, M. 2002. Identifying brand image dimensionality and measuring the degree of brand globalization: A cross-national study. *Journal of International Marketing*, 10(2), 46–67.

Hucker, C. 1995. *China's imperial past: an introduction to Chinese history and culture*. Stanford, CA: Stanford University Press.

Huston, E. 2006. *Sacred – New Orleans funerary grounds*. Raleigh, NC: Lulu.

Interbrand 2011. *Best in class to world class: Best China Brands 2011*. Available at: www.interbrand.com/en/Interbrand-offices/

Interbrand-Shanghai/BestChinaBrands2011.aspx [Accessed April 6 2013].

Interbrand 2012. Best Global Brands 2012. Available at: www.interbrand.com/en/news-room/press-releases/2012-10-02-7543da7.aspx [Accessed April 6 2013].

Iwabuchi, K. 2006. *Recentering globalization: popular culture and Japanese transnationalism*. Durham, NC: Duke University Press.

Jacobsen, K. A. 2004. Establishing ritual space in the Hindu diaspora in Norway. In K. A. Jacobsen and P. P. Kumar, eds. *South Asians in the diaspora: histories and religious traditions*. Leiden: Brill, pp. 134–48.

Jameson, F. 1991. *Post-modernism, or, the cultural logic of late capitalism*. Durham, NC: Duke University Press.

JayChouStudio.com 2010a. "Nun-Chuks," www.jaychoustudio.com/jay-chou-translations/nun-chuks/19.

JayChouStudio.com 2010b. "Chrysanthemum Flower Bed," www.jaychoustudio.com/jay-chou-translations/chrysanthemum-flower-bed/105.

Johansson, K. and Ronkainen, I. A. 2005. The esteem of global brands. *Journal of Brand Management*, 12(5), 339–54.

Joy, A. S. 2001. Gift giving in Hong Kong and the continuum of social ties. *Journal of Consumer Research*, 28(3), 239–56.

Joy, A. and Sherry, J. F. Jr. 2003. Speaking of art as embodied imagination: a multi-sensory approach to understanding aesthetic experience. *Journal of Consumer Research*, 30(2), 259–82.

Joy, A. and Sherry, J. F. Jr. 2004. Framing considerations in the PRC: creating value in the contemporary Chinese art market. *Consumption, Markets and Culture*, 7(4), 307–48.

Justice, L. 2012. *China's design revolution*. Cambridge, MA: MIT Press.

Kaiser, S. B. 1996. *The social psychology of clothing: symbolic appearances in context*, 3rd edition. New York: Fairchild.

Kapferer, J. N. 2006. The two business cultures of luxury brands. In J. Schroeder and M. Salzer-Mörling, eds. *Brand culture*. New York: Routledge, pp. 67–76.

Kapferer, J. N. 2012. *The new strategic brand management: advanced insights and strategic thinking*, 5th edition. London: Kogan Page.

Karababa, E. and Ger, G. 2011. Early modern Ottoman coffee-house culture and the formation of the consumer subject. *Journal of Consumer Research*, 37(5), 737–60.

Kartomi, M. J. 1990. *On concepts and classifications of musical instruments*. Chicago: University of Chicago Press.

Kates, S. M. 2004. The dynamics of brand legitimacy: an interpretive study in the gay men's community. *Journal of Consumer Research*, 31(3), 455–64.

Kates, S. M. 2006. Researching brands ethnographically: an interpretive community approach. In R. W. Belk, ed. *Handbook of qualitative research methods in marketing*. Cheltenham: Edward Elgar, pp. 94–103.

Kates, S. M. and Goh, C. 2003. Brand morphing: implications for advertising theory and practice. *Journal of Advertising*, 32(1), 59–68.

Kawamura, Y. 2004. *The Japanese revolution in Paris fashion*. Oxford: Berg.

Kawamura, Y. 2005. *Fashion-ology: an introduction to fashion studies*. Oxford: Berg.

Kay, M. J. 2006. Strong brands and corporate brands. *European Journal of Marketing*, 40(7/8), 742–60.

Kendall, G. and Wickham, G. 2001. *Understanding culture: cultural studies, order, ordering*. London: Sage.

Khan, N. and Balfour, F. 2011. Richemont's Shanghai Tang to double Chinese stores as luxury demand climbs, *Bloomberg.com*, October 6. Available at: www.bloomberg.com/news/2011-10-06/richemont-s-shanghai-tang-to-double-chinese-stores-as-luxury-demand-climbs.html [Accessed October 1 2012].

Kiday, G. 2008. AFI picks 'Moments of Significance'. *The Hollywood Reporter*, December 29. Available at: www.hollywoodreporter.com/news/afi-picks-moments-significance-124924 [Accessed September 29 2012].

Kidd, B. 2011. Human rights and the Olympic Movement after Beijing. In D. P. Martinez, ed. *Documenting the Beijing Olympics*. New York: Routledge, pp. 157–66.

Kjeldgaard, D. and Askegaard, S. 2006. The glocalization of youth culture: the global youth segment as structures of common difference. *Journal of Consumer Research*, 22(3), 231–47.

Kjeldgaard, D., Csaba, F., and Ger, G. 2006. Grasping the global: multi-sited ethnographic market studies. In R. W. Belk, ed. *Handbook of qualitative research methods in marketing*. Cheltenham: Edward Elgar, pp. 521–33.

Klein, J. G., Ettenson, R., and Morris, M. D. 1998. The animosity model of foreign product purchase: an empirical test in the People's Republic of China. *Journal of Marketing*, 62(1), 89–100.

Klein, N. 1999. *No logo: taking aim at the brand bullies*. London: Flamingo.

Kloet, J. 2010. *China with a cut: globalisation, urban youth and popular music*. Amsterdam: Amsterdam University Press.

Kornberger, M. 2010. *Brand society: how brands transform management and lifestyle*. Cambridge: Cambridge University Press.

Kozinets, R. V. 2001. Utopian enterprise: articulating the meanings of Star Trek's culture of consumption. *Journal of Consumer Research*, 28(2), 67–88.

KPMG 2007. *Luxury brands in China*. Available at: www.kpmg. com.cn/en/virtual_library/Consumer_markets/CM_ Luxury_brand.pdf [Accessed June 6 2013].

Lamb, C. W., Hair, J. F., and McDaniel, C. 2008. *Essentials of marketing*, 6th edition. Independence, KY: South-Western.

Lao-tzu, 1891. *Tao Te Ching*. Trans J. Legge. Available at: www. sacred-texts.com/tao/taote.htm [Accessed August 8 2009].

Latham, K. 2009. Media, the Olympics and the search for the 'real' China. *The China Quarterly*, 197(1), 25–43.

Latham, K. 2011. China's media viewed through the prism of the Beijing Olympics. In D. P. Martinez, ed. *Documenting the Beijing Olympics*. New York: Routledge. pp. 53–68.

Lee, Y. and Shen, S. 1999. *Chinese musical instruments*. Naperville, IL: Chinese Music Society of North America Press.

Lei, M. 2000. *Dingjian cehua: Zhongguo qiye zhuming cehua quan'an* [A collection of the best corporate strategic plans implemented in China]. Beijing: Enterprise Management Publishing House.

Leifer, M. 2000. *Asian nationalism.* London: Routledge.

Leslie, E. 1999. Souvenirs and forgetting Walter Benjamin's memory-work. In M. Kwint, C. Breward, and J. Aynsley, eds. *Material memories: design and evocation.* Oxford: Berg, pp. 107–22.

Leuthold, S. 1998. *Indigenous aesthetics: native art, media, and identity.* Austin: University of Texas Press.

Levitt, T. 1983. The globalization of markets. *Harvard Business Review,* 61(3), 91–102.

Liang, L. 2011. Framing China and the world through the Olympic opening ceremonies, 1984–2008. In D. P. Martinez, ed. *Documenting the Beijing Olympics,* New York: Routledge, pp. 75–88.

Liao, S.-H., Chen, J.-L., and Hsu, T.-Y. 2009. Ontology-based data mining approach implemented for sport marketing. *Expert Systems with Applications,* 36(8), 11045–56.

Ligas, M. and Cotte, J. 1999. The process of negotiating brand meaning: a symbolic interactions perspective. In E. J. Arnould and L. M. Scott, eds. *Advances in Consumer Research,* Volume 26. Duluth, MN: Association for Consumer Research, pp. 609–14.

Lipovetsky, G. and Sennett, R. 2002. *The empire of fashion: dressing modern democracy.* Princeton, NJ: Princeton University Press.

Liu, Y. 2001. *Zhongguo shichang yingxiao wuqu* [Fallacies in marketing in China], Beijing: Enterprise Management.

Lowenthal, D. 1985. *The past is a foreign country.* Cambridge: Cambridge University Press.

Lu, P. X. 2008. *Elite China: luxury consumer behavior in China.* Hoboken, NJ: Wiley.

Lu, T. and He, H. 2003. *Marketing in China – report 2003, no. 1.* Hangzhou: Zhejiang People's Publishing House.

Luedicke, M. K., Thompson, C. J., and Giesler, M. 2010. Consumer identity work as moral protagonism: how myth and ideology animate a brand-mediated moral conflict. *Journal of Consumer Research*, 36(6), 1016–32.

Luxury-insider.com 2011. From Shanghai with love – Shanghai Tang executive chairman talks to us. *Luxury-Insider.com*, October. Available at: www.luxury-insider.com/features/2011/interview-raphael-le-masne-de-chermont-for-shanghai-tang [Accessed October 3 2012].

Maclaran, P., Otnes, C., and Fischer, E. 2007. Maintaining the myth of the monarchy: how producers shape consumers' experiences of the British Royal Family. In A. Y. Lee and D. Somon, eds. *Advances in Consumer Research*, Volume 35. Duluth, MN: Association for Consumer Research, p. 68.

Maclaran, P., Saren, M., and Stern, B., eds. 2009. *Handbook of marketing theory*. London: Sage.

Maclaran, P. and Stevens, L. 1998. Romancing the utopian marketplace: dallying with Bakhtin in the Powerscourt Town House Centre. In S. Brown, A. M. Doherty and W. Clarke, eds. *Romancing the market*. London: Routledge, pp. 172–86.

Mandoki, K. 2007. *Everyday aesthetics*. London: Ashgate.

Manning, P. and Uplisashvili, A. 2007. 'Our Beer': ethnographic brands in post socialist Georgia. *American Anthropologist*, 109(4), 626–41.

Marcus, G. E. 1986. Contemporary problems in ethnography and in the modern world system. In J. Clifford and G. E. Marcus, eds. *Writing culture*. Berkeley: University of California Press, pp. 165–93.

Marcus, G. E. 1989. Imagining the whole: ethnography's contemporary efforts to situate itself. *Critical Anthropology*, 9, 7–30.

Marcus, G. E. 1995. Ethnography in/of the world system: the emergence of multi-sited ethnography. *Annual Review of Anthropology*, 24, 95–117.

Marcus, G. E. 1998. *Ethnography through thick and thin*. Princeton, NJ: Princeton University Press.

Marcus, G. E. 1999. What is at stake – and is not – in the idea and practice of multi-sited ethnography. *Canberra Anthropology*, 22(2), 6–14.

Martin, E. 1994. *Flexible bodies: tracing immunity in American culture from the days of polio to the age of AIDS*. Boston: Beacon.

Martin-Liao, T. 2008. China bends over backward during the Olympics to conceal the ugly truth. *The Daily News*, August 16. Available at: www.nydailynews.com/opinion/china-bends-olympics-conceal-ugly-truth-article-1.319127#ixzz27tFYc91J [Accessed September 29 2012].

McClary, S. and Walser, R. 1990. Start making sense! Musicology wrestles with rock. In S. Frith and A. Goodwin, eds. *On record: rock, pop, and the written word*. New York: Pantheon, pp. 277–92.

McCracken, G. 1986. Culture and consumption: a theoretical account of the structure and movement of the cultural meaning of consumer goods. *Journal of Consumer Research*, 13(2), 71–84.

McCracken, G. 1988a. *Culture and consumption*. Bloomington: Indiana University Press.

McCracken, G. 1988b. *The long interview*. Newbury Park, CA: Sage.

McKendrick, N. 1982. The consumer revolution of eighteenth-century England. In N. McKendrick, J. Brewer, and J. H. Plumb, eds. *The birth of a consumer society: the commercialization of eighteenth-century England*. London: Europa, pp. 3–33.

McLoughlin, D. and Aaker, D. A. 2010. *Strategic market management: global perspectives*. New York: John Wiley.

McRobbie, A. 1998. *British fashion design: rag trade or image industry?* London: Routledge.

Mead, A. 2011. Made in China. In L. Welters and A. Lillethun, eds. *The Fashion Reader*, 2nd edition. Oxford: Berg, pp. 556–63.

Melewar, T. C., Meadows, M., Zheng, W., and Rickards, R. 2004. The influence of culture on brand building in the Chinese market: A brief insight. *Journal of Brand Management*, 11(6), 449–62.

Meneley, A. 2007. Like an extra virgin. *American Anthropologist*, 109(4), 678–87.

Miles, M. B. and Huberman, A. M. 1994. *Qualitative data analysis*, 2nd edition. Thousand Oaks, CA: Sage.

Miller, D. 1987. *Material culture and mass consumption*. Oxford: Basil Blackwell.

Miller, D., Jackson, P., Thrift, N., Holbrook, B., and Rowlands, M. 1998. *Shopping, place, and identity*. London: Routledge.

Mills, A. J., Eurepos, G., and Wiebe, E., eds. 2010. *Encyclopedia of case study research*. Thousand Oaks, CA: Sage.

Mirambeau, C. 2004. *Moulin Rouge*. Paris: Assouline.

Moisander, J. and Valtonen, A. 2006. *Qualitative marketing research: a cultural approach*. London: Sage.

Moore, C. M. and Birtwistle, G. 2004. The Burberry business model – understanding a brand renaissance. *International Journal of Retail & Distribution Management*, 32(8), 412–22.

Morris, B. 1989. For spring, patches of strategically sited bare skin. *New York Times*. November 21. Available at: www.nytimes.com/1989/11/21/style/for-spring-patches-of-strategically-sited-bare-skin.html [Accessed September 28 2012].

Moy, E. 2009. Jay Chou to play Kato in 'Green Hornet.' *Examiner.com*, Arts & Entertainment, August 7. Available at: www.examiner.com/article/jay-chou-to-play-kato-green-hornet [Accessed October 2 2012].

Mukerji, C. 1983. *From graven images: patterns of modern materialism*. New York: Columbia University Press.

Muñiz, A. and O'Guinn, T. C. 2001. Brand community. *Journal of Consumer Research*, 27(4), 412–32.

Murray, J. 2002. The politics of consumption: a re-inquiry on Thompson and Haytko's 1997 "Speaking of Fashion". *Journal of Consumer Research*, 29(3), 427–40.

Nan, H. 1998. *Basic Buddhism: exploring Buddhism and Zen*. Newburyport, MA: Weiser Books.

Norris, P. 2000. Global governance and cosmopolitan citizens. In J. S. Nye and J. D. Donahue, eds. *Governance in a globalizing world*. Washington, DC: Brookings Institution Press.

O'Guinn, T. C., Allen, C., and Semenik, R. J. 2008. *Advertising and integrated brand promotion*. Independence, KY: South-Western.

O'Guinn, T. C. and Belk, R. W. 1989. Heaven on earth: consumption at Heritage Village, USA. *Journal of Consumer Research*. 16(3), 227–38.

Olins, W. 1989. *Corporate identity: making business strategy visible through design*. London: Thames & Hudson.

Ostwalt, C. 2003. *Secular steeples: popular culture and the religious imagination*. Valley Forge, VA: Trinity Press International.

Özsomer, A. and Altaras, S. 2008. Global brand purchase likelihood: a critical synthesis and an integrated conceptual framework. *Journal of International Marketing*, 16, 1–28.

Palls, B. P. 2008. *Cultural portraits: a synoptic guide*. Clearwater Beach, FL: B & B Educational Consultants.

Pandit, S. 2005, *Exemplary CEOs: insights on organizational transformation*. New York: McGraw-Hill.

Pargament, K. I., Magyar-Russell, G., and Murray-Swank, N. A. 2005. The sacred and the search for significance: religion as a unique process. *Journal of Social Issues*, 61(4), 665–87.

Peñaloza, L. and Gilly, M. C. 1999. Marketer acculturation: the changer and the changed. *Journal of Marketing*, 63(3), 84–104.

Pensky, M. 2004. Method and time: Benjamin's dialectical images. In D. S. Ferris, ed. *The Cambridge companion to Walter Benjamin*. Cambridge: Cambridge University Press, pp. 177–98.

Peterson, T. 2004. The branding of China. *Business Week*. November 9. Available at: www.businessweek.com/bwdaily/dnflash/nov2004/nf20041110_0338_db053.htm.

Pieterse, N. 1995. Globalization as hybridization, in M. Featherstone, S. Lash, and R. Robertson, eds. *Global modernities*. London: Sage, pp. 45–68.

Pongsakornrungsilp, S. and Schroeder, J. E. 2011. Understanding value co-creation in a co-consuming brand community. *Marketing Theory*, 11(3), 303–24.

Price, E. G. 2006. *Hip hop culture*. Santa Barbara, CA: ABC-CLIO.

Puntoni, S., Schroeder, J. E., and Ritson, M. 2010. Meaning matters: polysemy in advertising. *Journal of Advertising*, 39(2), 51–64.

Qing, L., Chen, C. C., Colapinto, C., Akihiko, H., Yun'il, H., and Miko, K. 2010. Attitudes towards China before and after the Beijing Olympics. *International Journal of the History of Sport*, 27(9/10), 1419–32.

Qiu, S. 2003. *Success from brands.* Beijing: Central Compilation and Translation Press.

Quelch, J. A. 1999. Global brands: taking stock. *Business Strategy Review*, 10(Spring), 1–14.

Quelch, J. A. 2007. *Readings in modern marketing.* Hong Kong: Chinese University Press.

Ranciere, J. and Rockhill, G. 2006. *The politics of aesthetics.* London: Continuum.

Reckert, S. 1993. *Beyond chrysanthemums: perspectives on poetry East and West.* Oxford: Oxford University Press.

Rein, S. 2012. *The end of cheap China: economic and cultural trends that will disrupt the world.* New York: Wiley.

Roll, M. 2006. *Asian brand strategy: how Asia builds strong brands.* Basingstoke: Palgrave Macmillan.

Roth, M. S. 1992. Depth versus breadth strategies for global brand image management. *Journal of Advertising*, 21(2), 23–36.

Roth, M. S. 1995. The effects of culture and socioeconomics on the performance of global brand image strategies. *Journal of Marketing Research*, 32(May), 163–75.

Savage, A. 2008. *The ecology: a "new to you" view – an orthodox theological ecology.* Birmingham, AL: CreateSpace.

Schmitt, B. and Simonson, A. 1997. *Marketing aesthetics: the strategic management of brands, identity, and image.* New York: The Free Press.

Schouten, J. and McAlexander, J. 1995. Ethnography of the new bikers. *Journal of Consumer Research*, 22(1), 43–61.

Schroeder, J. E. 2002. *Visual consumption.* New York: Routledge.

Schroeder, J. E. 2005. The artist and the brand. *European Journal of Marketing*, 39(11), 1291–305.

Schroeder, J. E. 2006. Critical visual analysis. In R. W. Belk, ed. *Handbook of qualitative research methods in marketing.* Cheltenham: Edward Elgar, pp. 303–21.

Schroeder, J. E. 2007. Brand culture. In G. Ritzer, ed. *Encyclopedia of sociology.* Oxford: Blackwell, pp. 351–53.

Schroeder, J. E. 2009. The cultural codes of branding. *Marketing Theory*, 9, 123–26.

Schroeder, J. E. 2012. Style and strategy: snapshot aesthetics in brand culture. In C. McLean, P., Quattrone, F-R. Puyou, and N. Thrift, eds. *Imagining organisations: performative imagery in business and beyond.* London: Routledge, pp. 129–51.

Schroeder, J. E. and Borgerson, J. L. 2002. Innovations in information technology: insights into consumer culture from Italian renaissance art. *Consumption, Markets & Culture*, 5(2), 154–69.

Schroeder, J. E. and Salzer-Mörling, M., eds. 2006. *Brand culture.* New York: Routledge.

Schuiling, I. and Kapferer, J. N. 2004. Real differences between local and international brands: strategic implications for international marketers. *Journal of International Marketing*, 12(4), 97–112.

Schultz, M. and Hatch, M. J. 2006. A cultural perspective on corporate branding: the case of LEGO Group. In J. Schroeder and M. Salzer-Mörling, eds. *Brand culture*, London: Routledge, pp. 15–33.

Scott, L. M. 1994. Images in advertising: the need for a theory of visual rhetoric. *Journal of Consumer Research*, 2, 252–73.

Segal, R. 2004. *Myth: a very short introduction.* Oxford: Oxford University Press.

Shanghai Tang 2009. *Catalog.* Available at: www.shanghaitang.com/pdf/AW09%20Catalogue%20PDF%20-%20FINAL.pdf.

Shanghai Tang 2010b. *Mandarin collar society.* Available at: www.shanghaitang.com/mcs.

Shanghai Tang 2010c. *Shanghai Tang cafe.* Available at: www.shanghaitang.com/shanghai-tang-dining-destination.

Shanghai Tang 2010d. *About us.* Available at: www.shanghaitang.com/shanghaitang-modern-chinese-chic-ambassador.

Shanghai Tang 2013. *Find a store*. Available at: www. shanghaitang.com/stores.html.

Shin, H. B. 2012. Looking back and ahead: lessons from the 2008 Beijing Olympic Games, *British Politics and Policy at LSE* [London School of Economics blog], August 1. Available at: http://blogs.lse.ac.uk/politicsandpolicy/2012/08/01/ looking-back-2008-beijing-olympic-games-shin/.

Skelton, T. and Valentine, G., eds. 1997. *Cool places: geographies of youth culture*. London: Routledge.

Solomon, M., Bamossy, G. Askegaard, S., and Hogg, M. 2006. *Consumer behaviour: a European perspective*, 3rd edition. Upper Saddle, NJ: Financial Times/Prentice Hall.

Song, W. and Buchanan, M. 2012. The Beijing Olympics (2008) – looking for positives despite the global financial crisis. *Goldman Sachs global economics, commodities and strategy research* (July), 26–27. Available at: www.goldmansachs.com/ our-thinking/archive-pdfs/olympics-and-economics-.pdf.

Spielberg, S. 2008. Person of the year: runners up: Zhang Yimou. *Time*, December 17. Available at: www.time.com/time/ specials/packages/article/0,28804,1861543_ 1865103_1865107,00.html [Accessed September 29 2012].

Spies, K., Hesse, F., and Loesch, K. 1997. Store atmosphere, mood and purchasing behaviour. *International Journal of Research in Marketing*, 14(1), 1–17.

Spindler, G., Spindler, L., Trueba, H., and Williams, M. 1990. *The American cultural dialogue and its transmission*. New York: Falmer.

Steenkamp, J.-B. E. M., Batra, R., and Alden, D. 2003. How perceived brand globalness creates brand value. *Journal of International Business Studies*, 34(1), 53–65.

Stelter, B. 2008. Networks fight shorter Olympic leash. *New York Times*. July 21. Available at: www.nytimes.com/2008/ 07/21/sports/olympics/21nbc.html?pagewanted=2 [Accessed September 29 2012].

Stern, B. B. 1992. Historical and personal nostalgia in advertising text: the fin de siècle effect. *Journal of Advertising*, 21(4), 11–32.

Strizhakova, Y., Coulter, R., and Price, L. 2008. Branded products as a passport to global citizenship: perspectives from developed and developing countries. *Journal of International Marketing*, 16(4), 59–87.

Swystun, J. 2006. Branding in China: Strategies and Responses. *BrandChannel white paper*, June 22. Available at: www.brandchannel.com/papers_review.asp?sp_id=1255 [Accessed October 2 2012].

Tai, S. H. C. 1997. Advertising in Asia: localize or regionalize? *International Journal of Advertising*, 16(1), 48–61.

Temporal, P. 2001. *Branding in Asia: the creation, development and management of Asian brands for the global market.* Singapore: Wiley Asia.

Temporal, P. 2006. *Asia's star brands.* New York: Wiley.

Thompson, C. J. and Arsel, Z. 2004. The Starbucks brandscape and consumers' (anti-corporate) experiences of glocalization. *Journal of Consumer Research*, 31(3), 631–42.

Thompson, C. J. and Haytko, D. L. 1997. Speaking of fashion: consumers' uses of fashion discourses and the appropriation of countervailing cultural meanings. *Journal of Consumer Research*, 24(2), 15–42.

Thompson, C. and Tian, K. 2008. Reconstructing the South: how commercial myths compete for identity value through the ideological shaping of popular memories and counter-memories. *Journal of Consumer Research*, 34(5), 595–613.

Thompson, C. J., Locander, W. B., and Pollio, H. R. 1989. Putting consumer experience back into consumer research: the philosophy and method of existential phenomenology. *Journal of Consumer Research*, 16(3), 133–47.

Thompson, C. J., Pollio, H. R., and Locander, W. B. 1994. The spoken and the unspoken: a hermeneutic approach to understanding the cultural viewpoints that underlie consumers' expressed meanings. *Journal of Consumer Research*, 21(4), 432–52.

Thompson, C. J., Rindfleisch, A., and Arsel, Z. 2006. Emotional branding and the strategic value of the doppelgänger brand image. *Journal of Marketing*, 70(1), 50–64.

Thompson, J. B. 1995. *The media and modernity: a social theory of the media.* Cambridge: Polity.

Thompson, L. G. 1996. *Chinese religion*, 5th edition. Belmont, CA: Wadsworth.

Tian, K. and Dong, L. 2011. *Consumer-citizens of China: the role of foreign brands in the imagined future China*. New York: Routledge.

Tischler, L. 2006. The Gucci Killers. *Fast Company* (January–February), 1–4. Available at: www.fastcompany.com/magazine/102/shanghai.html?page=0%2C3.

Tomlinson, J. 2001. *Cultural imperialism: a critical introduction*. London: Continuum International Publishing Group.

Tran, Y. 2008. *Fashion in the Danish experience economy: challenge for growth*. Odder, Denmark: Narayana Press.

Tse, D. K., Belk, R. W., and Zhou, N. 1989. Becoming a consumer society: a longitudinal and cross-cultural content analysis of print advertisements from Hong Kong, People's Republic of China, and Taiwan. *Journal of Consumer Research*, 15(3), 457–72.

Tu, Y. 2008. Beijing Olympic opening demonstrates high-tech Olympics. *China Radio International*, August 13. Available at: http://english.cri.cn/4026/2008/08/13/1881s393182.htm [Accessed October 12 2008].

Tuan, I. H.-C. 2011. Zhang Yimou's *Turandot* in Taiwan: intercultural spectacle, aesthetic of excess, and cross-strait sensibility. *Theatre Topics*, 21(2), 175–83.

Tumasoff, V. 2008. *The Olympics of fashion: Opening Ceremony*. Available at: http://tumasoff. blogspot.com/2008/08/olympics-of-fashion-opening-ceremony.html [Accessed September 29 2012].

Tungate, M. 2008. *Fashion brands: branding style from Armani to Zara*, 2nd edition. London: Kogan Page.

Udehn, L. 2001. *Methodological individualism: background, history and meaning*. New York: Routledge.

Usunier, J. 2000. *Marketing across cultures*, 3rd edition. London: Pearson Education.

Venkatesh, A. and Meamber, L. A. 2008. The aesthetics of consumption and the consumer as an aesthetic subject. *Consumption Markets & Culture*, 11(1), 45–70.

Wan, L. 2001. *Zhongguo mingpai zhanlue* [Strategies of 35 well-known Chinese brands]. Beijing: Chinese Commerce Publishing House.

Wang, J. 2000. *Foreign advertising in China: becoming global, becoming local.* Ames: Iowa State University Press.

Wang, J. 2008. *Brand new China: advertising, media, and commercial culture.* Cambridge, MA: Harvard University Press.

Wang, Y. 2001. *A paradise lost: the imperial garden Yuanming Yuan.* Honolulu: University of Hawaii Press.

Webster, R. 2008. *Flower and tree magic: discover the natural enchantment around you.* Woodbury, MN: Llewellyn.

Weng, X. 2002. *Branding strategy in China.* Hangzhou: Zhejiang People's Publishing House.

Whitelock, J. and Fastoso, F. 2007. Understanding international branding: defining the domain and reviewing the literature. *International Marketing Review*, 24(3), 252–70.

Whitfield, S. 2004. *The Silk Road: trade, travel, war and faith.* Chicago: Serindia.

Williams, R. H. 1982. *Dream worlds: mass consumption in late nineteenth-century France.* Berkeley: University of California Press.

Williams, R. 1994. Selections from "Marxism and literature." In N. Dirk, G. Eley, and S. B. Ortner, eds. *Culture/power/history.* Princeton, NJ: Princeton University Press, pp. 585–608.

Wilson, E. 2005. Fashion and modernity. In C. Evans and C. Breward, eds. *Fashion and modernity.* Oxford: Berg, pp. 9–17.

Wilson, E. 2008. Opening Ceremony fashions [narrated slide show]. *New York Times online.* August 8. Available at: www.nytimes.com/interactive/2008/08/08/sports/olympics/20080808-olympic-fashion2/ [Accessed September 29 2012].

Wu, X. 2001. *Da baiju* [Big failures]. Hangzhou: Zhejiang People's Publishing House.

Xie, D. F. 2009. *Beijing Games will further boost China's opening-up drive: Belgian scholar.* China Radio International. Available at: http://big5.cri.cn/gate/big5/english.cri.cn/

6066/2008/08/21/1821s397196.htm [Accessed September 26 2012].

Xing, Z. Y. and Xin, W. J. 1998. *Republic of China yearbook.* London: Routledge.

Xu, G. G. 2007. *Sinascape: contemporary Chinese cinema.* Lanham, MD: Rowman & Littlefield.

Xu, J. 1999. Body, discourse, and the cultural politics of contemporary Chinese Qigong. *The Journal of Asian Studies,* 58(4), 961–91.

Xu, X. 2006. Modernizing China in the Olympic spotlight: China's national identity and the 2008 Beijing Olympiad, *The Sociological Review,* 54(S2), 90–107.

Yahuda, M. 2000. The changing faces of Chinese nationalism. In M. Leifer, ed. *Asian Nationalism.* London: Routledge, pp. 21–37.

Yang, B. 1987. *Qingdai Guandong Gongpin: tributes from Guangdong to the Qing court.* Hong Kong: Art Museum, City University of Hong Kong.

Yang, M. 2002. *Chenggong yingxiao guoji zhiming pinpai zai Zhongguo* [Successfully marketing well-known international brands in China]. Shanghai: East China University of Science and Technology Press.

Ye, M. 2003. *The power of ideas.* Beijing: China Machine Press.

Yin, J. 1999. International advertising strategies in China: a worldwide survey of foreign advertisers. *Journal of Advertising Research,* 39(6), 25–35.

Yin, R. K. 1994. *Case study research: design and methods,* revised edition. Thousand Oaks, CA: Sage Publications.

Yip, G. S. 1995. *Total global strategy: managing for worldwide competitive advantage.* Upper Saddle River, NJ: Prentice Hall.

Zhang, B. 2001. *Branding no more?* Guangzhou: Guangdong Economy Publishing House.

Zhang, S. and Schmitt, B. H. 2001. Creating local brands in multilingual international markets. *Journal of Marketing Research,* 38(3), 313–25.

Zhang, Y. 2003. *Variability conjuncture.* Beijing: China Workers' Publishing House.

Zhao, X. and Belk, R. W. 2008. Politicizing consumer culture: advertising's appropriation of political ideology in China's social transition. *Journal of Consumer Research*, 35(2), 231–44.

Zhou, N. and Belk, R. W. 2004. Chinese consumer readings of global and local advertising appeals. *Journal of Advertising*, 22(3), 63–76.

Zhou, R. 2010, Ja(y)ded time ahead. *China Daily online*, July 1. Available at: www.chinadaily.com. cn/china/2010-07/01/content_10050278.htm.

Zhu, Y. 2002. Chinese cinema's economic reform from the mid-1980s to the mid-1990s. *Journal of Communication*, 52(4), 905–21.

Zuo, X. 1999. *Old trademarks*. Shanghai: Shanghai Pictorial House.

Zwick, D., Bonsu, S., and Darmody, A. 2008. Putting consumers to work: co-creation' and new marketing governmentality. *Journal of Consumer Culture*, 8(2), 163–96.

Index

Printed and bound by CPI Group (UK) Ltd, Croydon, CR0 4YY

Berkeley College

CAMPUSES: Brooklyn, NY * New York, NY * White Plains, NY
Newark, NJ * Paramus, NJ * Woodbridge, NJ * Woodland Park, NJ
Clifton, NJ * Dover, NJ * Berkeley College Online *

PLEASE KEEP DATE DUE CARD IN POCKET